THE POWER OF TEACHER LEADERS

Co-published with Kappa Delta Pi, *The Power of Teacher Leaders* provides a comprehensive resource for understanding the ways that teacher leaders foster positive change in their schools. Distinct from school administrators, teacher leaders are professionals who remain in the classroom and use their specialized knowledge and skills to improve student achievement, influence others, and build organizational capacity.

Written by leading educational researchers, each chapter of *The Power of Teacher Leaders* describes a different way that teachers are leading. Moving beyond the question of why teacher leaders are important and how such work is implemented, the contributing scholars to this collection offer a critical examination of the field by presenting original research, case studies, and programs in practice. Topics covered include how teachers become leaders, their wide-ranging leadership roles, and the effects of teacher leadership on student academic success and school communities. A cohesive edited collection, this book demonstrates how teacher leaders play an increasingly active role in the improvement of student learning, teacher professional development, and school climate.

Nathan Bond is Associate Professor of Curriculum and Instruction at Texas State University, USA.

THE POWER OF TEACHER LEADERS

Their Roles, Influence, and Impact

Edited by Nathan Bond
Foreword by Andy Hargreaves

KAPPA DELTA PI
INTERNATIONAL HONOR SOCIETY IN EDUCATION

Routledge
Taylor & Francis Group

NEW YORK AND LONDON

First published 2015
by Routledge
711 Third Avenue, New York, NY 10017

and by Routledge
2 Park Square, Milton Park, Abingdon, Oxon, OX14 4RN

Routledge is an imprint of the Taylor & Francis Group, an informa business

Library of Congress Cataloging-in-Publication Data

The power of teacher leaders : their roles, influence, and impact / edited by
   Nathan Bond.
      pages cm
   Includes bibliographical references and index.
   1. Teaching.   2. Educational leadership.   I. Bond, Nathan.
   LB1025.3.P685 2014
   371.102—dc23
   2014005625

ISBN: 978-0-415-74164-4 (hbk)
ISBN: 978-0-415-74165-1 (pbk)
ISBN: 978-1-315-81520-6 (ebk)

Typeset in Bembo
by Apex CoVantage, LLC

To my family, Bobbie, Jerry, Joe, and Patio, for their unwavering support as I worked on the book during those early morning hours.

CONTENTS

FOREWORD

Little of value occurs in any classroom without excellent teacher preparation in how to lead students. It is also true that lasting value rarely occurs in any organization without excellent leadership. To some, these two statements lead to a hierarchical conclusion: Individual leaders of organizations, including schools, must lead many directly beneath them in order to lead the rest. To others, leadership is at its best when it is distributed throughout a workplace, a classroom, or a school.

In education, teacher leadership emerges and exists among these competing principles and beliefs. Teacher leadership also rests on acknowledgment that no matter how high-handed or finely tuned the implementation of any reform might be, it will ultimately have no significant impact if teachers do not understand it, do not agree with it, or (because of limited time, resources, or skill) are unable to execute it. Behind the classroom door, in front of their own students, teachers are more powerful than the most senior policymakers.

Teacher leadership is, at one level, an inescapable reality. All teachers already are leaders of students, of people large and small. By design or default, teachers also are leaders of change, whether they promote it, support it, resist it, or ignore it. The question is, therefore, not whether teacher leadership is needed, but whether this leadership can and should extend in deliberate and positive ways to include the adults inside and outside individual schools.

This important volume from Kappa Delta Pi, an international society that truly honors the best of teachers and teaching, embraces the idea that leadership is shared and extends beyond the classroom. *The Power of Teacher Leaders* brings together current research on teacher leadership and sets out the ways that teacher leaders can and do become engaged with areas such as curriculum, special education integration, university–school partnerships, coaching and mentoring, and innovation and reform. Written accessibly in a way that practicing professionals will enjoy, the chapters are grounded in a clear body of literature and solid research. *The Power of Teacher Leaders* highlights some of the best of what is known about teacher leadership among experienced and emerging scholars in the field.

One of the most significant themes running throughout the book is the importance of professional culture among teachers in determining whether and how teacher leadership emerges in a formal or recognized sense. The impact of this culture is always evident in areas of work such as coaching and mentoring, leading professional learning communities, and even in the seemingly highly individualized domain of self-mentoring, as explored in Chapter 3 by Marsha L. Carr. The surrounding culture of teaching remains influential—even and especially when it does not actively support professional collaboration.

Professional culture has always had an impact on teachers' perspectives, practices, and beliefs. From the 1990s, though, schools and school systems around the globe began to act on the evidence of the benefits of teacher collaboration. Deliberate efforts were made to establish professional communities where teachers worked together to inquire about student learning topics and solve problems of professional practice. Strong professional learning communities, such as those described by Nathan Bond in Chapter 5, have clearly made a positive impact on student achievement. Many early communities, however, were micromanaged by school principals who dictated the goals and focus and also drove the details of professional conversations—especially in relation to analyses of student achievement data. In these instances, teachers were given little or no opportunity to take the lead, and collegiality was mostly contrived (Hargreaves, 2003).

Today, we can point to many examples of successful teacher collaborations led by classroom teachers. In Chapter 1 of *The Power of Teacher Leaders,* Ann Lieberman describes three programs in which teachers lead in formal and informal ways. In one example, she records how many thousands of teachers in Ontario, Canada, worked in partnership with their union and government to instigate innovations in their own schools and share them with colleagues across the province.

Quality teachers who lead and collaborate are deliverers of high-quality teaching. Individuals of this caliber are characteristic of high-performance school systems. They make up the *human capital* in teaching—the many individual teachers with good university degrees, prepared in strong university programs, and with high levels of knowledge and skill (Mourshed, Chijioke, & Barber, 2010; OECD, 2011). Official accounts of teacher quality, however, tend to underemphasize the presence and impact of a second kind of capital on teaching—*social capital* (Leana, 2011). Social capital refers to the quality that teachers produce together through shared trust and effective collaboration, and its benefits appear to outweigh even those of human capital.

Quality social capital among teachers is closely related to educational success, even though social capital may take different forms in various cultures and systems. Teachers lead and collaborate with colleagues in many different ways, and they assume a variety of roles, many of which are explored throughout the chapters of *The Power of Teacher Leaders*. Moreover, quality teachers aspire to assume these leadership roles. A recent Metlife® survey revealed that large numbers of teachers in the United States do not want to be principals but are hungry for leadership opportunities (Markow & Pieters, 2012). After years of overtesting and standardization that have tried to bypass the principal's and the teacher's influence by prescribing the instruction, teacher leadership matters now more than ever.

While the standards are prompting some overburdened administrators to simply download curricula from one another's states, teachers in other schools and school districts are combining their knowledge and leadership to develop new units of work that suit their students and fit the standards. Opportunities for teachers to lead are presenting themselves. More and more U.S. cities and regions are starting to countenance a strategy of school turnaround that does not depend on top-down intervention teams composed of outsiders, but uses networks of school principals and teachers committed and also funded to assist one another and assume responsibility for the success of children in everyone's school, not just in their own.

These are genuine efforts to elevate the teaching profession, as cycles of imposed and contradictory reforms have driven good teachers from the profession and discouraged new ones from entering it. At the top, bureaucrats are still reluctant to give teaching back to teachers and enable them to exercise collective autonomy in their work. But on the ground, in the United States and globally, teacher leadership is emerging as the best and most honorable way to provide equity and excellence for all students, by galvanizing the collective abilities, the shared professional capital of the people who know these students best and care for them the most—our teachers.

The Power of Teacher Leaders is therefore an incredibly timely book by authors who come from the teaching profession, have the highest regard for it, know how to work closely within it, and also are uncompromising in delivering the highest quality teaching for all students. Through their combined efforts, they set out evidence of the high performance secured when teachers lead and work with other teachers, within their own schools and beyond, and everyone is committed to improving all students' well-being and success.

Andy Hargreaves
Thomas More Brennan Chair in Education
Lynch School of Education
Boston College

References

Hargreaves, A. (2003). *Teaching in the knowledge society: Education in the age of insecurity.* New York, NY: Teachers College Press.

Leana, C. R. (2011, Fall). The missing link in school reform. *Stanford Social Innovation Review*, 30–35. Retrieved from www.ssireview.org/articles/entry/the_missing_link_in_school_reform

Markow, D., & Pieters, A. (2012, March). *The Metlife survey of the American teacher: Teachers, parents and the economy.* New York, NY: Metlife.

Mourshed, M., Chijioke, C., & Barber, M. (2010). *How the world's most improved school systems keep getting better.* London, UK: McKinsey & Company.

OECD. (2011). *Lessons from PISA for the United States: Strong performers and successful reformers in education.* Paris, FR: OECD Publishing. doi: 10.1787/9789264096660-en

PREFACE

The genesis of this book came when two areas of my professional life merged. The first area pertains to my work as a professor and researcher at Texas State University. Since 2006, I have taught a graduate course to a group of outstanding practicing teachers in a school district near my university. The course, titled Teacher Leadership, is the first course in a specialized graduate program intended to help the teachers become teacher leaders on their home campuses. Since the first time that I taught the course, I have been impressed with the high caliber of the teachers and the district. They are truly remarkable! In an age when the teaching profession seems to be under attack from all sides, this district serves as a fortress of hope for other educators. The district's administrators regard classroom teachers as the most important component in a child's education and respect them for their knowledge, experience, work ethic, and ingenuity. Working with these teachers is an incredible honor. As I developed the course, I noticed gaps in the scholarly literature. It seemed that quite a few publications regarding teacher leadership were anecdotal articles that offered occasional glimpses into the impact of teacher leaders. My search left me wanting a book that would provide a more scholarly and critical examination of teacher leadership.

The second area relates to my service on the Executive Council of Kappa Delta Pi (KDP), International Honor Society in Education. While teaching my courses at Texas State University, I also was serving as the president of the organization. The other leaders on the Council and I regularly faced the challenge of helping our members, who included both preservice and inservice teachers, to become more positive forces in their schools, in their communities, and in the teaching profession as a whole. We wanted to empower teachers. We wanted them to be proactive, instead of reactive, to the nonstop challenges they faced. What emerged from our discussions was a series of initiatives aimed at helping teachers to become agents of positive change. Working closely with the KDP Executive Director, we launched iLead, a one-day workshop that would introduce KDP members to teacher leadership and equip them with some useful knowledge and skills related to leadership. The organization also granted me the authority to form a commission to examine the issue of teacher leadership from multiple perspectives and offer a reasoned voice in educational discussions. This book brings together these experts to share their insights about teacher leadership.

—Nathan Bond

ACKNOWLEDGMENTS

I want to thank the practicing teachers whom I have taught in my graduate course on teacher leadership. You have inspired me through your words and actions to lead where I can. I also want to thank Drs. Jennifer Battle and Emily Summers, my colleagues at Texas State University, for offering detailed and insightful feedback on the chapter proposals. Your friendship and collegiality mean a lot to me. I am grateful to my graduate students, Marc Alpert, Kyndra Bowerman, Maggie Camarillo, Michelle Crain, Isaac Lim, and Jeff Nixon, for reviewing some of the proposals. You all are the reason that I teach. My sincerest thanks go to Kathleen Magor for reading early drafts of the book and suggesting specific ways to improve each chapter. Finally, words cannot express how appreciative I am of Kathie-Jo Arnoff, the Director of Publications at Kappa Delta Pi, and Faye Snodgress, the Executive Director of Kappa Delta Pi, for giving me the opportunity to edit this book and then working closely with me to ensure that it was of the highest quality. You and Kappa Delta Pi have played such an integral role in my life as an educator. Thank you!

INTRODUCTION

Nathan Bond

Teacher leadership is not a new idea. In fact, it has been around for a long time. In their sociological studies of the teaching profession, Waller in 1932 and later Lortie in 1975 noted the informal ways that teachers serve as leaders in schools. Scholars often mark the school reform movement of the 1980s as the time when teacher leadership rose to prominence as a field of study. Working independently in 1986, the Holmes Group and the Carnegie Forum on Education and Economy sought ways to raise the status of teaching and make it more professional. As part of their solution, both groups proposed a ladder system for teachers, with the top rung occupied by what they respectively called "career professionals" and "lead teachers." Teachers at these highest levels would remain in the classroom and assume various responsibilities in the school.

Since the 1980s, there has been an increasingly steady stream of journal articles and books on teacher leadership. The most frequently cited experts include Lieberman (1988), Wasley (1991), Barth (2001), Lieberman and Miller (2004), York-Barr and Duke (2004), and Danielson (2006). The Teacher Leadership Exploratory Consortium released the teacher leadership standards in 2011 to codify, promote, and support teacher leadership as a way to transform schools for the 21st century.

In all of these publications, scholars have defined teacher leadership, proposed models and guidelines for preparing preservice and inservice teachers as leaders, reviewed the published literature, and recommended practical ways for teachers to lead. *The Power of Teacher Leaders: Their Roles, Influence, and Impact* builds on the previous scholarship and contributes to the evolving field. The authors in this collection identify some of the many ways that teachers are leading and begin to examine critically the impact of teacher leaders' efforts on schools and children.

The book is divided into three parts. In Part I, Becoming a Teacher Leader, the authors describe ways that teachers can become leaders in their schools and ways that aspiring teacher leaders can develop the knowledge, skills, and dispositions for the role. The authors are distinguished scholars who share their unique insights and firsthand experiences with teacher leadership. They represent various viewpoints as a distinguished researcher and writer in the field, a professor of a university-level graduate program on teacher leadership, a provider of professional development for inservice teachers, and a public school administrator who worked with practicing teacher leaders.

Part II, Roles of Teacher Leaders, highlights some of the many roles in which teachers can serve as leaders. The roles cover a broad spectrum ranging, for example, from professional developer of inservice teachers to mentor of preservice teachers, from first-year teacher leader to nationally board certified teacher with many years of experience, and from teacher leader as reformer of a school district to reformer of the education profession. The authors in this section are experienced researchers and teacher leaders in their own right. They weave together the previously published scholarship with their critical examination of present cases of teacher leaders to offer practical advice for educators who want to serve in this role in the future.

Part III explores the influence and impact of teachers who lead. Although each chapter in the book includes a section on the impact of teacher leaders, the chapters in the last part of the book delve more deeply into the subject. These authors, all of whom are experienced researchers and thinkers in the field, provide readers with various ways to measure teacher leadership, whether exploring our conscience for the moral reasons for leading, questioning the results of our teaching, or measuring our efforts using quantitative measures. They also challenge us to look at the impact of teacher leaders on new teachers, colleagues, and the communities where teacher leaders work. Of course, the focus for all teacher leaders is to improve the learning experiences of our K–12 students, and the authors emphasize this point in each chapter.

The book is designed to give readers representing a wide audience maximum flexibility in their approach to the material. Colleagues who are new to teacher leadership may want to start at the beginning and move sequentially through each chapter. Experienced teacher leaders who want to explore a new role or who want to increase their impact may want to start with specific chapters that pique their interest. University professors of teacher leadership courses are advised to work sequentially through the first part, give students a choice in what they read in the second part, and then work with students as a group for the third part. A study guide with questions and in-class activities accompanies the book and helps readers to think more deeply about the information in each chapter.

Teacher leadership is a fascinating topic. In my professional opinion, we have only begun to explore the possibilities of teacher leadership. This book captures what teacher leaders are currently doing and offers guidance for the future.

References

Barth, R. S. (2001). Teacher leader. *Phi Delta Kappan, 82*(6), 443–449.

Carnegie Forum on Education and Economy. (1986). *A nation prepared: Teachers for the 21st century. The report of the task force on teaching as a profession.* New York, NY: Carnegie Corporation.

Danielson, C. (2006). *Teacher leadership that strengthens professional practice.* Alexandria, VA: ASCD.

Holmes Group. (1986). *Tomorrow's teachers: A report of the Holmes Group.* East Lansing, MI: Author.

Lieberman, A. (Ed.). (1988). *Building a professional culture in schools.* New York, NY: Teachers College Press.

Lieberman, A., & Miller, L. (2004). *Teacher leadership.* San Francisco, CA: Jossey-Bass.

Lortie, D. C. (1975). *Schoolteacher.* Chicago, IL: University of Chicago Press.

Teacher Leadership Exploratory Consortium. (2011). *Teacher leader model standards.* Carrboro, NC: Center for Teaching Quality. Retrieved from http://www.teachingquality.org/content/teacher-leader-model-standards

Waller, W. W. (1932). *The sociology of teaching.* New York, NY: Wiley.

Wasley, P. A. (1991). *Teachers who lead: The rhetoric of reform and the realities of practice.* New York, NY: College Teachers Press.

York-Barr, J., & Duke, K. (2004). What do we know about teacher leadership? Findings from two decades of scholarship. *Review of Educational Research, 74*(3), 255–316. doi: 10.3102/00346543074003255

PART I

Becoming a Teacher Leader

1

TEACHERS AT THE FOREFRONT

Learning to Lead

Ann Lieberman

Teachers have assumed both formal and informal leadership roles in schools and have been studied by scholars in these roles for more than two decades. Several important collections of research on teacher leadership (Smylie & Denny, 1990; York-Barr & Duke, 2004), as well as some interesting data on a variety of teacher leadership programs, are currently available. This research and data show that teacher leadership is an important idea that is gaining popularity throughout the world. In spite of the progress, though, we still need to understand *how* teachers learn to lead and the different kinds of *organizational conditions* that are developed as teachers assume a professional orientation for leadership in mostly bureaucratic school settings (Talbert, 2010).

The purpose of this chapter is to analyze three programs that have created organizational arrangements that support teacher leaders as they learn to negotiate the inevitable tensions of this new role. All of these programs create opportunities for leading and provide unique arrangements for teacher learning. All have a core set of identifiable strategies, tools, and structures, and all are able to disseminate their work to different contexts without losing the essence of their programs. By looking at these programs in some depth, I hope to showcase how teachers engage in particular types of activities and what it takes to support them as they are learning to lead. These programs can help us understand what it takes to organize and support teachers to supplant a haphazard way of simply announcing new teacher leadership roles without the necessary intellectual, emotional, and organizational supports needed to do the job well. The programs are the National Writing Project (NWP), the New Teacher Center (NTC), and the Teacher Learning and Leadership Program (TLLP). The first two are primarily American, while the last is Canadian.

The National Writing Project

The National Writing Project was started in 1974 by Jim Gray, who had been a secondary English teacher for many years. Gray's principal periodically provided professional development workshops led by outside consultants for the teachers in his school. After attending one of these events, Gray commented that the English department at his school already was doing many interesting things in their classrooms. Why couldn't the professional development be done by the teachers themselves? During the summer of 1974, Gray became a supervisor of student teachers at the University of California Berkeley and garnered some support from his administrators to start the Bay Area Institute, which focused on the teaching of writing (Lieberman & Wood, 2003).

He invited 29 colleagues to attend the first summer institute, which was held on the Berkeley campus. He and his fellow teachers now had an opportunity to think differently about professional development. The big idea guiding the development of the institute was that *"teacher knowledge was to be the starting point for learning"* (Lieberman & Wood, 2003, p. 7, emphasis in original). This idea, along with several other propositions, became known as the core principles of the Bay Area Institute, which subsequently developed into the NWP. The propositions are the following:

- Teachers teach one another their best practices.
- Teachers write and present their work for feedback and critique.
- Teachers read, discuss, and analyze research, reforms, and other literature during the institute.
- Teachers form a "site," which is a group of local teachers in partnership with a college or university.

The first site attracted immediate attention, and within a year or two, there were as many as 18 sites in California. NWP started out as a way for teachers to share professional development with colleagues and then evolved over the next 30 years into a group of teachers devoted to improving student writing. Despite the removal of federal funds, there are still 200 sites throughout the United States.

From 1998 through 2000, Diane Wood at Towson University and I studied two sites of the NWP in an effort to get an inside view of how the learning took place and to understand firsthand the kinds of conditions created by the NWP that made teachers describe going to the summer institute as "magical" (Lieberman & Wood, 2003, p. 14).

Social Practices

After sitting through two summer institutes, one in Los Angeles at the University of California at Los Angeles (UCLA) and another at Oklahoma State University (OSU) in Stillwater, we had collected a lot of data. UCLA was an older site, and

OSU a relatively new one. One was clearly in an urban area and the other a more rural and suburban site. We called the important ideas we observed a set of *social practices.*

When brought together in the institute setting, teachers literally changed the way they thought about their teaching, one another, and themselves. They gained a professional learning community that for many became a lifelong connection. Also, for many, the professional development activities became so powerful that they not only changed the way they taught in their own classrooms, but also felt empowered to provide this type of learning experience for their peers. Many became teacher consultants (TCs) who took responsibility for professional development, not only in their own schools, but in their districts as well.

This approach to learning leadership clearly showed the power of "learning by doing," an idea first written about by John Dewey almost a century ago. During the institutes, we witnessed the following social practices:

- approaching each colleague as a potentially valuable contributor;
- honoring teacher knowledge;
- creating public forums for teacher sharing, dialogue, and critique;
- turning ownership of learning over to learners;
- situating human learning in practice and relationships;
- providing multiple entry points into the learning community;
- guiding reflection on teaching through reflection on learning;
- sharing leadership;
- promoting a stance of inquiry; and
- encouraging a reconceptualization of professional identity and linking it to a professional community.

What we learned was that these social practices, when integrated into a three- to five-week institute, were so powerful because the teachers in the institute, rather than an outside developer, were the knowledge givers. All teachers were accepted no matter why they had come or from where and, in a short time, a community developed in which teachers were both learners and leaders in a variety of activities. As quickly as the second day, some teachers were teaching their best lesson to a group, while others were writing, reading their writing aloud, and receiving feedback. At the same time, still other teachers were discussing books and research articles they had read. It slowly felt as if the teachers, rather than the directors, were leading the institute.

The participants were the teachers of others some of the time and learners at other times. There were experiences where the teacher could be a leader in the morning teaching his or her best lesson and a learner in the afternoon listening to a presentation or reading research. This trading of roles was both exciting and educative! Teachers clearly learned that engagement is a powerful form of teaching. More than that, teachers felt respected, trusted, and supported in what they had learned as teachers!

Going public with their teaching became the norm of the institute, and teaching one another and giving feedback to colleagues was at the heart of the days and weeks in the institute. Many vowed on the spot that they were going to create such activities in their own classrooms. It was not difficult to see that teachers realized the enormous power of engaging learners and building a community rather than directly teaching them as individuals.

From Institute to Classroom

In our study, we visited three teachers at each site: one brand new teacher who had recently completed the summer institute and two who had taken it a while ago. We did indeed see that the teachers used many of the strategies they had learned in the summer institute. We realized that we got close to how the teachers were learning and that the summer institute with its social practices was clearly the organizing strategy. It worked in Los Angeles as well as in Stillwater, and history has shown that the core ideas travel well without being distorted by differences in context.

We also realized that, in addition to being armed with the social practices, the teachers felt that their knowledge was important, respected, and honored for its complexity and authenticity. The fact that *their* lessons and *their* writing and *their* discussions of books and research were central was of critical importance to their learning and the development of leadership.

The New Teacher Center

More than 15 years ago, in 1998, Ellen Moir, who had been a K–12 teacher in Santa Cruz, California, imagined that there had to be a better way to support new teachers for their first few years. Many new teachers often quit early in their careers because they struggle, alone, to figure out how to improve and learn how to teach their students well—regardless of their students' socioeconomic backgrounds. The goal to support new teachers became the centerpiece of the New Teacher Center (NTC), which specializes in the induction years, or the first two years of a teacher's life. Moir was an important participant in the policy discussions as the state of California voted to mentor teachers during these years.

Moir and her colleagues built a program that, like the NWP, has some core pieces that have developed over time. Since the founding of the NTC, these core programmatic structures have been introduced to different districts throughout the United States (Moir, Barlin, Gless, & Miles, 2009). Over the years, the program has developed in an interesting way. Not only have the core pieces improved, but Moir involved Susan Hanson, a researcher, to learn what mentors struggle with as they develop into teacher leaders.

Hanson interviewed mentors for their first four years to find out how they were supporting their mentees. Janet Gless, one of the founders of the NTC, and

I were invited to look with Hanson at the data from these years and, together, we wrote a book about mentors as they learn to lead (Lieberman, Hanson, & Gless, 2012). These data taught us that mentors negotiate a series of tensions as they learn to lead. These tensions include building a new identity, developing trusting relationships, accelerating teacher development, mentoring in challenging contexts, and learning leadership skills.

For mentors, these themes represent the *how* of how they learn to lead. Mentors struggle with what it means to teach someone else how to teach even though they are selected because they have been excellent teachers themselves. Somehow, mentors feel confident about what they have learned from their classroom experience; yet when they are faced with learning about the cultures of the many new schools where they will be mentoring, they become uneasy about claiming their new identity as mentors.

Because most mentors in the United States work in several different schools, they must learn how to build trust with principals, veteran teachers, and other personnel in the schools, not to mention their mentees. Mentors very quickly learn that they must play a supportive role with their mentees, who are facing increased demands in this era of school reform. Building trust among the various players in the schools is a corollary, but a necessary one, to their central work of helping novices learn how to teach.

Another main job for mentors is to learn to accelerate the development of their mentees. Identifying a starting point for where to begin helping the mentee requires sensitivity and can be difficult when the mentee has a number of problems. At the NTC, mentors learn to start with the problems as the mentee describes them. In the face of different subject areas, school cultures, and personalities, even getting the mentee to describe the problems can be complicated.

Many mentors work in dysfunctional schools. Supporting beginning teachers in depressing situations with nonsupportive principals or fellow teachers not happily engaged with their students is an incredible challenge. Somehow, the mentors must figure out how to support their mentees and make the profession worth the struggle, despite the difficult context.

Their positions as mentors put them in places where they must learn to broker resources for their mentees, support their mentees in difficult situations not of their making, and help create communities of practice where their mentees can learn to teach as the mentors learn to lead. Supporting, organizing, negotiating, teaching, and collaborating are parts of leadership that mentors learn in the NTC (Lieberman et al., 2012).

Mentor Academy Series

What makes the NTC a significant program is that it has a number of organizational tools and structures that have been developed over time. These are as important to the mentors and their leadership as they are to the mentees who are learning to teach. As with those of the NWP, the tools support the mentor's growth as a leader. As the NTC has grown, so has the sophistication and importance of the ideas that lie at the center of the support for teachers during their induction years.

Mentors use what the NTC calls the Formative Assessment System during the development of the relationship of mentors to their mentees. Within this system is a most important organizational structure in the NTC, called the Mentor Academy Series, actually a curriculum that has been developed over many years. This series of sessions helps mentors with a complex array of practices that they need to understand and internalize as they work with a variety of mentees in different contexts throughout the United States.

The Mentor Academy Series is divided into three years consisting of eight three-day sessions during the first two years, followed by three two-day sessions in year three. In the first year, mentors learn how to *inquire into practice*. These sessions consist of understanding what is meant by instructional mentoring and formative assessment. The mentors learn how to assess growth in the mentees while they help them deepen their practice. During the second year, academy sessions are concerned with *equity in education*. In these sessions, mentors learn about language development and how to reach *all* students. In the third year, mentors learn how to inquire into their own practices and how to read and inquire into research.

Formative Assessment Tools

A number of tools have been created by NTC that serve as part of the Formative Assessment System. They include the following:

- **The Collaborative Assessment Log (CAL).** This helps the mentor guide the structure of the session he or she will hold with the mentee.
- **Assessing Student Work (ASW).** This shows the mentee how to measure progress when examining student work.
- **Co-assessing Teacher Practice in Core Capabilities.** This helps the teacher assess his or her own practice and identify the strengths as well as next steps in improving practice. (Reference the New Teacher website at www.newteachercenter.org for more details.)

Helping mentors learn the complexities of how to organize their approach to their mentees and attend to teachers in their first two years is an incredibly complex process. The mentors not only are learning how to approach new teachers and slowly helping them learn to teach well, but also are learning how to negotiate different school cultures and work with principals and veteran teachers. Mentors themselves are moving from being excellent teachers to holding leadership roles in sometimes fractious and complicated schools. Learning how to mentor successfully demands a serious curriculum with built-in supports (Moir et al., 2009).

The NTC is successful precisely because it has a *core* curriculum that embraces both an organizational and a curricular structure as mentors learn leadership and their mentees learn to teach well.

Whereas the NWP has a summer institute that serves as the core organizing structure, the NTC has the Formative Assessment System with its Mentor Academy Series and opportunities to learn in a community of practice. Each program has shown that the core ideas can be disseminated and learned in other districts, states, and now even in international settings. Each supports teachers with a core set of knowledge and practice. The final program we will look at is different from the first two in that the learning is self-directed, while the supports are developed and run by a collaboration of the Ministry of Education and the Ontario Teachers Federation.

Teacher Learning and Leadership Program

The Teacher Learning and Leadership Program (TLLP) is much younger than either of the two programs discussed previously. This program attempts to provide opportunities for both learning and leadership of teachers. In 2005, the Ministry of Education in Toronto and the Ontario Teachers Federation (OTF), which is comprised of several teacher unions, established a Working Table on Teacher Development. The new Minister of Education announced that teachers are professionals, and the Working Table created an opportunity for the teachers and ministry officials together to develop a program of teacher learning. The group met periodically for two years and developed a proposal for teachers to learn and take leadership positions.

In 2007, the first TLLP was announced to the public. Its goals were straightforward:

- support experienced teachers to undertake self-directed professional development;
- help teachers develop leadership skills in sharing their learning and spreading exemplary practices; and
- facilitate knowledge exchange by working and collaborating with others.

Professional development was to be initiated by and run by teachers. Teachers who wanted to participate were to write a short proposal of their intention to organize professional development in their own schools or within their province. Suggestions were made by those who represented the Ministry and the OTF to encourage collaboration with another person or a team, but teachers essentially would be in charge of their own learning. All proposals were required to include a budget of up to $10,000 for one year's efforts. If the program needed more financial support, the door was open for continuous discussion during the year.

Developing a Proposal

To gain approval, the proposal was required to address five characteristics put forth by the Working Table. The characteristics included the following:

- coherence built on the three Rs of respect, responsibility, and results;
- attention to adult learning styles including choice, collaboration, and differentiation;
- goal orientation that was job-embedded and connected to student learning;
- sustainability with supports over time; and
- evidence-based stance built upon current research as well as formal and informal data to be collected.

Choosing a Topic

Topics for proposals could include such areas as teaching and learning strategies across the content areas, innovative approaches of all kinds, community partnerships, technology integration, professional learning communities, competencies and strategies for teaching in minority contexts, and other ideas created by teachers. Over time, the funding became more flexible. Technology equipment can now be funded as well as other resources needed in the professional development program being proposed. Also, the proposal requires an explanation of the quality of the idea, the proposer's background and experience, the idea's potential and impact on students, and a plan for sharing outcomes.

Gaining Approval

A school board committee in Ontario involving a board member and a member of OTF reads and selects at least two proposals for each board, which is like a district in the United States. The choices are then sent for final approval to the provincial representatives, who include a Ministry of Education representative and an OTF representative. After the awards are announced, teachers whose proposals were accepted are invited to the first of two gatherings to meet, learn, and start thinking about launching their project. About 100 to 125 awards are made each year.

Providing the Supports

After a cohort is selected, teachers are invited to the first conference, titled *Leadership Skills for Teachers,* which includes a few speakers, an introduction to the program, and a series of carousels that include budget knowledge, conflict resolution, project initiation, and more. Toward the end of the year, teachers are invited to the *Sharing the Learning Summit* to provide posters and any other demonstrations of their work. Teachers walk around the room, learn from one another, and get to see themselves in a growing community of teachers who have developed, organized, and run professional development in their schools and beyond.

Providing Research Evidence

To date, 600 projects have been developed, and 3,300 teachers in seven different cohorts have created and developed projects of all kinds. In 2012, a small research study on the TLLP (Campbell, Lieberman, & Yashkina, 2013) collected data on a few key questions that included:

- What is the value of TLLP for teachers?
- What can we learn about professional development organized the TLLP way?
- To what extent have the overall goals of TLLP been realized?
- What lessons can be learned so far?

In observing the events, interviewing both Ministry and OTF representatives, analyzing a percentage of the final reports (20%), and reviewing descriptive data, some important data were collected to answer these questions. (Reference the Stanford Center for Opportunity Policy in Education [SCOPE] website for the final report on TLLP [Campbell et al., 2013].)

Teachers overwhelmingly said that this form of professional development was important and meaningful in helping them learn as well as supporting them in learning how to organize professional development with their peers. The average number of people on a project team was approximately four. Of 302 projects, 53 were one-person projects even though the program encouraged teachers to work with others. In more than 85% of those projects in the first four cohorts, teachers worked with at least two people, and sometimes with a team. While the projects were teacher initiated, they were also aligned with school board and ministry priorities.

Organizational Supports for Teacher Leaders

Perhaps the most interesting support in the TLLP is that the Ministry of Education (the policymakers) and the OTF (representing practicing teachers) have truly collaborated on this program. The policies for the TLLP enable the growth and development of both learning and leadership. Both groups created the program, and both also facilitate, troubleshoot, and make themselves available for help throughout the year. The two large meetings, *Leadership Skills for Classroom Teachers* at the beginning of a project and *Sharing the Learning Summit* showcasing the completed projects, provide support that teachers rarely get. The teachers are given money, time, and support for self-directed learning and firsthand knowledge and practice in how to develop leadership. More than 95% of the participants reported that they were satisfied or very satisfied with these meetings.

Development of Teacher Leadership

In TLLP, the experience of actually organizing a project—figuring out how to create activities, materials, and structures for learning—all put the teachers in a position to learn. They must work with their peers to determine how to improve a particular area of the curriculum, find the time to meet, establish a way of working, find a focus for the work, and produce not only knowledge, but also a way of operationalizing it in practice. Many teachers for the first time learn how to spend money, keep within a budget, organize a scope of work that is doable in a year, create materials together and try them out in their classrooms, lead their peers in activities that push ideas forward, share these ideas with a growing number of teachers, and collaborate to improve in a given area. Some teachers are knowledgeable in a given area and want to do more, while others pick areas where they need or want to know and do more. The respect and dignity that teachers feel in the TLLP is palpable.

This program, like the NWP, provides opportunities for the teachers who write successful proposals to learn leadership by actually being leaders and by organizing their peers to participate together in some improvement area. In the study mentioned earlier (Campbell et al., 2013), teachers overwhelmingly reported that this program provides powerful professional development, and many also spoke about their opportunities to learn leadership. So far, the goals of the program have been realized.

There have been challenges, too. Most teachers state that there is not enough time to do the work, but many figure out how to organize their time so that they can teach and also do the project. Many learn that some teachers are resistant to change and that it is more difficult than they thought to gain other teachers' commitment to engage in a professional development effort even though it is sponsored by one of their peers. Despite these challenges, the program appears to be a raging success.

What Can We Learn From These Development Efforts?

All three of these programs put an emphasis on the teacher as primary learner even though student learning is the ultimate goal. The NWP does it by having the institute focus on teachers as writers as well as teachers teaching other teachers their best lesson and generally learning together. The NTC puts its emphasis on the new teacher during his or her first two years, but focuses much time on the mentor as leader, constantly using problems encountered in the field, even as the Mentor Academy focuses on building a system and tools for the mentor to use with the mentees. The TLLP focuses on teachers as the professional developers. The programs are their ideas, their organization of the ideas, and their mode of working on professional development—whether it be creating materials, learning technology, advancing knowledge in a given area, or organizing their communities.

All three of these programs also support teachers even though they give the support in different ways. The NWP offers the summer institute, and in all areas where there is a site, there are meetings throughout the year to keep people connected. The NTC offers the Formative Assessment System, which systematically teaches new mentors even as they are working with their mentees. Teachers in the NTC are constantly learning about new tools to use in their work. The TLLP provides money to enact a proposal and builds confidence in teachers who write successful proposals to do professional development in their own schools. The partnership of the Ministry and OTF and the boards are all involved in support of these projects and, when troubleshooting is necessary, all are available for help.

Ultimately, what we learn is there are many different ways to support teachers in their efforts to improve and eventually take on leadership responsibilities. A key idea is for teachers to have opportunities to learn in the practice of *doing* professional development or mentoring or writing as they are being supported by outside knowledge. In this way, experiences of inside knowledge of classroom and school practice are mated with outside knowledge of research.

In the process of paying attention to teacher learning *first,* teachers feel respected and raise their expectations of themselves beyond *I am just a teacher* and get opportunities to think and act differently. It is not only about their own learning, but about their work with others as well as their growing leadership responsibilities and the possibilities of building a community with their peers.

These programs provide us with a different way of thinking about professional development, the growth of teachers as leaders, and the kinds of organizational support that must accompany real changes in schools and classrooms. The successes of these programs lead us to think hard about *how* teachers learn and the variety of organizational conditions that must accompany good and lasting teacher development efforts. The impact of these three programs shows us examples of *how* teachers learn to lead and of the different kinds of conditions that support their new roles and responsibilities as teacher leaders. Each program has helped both novice and experienced teachers to become teacher leaders, and the success of the programs is measured in their growing acceptance by additional districts and states.

References

Campbell, C., Lieberman, A., & Yashkina, A. (2013). *Teacher learning and leadership program: Research report.* Stanford, CA: Stanford Center for Opportunity Policy in Education. Retrieved from http://edpolicy.stanford.edu/publications/pubs/751

Lieberman, A., Hanson, S., & Gless, J. (2012). *Mentoring teachers: Navigating the real-world tensions.* San Francisco, CA: Jossey-Bass.

Lieberman, A., & Wood, D. R. (2003). *Inside the National Writing Project: Connecting network learning and classroom teaching.* New York, NY: Teachers College Press.

Moir, E., Barlin, D., Gless, J., & Miles, J. (2009). *New teacher mentoring: Hopes and promise for improving teacher effectiveness.* Cambridge, MA: Harvard Education Press.

Smylie, M. A., & Denny, J. W. (1990). Teacher leadership: Tensions and ambiguities in organizational perspective. *Educational Administration Quarterly, 26*(3), 235–259. doi: 10.1177/0013161X90026003003

Talbert, J. E. (2010). Professional learning communities at the crossroads: How systems hinder or engender change. In A. Hargreaves, A. Lieberman, M. Fullan, & D. Hopkins (Eds.), *Second international handbook of educational change* (pp. 555–571). New York, NY: Springer International Handbooks of Education.

York-Barr, J., & Duke, K. (2004). What do we know about teacher leadership? Findings from two decades of scholarship. *Review of Educational Research, 74*(3), 255–316. doi: 10.3102/00346543074003255

2

STEPPING UP

How Teachers' Definitions of Teacher Leadership Change

Robin Haskell McBee

The work of teachers lies at the core of effective learning and academic growth, and teacher leaders often set the pace and standard for other teachers. Productive change in schools emerges naturally from the daily practice of outstanding teachers who are willing to share their successful practices with other teachers who, in turn, are willing to learn from them. This organic and often informal approach to field-based teacher development and educational change is critical to promoting meaningful improvements in students' social, emotional, and academic performance.

In the scholarly literature, teacher leaders are typically recognized for their success with students, their effectiveness in helping to lead new initiatives, and their strength as mentors to other teachers (Danielson, 2006; Lieberman & Miller, 2005; Martin, 2007; Morehead & Sledge, 2006; Patterson & Patterson, 2004; Reeves, 2008). Their strong content and pedagogical expertise, interpersonal skills and credibility among peers and administrators, child-centered orientation, and willingness to do what it takes for students to learn are consistently noted qualities. Teacher leaders are seen as problem solvers who can step outside of their own classroom perspectives, view things from a whole-school orientation, and collaborate effectively in teams. They are pivotal to the educational change process. Yet it is the informality of the teacher leader role that makes it work. As Danielson (2006) wrote, "Teacher leaders don't gain their authority through an assigned role or position; rather they earn it through their work with both their students and their colleagues" (p. 1). Teachers who are viewed as leaders are go-to anchors for school principals and other teachers. Patterson and Patterson (2004) explained, "[I]n tough times, teachers turn to teacher leaders for help—and teacher leaders rise to the occasion" (p. 78).

Since teacher leaders play a critical role in moving change initiatives forward successfully, and in strengthening teaching and learning generally, it is incumbent on the education profession to find ways to develop greater leadership skills on the part of more teachers. There are various means of cultivating teacher leaders that range from initial teacher preparation to school-based professional development to university graduate level programs. Graduate programs in teacher leadership, such as the one that is the focus of this chapter, acknowledge the key role that teacher leaders play in affecting needed educational change. Furthermore, this program, in particular, promotes the development of new teacher leaders who wish to help lead change efforts from the classroom rather than assume administrative leadership roles. The purpose of this chapter is to examine how notions of teacher leadership evolve for the practicing teachers who take part in this program and the implications of that evolution for strengthening teaching and learning.

Description of Program and Students

Practicing teachers, who are the focus of this chapter and who are graduate students at a mid-Atlantic state university's Master of Education in Teacher Leadership program, pursue two threads of study: a four- to six-week course sequence in a chosen academic area of specialization, for which they earn a Certificate of Graduate Study (COGS), and a core of six courses that closely examines and modifies their own classroom practices to reflect learning community theory, theories of learning, curriculum development, action research, and educational change. As they progress through this series of master level courses, they are asked to

- delve deeper into an area of content teaching (mathematics, reading, writing, science, history) or pedagogy (educational technology, special education, English as a second language);
- experiment with innovative approaches designed to increase student engagement and motivation through responsive practices;
- develop leadership skills in curriculum development and instruction;
- foster and strengthen classroom and professional learning communities;
- analyze their classroom practices;
- conduct action research; and
- pursue change within their schools and districts.

At the end of the program, the teachers complete a reflective portfolio in which they analyze their progress in meeting the standards and indicators that guide the program. They also present a 20-minute slide show on their emerging leadership skills.

The program has operated for 8 years, with the first students graduating in 2008. Twenty students complete the 2-year program each year, with 100 having already graduated from the program and 40 students currently enrolled (numbers are approximate). Eighty-five percent of the students are practicing teachers with 1 or more years of classroom experience, some having up to 15 years of experience. Over the last 5 years, a special grant-funded program has also included four beginning teachers each year who were part of an Urban Teacher Residency Program, and they completed their coursework concurrently with a full-time teaching internship. Because the core courses and some of the COGS courses are offered completely online, the program draws early childhood, elementary, middle school, and high school teachers from publicly and privately funded schools, including charter and parochial, in urban, suburban, and rural communities across the state and from neighboring states.

Three years ago, a program evaluation process was initiated to examine the impact of the program on teachers' definitions of teacher leadership. The teachers were asked to provide their definitions of teacher leadership in application essays. Then, as they completed the program, they were again asked to write essays defining teacher leadership and discussing how it is manifested in their work. These two essays are two of the sources for data used in this chapter, along with a survey of current students and graduates.

Using these essays and a survey as data sources, this chapter examines the shifts that occur in the teachers' perspectives on teacher leadership from entrance to completion of this graduate program on teacher leadership and then in the years following graduation. After considering the changes reflected in the data and their implications, the chapter concludes by questioning whether these changes are sufficient to effect meaningful transformation in the education of students.

The Study and Its Participants

A survey consisting of open-ended and selected-response questions was e-mailed to 80 graduates and 30 students who were currently enrolled in the program. To increase the survey response rate, the request to participate in the study was sent four times across a 4-month period.

The survey's two open-ended questions asked the teachers to describe how they feel their program studies helped them become more effective classroom teachers and school or district leaders and what they are doing differently as a result of their graduate studies. The survey also asked the teachers to look at a list of teacher leader characteristics and check off those that applied to their work now but would not have applied to their work before their participation in the program. The list of characteristics was developed from an earlier pilot study as well as from the literature on teacher leadership. The list included student-centeredness, building learning communities, content knowledge, differentiation, advocacy for students, use of new ideas and innovations, greater confidence, increased technology use, reflectivity, willingness to learn more, passion, speaking up more at meetings, taking action to change and improve circumstances, being asked by the principal to lead efforts, increased awareness of school and district concerns, collaborating with others, mentoring others, problem solving, motivating others, and being someone to whom others come for advice and help.

Thirteen graduates and seven current students returned consent forms to participate and use their essays; however, one graduate and one current student did not complete the survey, so there were a total of 18 surveys. Because of when they had completed the program, very few of these study participants had actually written the application essays, and not all had written the exit essays either. Therefore, only five application essays and ten exit essays were used for this study.

The 20 teachers in this study included current students and graduates from each year going back to 2008. All but one were from the public schools, and their teaching experiences ranged from beginning teacher residents to 10 years in the profession. Eight taught in urban settings, twelve in suburban settings. Five were high school teachers, six middle school, and nine elementary. The subject matter specializations included foreign language, English as a second language, physical education and health, science, English, social studies, and mathematics. The remainder of this chapter examines the themes and patterns that emerged from the pre- and post-program essays on teacher leadership and from the survey responses. The teachers' definitions of their leadership work at the beginning of the program, during the program, at the end of the program, and 1 to 5 years after graduation are considered. The analysis focuses on how these budding teacher leaders ventured into more and more leadership roles and what they said about how they see themselves as leaders at these four different points. These findings are also considered both in light of how teacher leaders are defined in the literature and in response to calls for teacher education programs to increase teacher leaders' sense of efficacy, influence, activism, and agency (Katzenmeyer & Moller, 2009; Neumann, Jones, & Webb, 2012) as they become vested agents of transformation and change.

Patterns and Trends in the Data

Three sources of qualitative data informed this study: pre-program essays, end-of-program essays, and surveys of current students and graduates 1 to 5 years after program completion. The data were coded using 30 teacher leader characteristics that had emerged from an earlier pilot study of program graduates combined with characteristics from the literature (Danielson, 2006; Lieberman & Miller, 2005; Martin, 2007; Morehead & Sledge, 2006; Reeves, 2008). After the analysis, these characteristics were distilled down to the 17 that occurred most frequently, which were then categorized by qualities, orientations, behavior, and actions. These 17 codes are presented in Table 2.1 for each of the four periods under study. The frequency is also presented in terms of percentage of respondents who mentioned the characteristic in their essays or surveys.

A more careful analysis comparing pre-program responses to graduates' responses reflects the potential long-term effects of the program. The characteristics of reflecting, becoming a go-to person for others, developing more confidence as a teacher and teacher leader, and speaking up about issues and concerns were not noted at all in pre-program essays. Yet they were noted by 75% to 100% of

TABLE 2.1 Code Frequency by Percentage of Respondents Mentioning at Different Stages

Code	Pre-Program (N = 5)	Current Students (N = 6)	End of Program (N = 10)	One- to Five-Year Graduates (N = 12)
Qualities				
Go-To Person	0	67%	20%	92%
Confidence	0	100%	50%	83%
Creative	40%	83%	90%	83%
Teaching Strength	40%	67%	100%	67%
Orientations				
Whole School/ District Perspective	20%	100%	60%	75%
Willing to Learn, Lifelong Learner	80%	33%	80%	8%
Behavior				
Reflects	0	83%	70%	100%
Differentiates	0	50%	70%	67%
Student-Centered Instruction	0	67%	30%	58%
Uses Data, Research	40%	67%	100%	17%
Actions				
Leads	20%	17%	60%	83%
Speaks Up	0	33%	20%	75%
Learning Community	0	83%	80%	67%
Collaborates	60%	83%	90%	67%
Acts	40%	83%	100%	67%
Mentors	80%	33%	30%	58%
Models	40%	33%	50%	8%

those who graduated in the last 1 to 5 years. These seem to be qualities and skills that are acquired and sharpened as teacher leaders become more and more comfortable with their growing expertise, their recognition of that expertise, and their shifting roles in sharing that expertise.

Conversely, two teacher leader qualities were mentioned much less frequently in the post-graduation essays than in the pre-program essays. Eighty percent of pre-program candidates noted mentoring and a willingness to learn or lifelong learning as important features of teacher leadership. Among the graduates, however, the number of respondents noting these two qualities dropped to 58% and 8% respectively. Apparently, those just beginning their study of teacher leadership, more so than those who have been leaders for a while, tend to view teacher leaders as mentors who collaborate and encourage learning. This finding makes sense in terms of the respondents' early teaching experiences having been formally mentored by a veteran teacher for the first 3 years of their teaching, a state- and union-backed mandate that establishes mentoring as a norm in the schools where these teachers work.

Large discrepancies sometimes appeared between end-of-program theme percentages and graduates' survey perspectives. For the numbers that went up, the change might be attributed to the fact that the survey offered a list of all codes that may have prompted respondents to select characteristics that they had not mentioned in the open-ended essay at the end of the program. For the numbers that went down, this might be attributed to the fact that the end-of-program essays were part of a larger task in which the candidates had to reflect on how they were meeting 8 standards and 34 indicators, thus prompting them to write about each of these topics as well as to focus much more on tasks and learning from the program courses. Once the active thinking about course work dissipated some, the teacher leaders may have been less likely to do or think about some of the things that were at the forefront of their minds at the end of their programmatic studies.

Changes in Views on Teacher Leadership

The data suggest that becoming a teacher leader in this graduate program is developmental. Teachers began with a cursory understanding of teacher leadership from what they had observed in their schools. Taking courses and experimenting with the application of concepts and insights gained in the program expanded and shifted that initial set of ideas. When asked at the end of the program to reflect on their learning and accomplishments in light of teacher leader standards that guide the program, the teachers had a wider set of personal experiences from which to draw and professional learning on which to base their comments. Once they moved well beyond courses, papers, and reflective assignments, and they were naturally implementing and further developing their notions of themselves as teacher leaders, there was a marked increase of comments that reflected many of the characteristics of teacher leaders that framed this study. Following is a more detailed consideration of the salient points that emerged for each of the four stages studied.

Views on Teacher Leadership at Program Entry

When teachers entered the graduate program in teacher leadership, they viewed teacher leaders as mentors who collaborated with others and acted as lifelong learners always open to learning new ideas. They saw leadership roles shaped by being members of a group and acquiring new ideas to bring back to colleagues. An elementary teacher explained in her admission essay:

> A teacher leader is someone who develops teaching processes that have never been tried before. It is also a person who is not afraid to take a risk in

different approaches to teaching. A teacher leader learns by trying and later teaches successful strategies to other staff members so that they can utilize them in their classroom.

Even though they mentioned improved teaching and trying new things in their classrooms, the details of building a learning community, student-centeredness, differentiation, and reflectivity were absent from their statements at that point. Confidence was not a quality that was discussed; nor did they indicate an expectation that they would speak up, lead groups, and become people to whom others might go for advice and help. These key aspects of teacher leadership were missing in the beginning.

Views on Teacher Leadership During the Program

At the point of completing their coursework, the teachers' definitions of teacher leadership expanded. Their survey descriptions of their own emerging leadership strengths included a greater confidence in their teaching skills. A high school teacher wrote, "I feel more confident and secure in my teaching role," while an elementary teacher explained, "My courses have helped me to feel more confident in taking on a role of a teacher leader among my colleagues to be a change agent." That confidence extended to educational views and an expanded understanding of educational issues beyond their own classrooms to whole-school and district-wide orientations. A middle school teacher described the changes in her thinking this way by saying, "I also think about the changes implemented by administration differently. I consider the need for the change from their perspective instead of solely focusing on the teacher's perspective."

Strong, innovative teaching with a student-centered, learning community focus, and constant reflection on and analysis of their work were more prominent in their discussions of their leadership. In their words, they were "more aware of the learning community in my classroom" and took the initiative "to reflect on my teaching and incorporate new strategies." A middle school teacher who struggled with the constraints of brief class periods said that she still tried to "implement as many things that lead to a learning community as possible" including "active students that have a strong relationship with the teacher."

They also described themselves as leaders who took actions to improve education in their schools and districts, including collaborating extensively with colleagues, becoming go-to people for others, and building strong classroom and professional learning communities. An elementary teacher explained, "I share strategies and ideas with colleagues to inspire change and help them in integrating new skills. . . . I also plan to run workshops next year to teach my colleagues about educational technology tools that they can use to enhance student learning."

The collaborative view of leadership was even stronger at this stage. However, mentoring was no longer emphasized as frequently as at the beginning of the program. The focus at this point tended to be on leaders as colleagues sharing what they were learning in their graduate program and organizing professional study of classroom teaching.

Views on Teacher Leadership at Program Completion

Once the teachers completed their coursework and built reflective portfolios through which they analyzed their work in terms of teacher leader standards, some characteristics of their teacher leader descriptions remained consistent with prior stages, and some shifted. The descriptions still clearly emphasized teacher leaders as strong, innovative, and reflective teachers as well as collaborative community builders who take actions to improve education in their schools or districts. According to one of the elementary teachers, "Great teachers are exceptional educators to their students. Great teacher leaders extend their expertise beyond the walls of the classroom."

At this point, however, there was less emphasis on increased confidence and mentoring and much more emphasis on leading others and suggesting changes. A high school teacher described efforts to motivate colleagues and administrators to make "meaningful changes" to their English language program. Similarly, an elementary teacher said that she pushed herself to "uphold" her role as a leader beyond school and district committees, "but also to the community and the families who reside within it." A middle school teacher expressed the idea succinctly by saying, "To me, a willingness to step up and help is one of the most essential qualities of a leader. . . . It is about doing your part and inspiring others to do theirs and more."

All of the teacher leaders during this stage of their development viewed themselves as strong teachers, and even though explicitly stated student-centered instruction was not a focus at this juncture, differentiated instruction and the active use of data and research were. An elementary teacher and a middle school teacher respectively noted in their surveys:

> As a researcher and reflector, I carefully think about my teaching methods, lessons, curriculum, and student needs. I make changes based on my reflections, and I research best practice methods and ideas to incorporate in my classroom to strengthen my teaching and student learning. I keep informed of best practices through blogs, conferences, and workshops.

> I try to look at the data that is available to us and adjust lessons so that they are geared towards raising the bar. I want students to be successful. . . . If I find methods that challenge students and help them understand the meaning, I then share that information with my colleagues.

Views of Post-Program Graduates About Their Teacher Leadership Skills

Once the teacher leaders completed the program and practiced their skills for 1 to 5 years, there were notable changes in how they characterized their work as leaders. Most survey respondents were highly reflective and confident in their knowledge and skills and what they had to share with their colleagues. A high school teacher stated that the program "encouraged me to research best practices and also analyze my current practices. I became more confident to try new instructional practices, utilize technology, and encourage my students to work as a community." Another found "my niche in education" and felt "confident expressing my ideas and philosophies to administrators, colleagues, and students alike."

During this stage of their development, the teacher leaders saw themselves as people to whom others went for support and assistance, and they took the lead on established committees and in creating new initiatives and curricular approaches. A high school teacher and a middle school teacher respectively commented:

> I find that many of our new, less-experienced department members often come to me for suggestions on effective lessons, or . . . how I form such strong relationships with my classes. This gives me great satisfaction to see how far I've come professionally . . . since receiving my [degree].

> I have presented and led discussions at teaching and learning meetings . . . a book study and a review of the science grading policy. I am currently involved in developing a new district professional development plan to match the new teacher evaluation system.

They still frequently described themselves as learning community builders and collaborators, but three quarters of them also indicated that they were speaking up about issues that concerned them. A middle school teacher remarked:

> I've written long letters and had meetings with curriculum supervisors about the poor state of our district in-services and the need to have better professional development. I've expressed my concerns to the principal, vice principal, and curriculum supervisor about the need to change the honors program in order to improve student learning.

Discussion and Implications of Emerging Teacher Leadership Traits and Skills

The traits and skills used to frame this study and examine emerging teacher leaders' views on their leadership work reflected a set of teacher leader characteristics put forth in the literature over the last two decades. The division of formal and informal roles, or "layers," as Martin (2007) called them, are often described in the scholarly literature (Danielson, 2007; Dozier, 2007; Lieberman, 2011; Patterson & Patterson, 2004) to differentiate between formally appointed and sometimes compensated roles, such as department or grade level chair, new teacher mentor, and literacy or math coach; and the informal roles based on recognition of expertise from the classroom. Danielson (2007) described these informal roles as emerging "spontaneously and organically from the teacher ranks" (p. 16).

The program examined in this study attracts teachers interested in the informal leadership roles, though several eventually moved into more formalized roles. The study's findings repeatedly documented a teacher leader orientation toward collaborative sharing of successes and organic blossoming of changed teaching practice both within the leaders' classrooms and across other classrooms, thus reflecting a move from Neumann et al.'s (2012) instructional or transactional domain of their classrooms to the professional development or transformational realm of their triadic teacher leadership model. Clearly the characteristics reflected in this study began within the leaders' classrooms, or their primary spheres of influence, and then moved to their next or secondary spheres of influence, which were other colleagues who were interested in learning from them about their successes within their classrooms. As they began to share and others listened, the teacher leaders' confidence grew. They began to see themselves, as did others, as people to go to for advice and help.

The study's findings suggest that by the time teacher leaders reached the graduate stage, they were speaking up about educational issues, taking action, and leading committees and initiatives at high rates of frequency, an overall marked change from earlier in the program. In some instances, these types of changes might have been at work in what Neumann et al. (2012) referred to as the "social responsibility" or "critical domain," though in other cases the actions were simply action to formally develop and share professional expertise in school or district workshops or learning communities. The teacher leaders moved into the third sphere of influence, which is of the whole school and district. This action took the teachers further from the comfort zone of their own classrooms and from the classroom focus of most of the program's core courses. In this third sphere of influence, the leaders simply sought to extend the professional development they felt empowered to provide. A high school teacher and an elementary teacher respectively explain this change:

> The M.Ed. program has given me the knowledge required to feel confident and willing to take on leadership roles within my department. I have offered to spearhead projects and/or discussions involving creating learning community classrooms and the importance/impact of doing so.

> When I deal with administrators, especially our director of curriculum, I try to encourage and suggest programs and processes that will enable the staff and students to grow and adapt most easily to the changes on the horizon.

Yet some reflected a potentially deeper commitment to the type of social justice change suggested by Neumann et al. (2012) in their triadic model. An elementary teacher noted:

> I have joined the local TESOL (Teachers of English to Speakers of Other Languages) chapter and volunteered to serve on a district RTI (Response to Intervention) committee as a representative for our school. These will both allow me to effect greater change and improvement of services for our students. Because I have been more vocal, I am seen as a resource and problem solver.

Implications for Teacher Leadership Programs

The field of teacher education should seek to cultivate strong field-based leadership by developing teacher leaders who initiate, share, collaborate, mentor, and generate solutions for education. Yet critical to teachers' willingness to share is an inner confidence in daily practice and a strength of conviction that their classroom successes are worthy of consideration by others. Teacher leadership programs must therefore nurture the development of such confidence and conviction and encourage teacher leaders to enter that third sphere of influence, the one that is twice removed from their classroom comfort zones.

The data from this study indicate that most graduates of the program developed that critical confidence to share their successes and expertise and have begun to do so. They moved into the second sphere of influence and are offering methodological ideas, support, and training on an informal basis to their peers. They are having the greatest impact influencing the classroom teaching of their colleagues through informal and formal method sharing. It also appears that the program graduates have begun to scratch the surface of the third sphere of influence beyond informal exchanges with peers by engaging in formal school and district committee work to effect change in areas where they feel they have expertise and by offering districtwide professional development. Some have also begun contributing to critical educational change by speaking up at district meetings, reaching out to parents and community groups, and advocating for student learning and success; but this inclination has not yet emerged as a consistent and meaningful outcome of the leadership preparation this program provides. For that to happen, the program needs to more systematically encourage and guide practicing teachers to step assuredly into that realm of the leadership role.

Because teacher leadership is central to educational change, the education profession needs more programs that prepare teachers for multifaceted leadership roles while also recognizing that it takes practice, time, and experience for teachers to move out of that first sphere of influence—their classrooms—into the second sphere of influence—informal work with colleagues—and then to the third sphere of more formal school and district structures. Even then the emergence of teachers as critical leaders and change agents (Neumann et al., 2012) who are at the forefront of action for social change may not necessarily manifest as a result of teacher leadership programs such as the one that is the focus of this chapter without putting into place additional catalysts and supports to inspire that dimension of leadership.

References

Danielson, C. (2006). *Teacher leadership that strengthens professional practice.* Alexandria, VA: Association for Supervision and Curriculum Development.

Danielson, C. (2007). The many faces of leadership. *Educational Leadership, 65*(1), 14–19.

Dozier, T. K. (2007). Turning good teachers into great leaders. *Educational Leadership, 65*(1), 54–59.

Katzenmeyer, M. H., & Moller, G. V. (2009). *Awakening the sleeping giant: Helping teachers develop as leaders* (3rd ed.). Thousand Oaks, CA: Corwin.

Lieberman, A. (2011, Fall). Can teachers really be leaders? *Kappa Delta Pi Record,* 16–18.

Lieberman, A., & Miller, L. (2005). Teachers as leaders. *The Educational Forum, 69*(2), 151–162.

Martin, B. (2007). Teacher leaders: Qualities and roles. *Journal for Quality and Participation, 30*(4), 17–18.

Morehead, P. A., & Sledge, J. (2006). Follow the teacher leaders: The potential of teacher leadership to close the achievement gap. In A. Salhi (Ed.), *Excellence in teaching and learning: Bridging the gaps in theory, practice, and policy* (pp. 69–78). Lanham, MD: Rowman and Littlefield Education.

Neumann, M. D., Jones, L. C. S., & Webb, P. T. (2012). Claiming the political: The forgotten terrain of teacher leadership knowledge. *Action in Teacher Education, 34*(1), 2–13.

Patterson, J., & Patterson, J. (2004). Sharing the lead. *Educational Leadership, 61*(7), 74–78.

Reeves, D. B. (2008). *Reframing teacher leadership to improve your school.* Alexandria, VA: Association for Supervision and Curriculum Development.

3

TEACHER LEADERS AND THE ART OF SELF-MENTORING™[1]

Marsha L. Carr

Leadership is a process, not an innate or taught set of individual skills. Lambert (2003), a scholar in the field of leadership development, stated that leadership includes problem solving, broad-based skillful participation, conversations and stories among colleagues, and task enactment in the environment. Teachers who aspire to become leaders and who are aware of these requirements still need encouragement and a structured approach to reach their full leadership potential.

A way to help educators become teacher leaders is through self-mentoring, which is a process for leadership development in any environment. Self-mentoring differs from other approaches in that individuals assume responsibility for their own leadership expectations and opportunities. While self-mentoring is not a component of mentoring or a replacement practice, it is a frame of reference for beginning the process of leadership development.

The Art of Mentoring

Mentoring has become a nationwide practice in the development of teacher leaders. As research increasingly suggests, professionals benefit from a mentor's guidance (Allen, Eby, O'Brien, & Lentz, 2008). Mentoring is a common practice to acclimate mentees who are new to an environment or a profession. Thomas and Saslow (2007) stated:

> Mentoring is a developmental partnership through which one person shares knowledge, skills, information, and perspective to foster the personal and professional growth of someone else. The power of mentoring is that it creates a one-of-a-kind opportunity for collaboration, goal achievement, and problem solving.

(p. 1)

Working with a mentor can be a rewarding experience for some professionals. However, having mentors who are unavailable due to time and cost restraints creates a burden for the mentee. Often mentors are assigned with no input from the mentee or consideration of personality or mentee needs. Mismatched relationships can produce negative mentoring results (Burk & Eby, 2010; Eby, Durley, Evans, & Ragins, 2008; Hansman, 2003). Negative mentoring is defined "in terms of dysfunctional mentoring outcomes, such as dissatisfaction" (Burk & Eby, 2010, p. 438). Negative mentoring does not imply malice on the part of the mentor but suggests that for various reasons the relationship experiences problems.

Five types of negative mentoring practice experiences exist. They are general dysfunctionality, mismatch within the dyad, lack of mentor experience, manipulative behavior, and distancing behavior (Eby et al., 2008; Scandura, 1998). General dysfuctionality is caused by the mentee's interfering personal problems, negative attitude to the work environment and individuals in the setting, or general lack of responsibility. Dyad mismatch occurs when both the mentor and mentee report a mismatch in personality or work ethic. Lack of mentor expertise is when the mentee believes the mentor lacks the necessary skills, whether interpersonal or knowledge driven, to serve in the mentoring role. Manipulative behavior exists when the mentoring position is used for power and influence or becomes political. The final type of negative mentoring is distancing behavior, which results when the mentor intentionally fails to provide proper guidance or devote sufficient time to the mentee. In most cases, when the mentoring relationship becomes negative, the mentor and mentee are ready to part ways. If the mentee perceives no benefits from the relationship, then the mentoring relationship is usually dissolved.

Formal mentoring practices often fail when the mentor is absent (Burk & Eby, 2010). If this situation occurs, then it becomes necessary to create a process in which the mentee can benefit from leadership practices that are embedded in existing experiences (Carr, 2012). This chapter explores the self-mentoring approach. The chapter's goal is not to discredit or dispel studies advocating for formal mentoring practices, but to introduce an approach that builds independent and capable teacher leaders who can thrive and succeed in any environment in the absence of a formal mentoring program.

The Art of Self-Mentoring

Self-mentoring is an art of leading oneself in unknown environments or even hostile settings if necessary. It is a formal process that unleashes the creative side, allowing the potential leader to emerge. By definition, a self-mentor is an

> achiever who is willing to initiate and accept responsibility for self-development by devoting time to navigate within the culture of the environment in order to make the most of opportunity to strengthen competencies needed to enhance job performance and career progression.
>
> (Carr, 2012, p. 7)

Stated another way, self-mentoring is the practice of building oneself into a leader who accepts responsibility for personal and professional growth through the identification and development of individual skills, aligning internal and external resources to meet expectations and goals, and applying social and professional networking to further support goals.

Self-mentors set goals that are closely aligned to their individual needs. To reach these goals, self-mentors choose the tools, such as collaborations, observations, one-on-one interactions, discussion groups, networking activities, and community clusters. For teacher leaders, self-mentoring occurs in the classroom or the school setting. While mentoring for the most part is a one-on-one interaction, self-mentoring encourages the person to invite a legion of colleagues to be involved. It is through this self-directed process that the teacher learns to lead in an ever-changing living environment and to develop efficacy in decision making as well as problem solving. Over time, the teacher gains confidence in her or his ability to lead.

Yarger and Lee (1994) suggested that "in the absence of conceptual frameworks for guiding program development and evaluation, teacher leadership programs will continue to be sporadic, idiosyncratic events" (p. 235). Self-mentoring is beneficial because it provides a structured process for inducting new teachers into an organization, providing leadership opportunities among existing teachers, and motivating experienced teachers to offer feedback or participate in peer-reflections with new teachers. Self-mentoring recognizes that each teacher brings different strengths and values to the process. Schools that implement a self-mentoring program observe heightened teacher confidence, efficacy in instructional practice in the classroom, and willingness to support colleagues to assume other leadership roles in the school setting.

Self-mentoring is not isolated to building teacher leaders; it can be applied to any profession or age group, including elementary or high school students. The process differs in content delivery as adjustments are necessary to accommodate the audience's maturity level and the specific needs as identified in a particular profession. For the purposes of this chapter, the focus is on teacher leaders.

Framework for Self-Mentoring

Self-mentoring as a formal process involves four stages of development: self-awareness, self-development, self-reflection, and self-monitoring. Each stage is explained in the following section. Figure 3.1 provides a map of how the self-mentor evolves through the stages.

Self-Awareness. The first stage, self-awareness, involves the teacher's learning about the environment and his or her own strengths and weaknesses. It is a process of identifying, sorting, and categorizing leadership traits that are essential for successfully navigating the environment. By using inventories and activities, teachers can sort specific leadership behaviors into two categories of necessary practices and unwanted practices. Through this process, teachers learn to recognize traits associated with great leadership and categorize their own skills to either maintain or target for change.

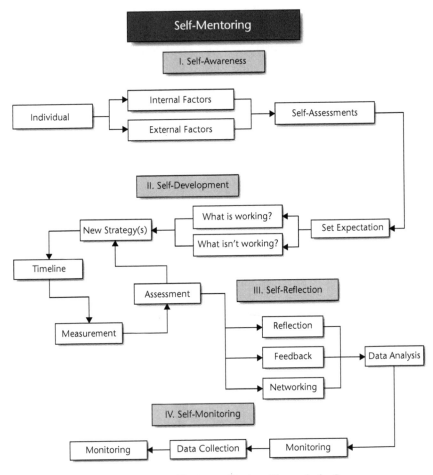

FIGURE 3.1 A Map of How the Self-Mentor Evolves Through the Stages

Organizations in which teachers work are complex systems consisting of living, breathing, and ever-changing networks of interlocked subcultures. A teacher immersed in a new culture requires the skills to navigate through what can be treacherous waters. To succeed in these and any other environments, a teacher needs to understand how a system operates. By definition, a system is a set or network of interdependent components that work together to accomplish the organization's goals (Lezotte & McKee, 2002). Teachers, as self-mentors, must first have an understanding of the culture in which they are embedded. They must identify implied or hidden expectations from the environment. This process can be challenging for even experienced teachers, but one method for helping self-mentors to succeed is using information obtained through peer conversations.

Conversations are crucial in every profession and are considered powerful tools in self-mentoring (Patterson, Grenny, McMillan, & Switzler, 2012). By talking to colleagues, the aspiring teacher leader identifies key staff in the new school. These interactions quickly shed light on the history and culture of the environment. Conversation topics may include political structures, operating procedures, schoolwide leadership, teacher and student expectations, and the chemistry of the community at large. Meeting with peers in the school setting uncovers the internal hierarchies of power. Some staff will come across as friendly; others, more distant. Some will share leadership roles while others hoard power. Knowing colleagues' expertise becomes a valuable resource for the self-mentor. This mental library of available resource specialists in the school is especially important for new teachers. Colleagues who are adept in a specific subject matter or who serve in positive leadership roles understand the school climate and are often willing to engage in professional conversations. Future collaborations often come from these encounters.

Self-mentoring thrives in a culture that respects differences of opinion and supports learning. This type of culture provides fertile ground for debate and dialog to test the boundaries of prior practices and extend one's thinking. Resilient self-mentors can overcome challenging environments that discourage differences and punish learning by employing the tools of collaborative conversations.

Self-Development. During the second stage of self-mentoring, the teacher articulates personal and/or professional expectations, develops measurable strategies, aligns activities, establishes a timeline for implementation, and applies measurement methods to meet the desired expectations. Although the teacher's expectations are numerous at first, they are eventually narrowed to one that becomes the focus for planning. This second stage is marked by organization, commitment, and dedication from the teacher.

There is some overlap between the second and third stages, both of which serve as the core of self-mentoring. Teacher leaders spend considerable time planning during these stages, and they learn to prioritize and independently develop measurable and realistic expectations.

Self-Reflection. In the third stage, the teacher begins to employ techniques to deepen data collection. Strategies are utilized from observable moments to pull data. Planning includes self- and peer-reflection with internal and/or external peers. External networking is also considered when needed. As Duke, Carr, and Sterrett (2013) stated, "Self-mentoring . . . involves videotaping. [Self-mentors] observe their own . . . practice privately and note areas for possible improvement. These areas for improvement then become foci for professional development and coaching by more experienced [colleagues]" (p. 149). The teacher leader acclimates to using observable data and identifying other strategies, which are both practices in leadership.

Self-Monitoring. The final stage is characterized by the continual process of leading in the absence of any formalized structure. Sustainability emerges during this stage. Teachers as self-mentors become more motivated and passionate in sustaining success. They maintain control over their own destiny, and they make their achievements their personal endeavor. Since a sense of accomplishment is motivating, they strive to sustain these skills for empowerment and self-efficacy.

An Investigation of Self-Mentoring and Teacher Leaders

Another researcher and I conducted an empirical study in a rural North Carolina public school system to explore the idea of self-mentoring as a way to develop teacher leaders. We asked district administrators to select participants. Chosen were eight females who taught in Grades 1–3 and 6–12. The sampling represented teachers from the elementary, middle, and high schools in the school system. On average, the participants had 4.3 years of teaching experience. Their ages varied. Four were in their twenties, three in their thirties, and one in her fifties. All lived in the county. None held graduate degrees. In terms of mentoring experiences, seven had 3 years of prior mentoring while one had 4 years. All names used in this chapter are pseudonyms.

The primary question driving this qualitative inquiry was *In what ways does self-mentoring serve to support and encourage teacher leaders?* Because self-mentoring is an evolving field, this study used a grounded theory approach that draws from rich descriptive data captured in qualitative interviews. Grounded theory relies on the researcher's interpretation of the data. In this study we searched for segments of interview transcriptions that generated and illustrated categories of meaning. This qualitative inquiry method was most suited to uncovering the unexpected or exploring new avenues (Marshall & Rossman, 1999).

Over a period of 9 months, the participants met four times, with each seminar lasting 2 or more hours. Each seminar focused on one of the four stages of self-mentoring while incorporating information from the previous meetings. Data for this study consisted of observations, video, journals, photos, reflection notes, small group discussions, interviews, email exchanges, and written responses to surveys.

The participants were not isolated in their efforts to self-mentor. While they were assigned to different schools and grade levels, they were able to interact during and between the seminars and to contact the school officials for additional guidance. Although this type of group internal support may have been beneficial, the impact of this type of support was not considered in the study. Self-mentoring does encourage, however, the use of internal and external resources; it does not limit the interactions to single contact. In most cases, a self-mentor may be self-mentoring outside a group format.

Each participant signed a contract as a testament of commitment to self-mentoring. During the first seminar, the participants used leadership inventories and tools to discuss leadership processes and traits and to describe and identify the school system's culture. Although the participants came from different schools with unique climates, the overarching culture for the county was supportive. At the end of each seminar, the participants compiled a list of individual expectations before choosing a primary focus for the next meeting.

During the second seminar, the participants discussed their individual expectations and developed activities or strategies to monitor and assess progress. Group discussions provided activity selection feedback to each participant. Measurable strategies were developed for the individual expectations, and timelines were established for implementation and data collection. Each participant committed to a specific amount of time each week to working on strategy implementation.

The third seminar applied the previous work in more depth. The participants determined what professional and social networking was necessary to reach their expectations. Peer- and self-reflection guided the participants.

The final seminar was a culmination of all previous work. The participants took time to reflect in groups by sharing results from reviewing recommendations and data, a process that resulted in future modifications. The participants planned for continual monitoring and developed new expectations for the upcoming year.

We researchers coded the data manually by using In Vivo software during the first coding cycle and pattern coding in the second (Saldaña, 2009). We gathered analytical data from memos; observations; journal entries; open-ended questioning during seminars; individual and group interviews; and available documents such as teacher evaluations, teacher improvement plans, and school improvement plans.

During the first coding cycle, the initial review was laden with emotional, value-laden, and evaluative phrases or words, primarily categorized as the affective domain in comparison to the cognitive and psychomotor. Two categories of leader and teacher were established by the researchers, with confidence emerging as the most prominent theme. The second cycle coding yielded similar patterns that related to teacher and leader confidence during the data reviews. Positioning theory emerged from this cycle of data analysis. Reflective and interactive positioning were dynamics at work within participants and among participants and their peers. According to positioning theory, learners make decisions as information becomes available and reflect on data to alter decisions, hence becoming more confident through practice (Harré & Van Langenhove, 1999).

The Findings

Two primary teacher expectations emerged from the data: Teachers wanted to assume more prominent leadership roles in the school, and teachers wanted to become more effective instructional leaders in the classroom. By participating in self-mentoring, the teachers claimed that they experienced improvements in both areas.

Classroom Leadership

The self-mentoring teacher leaders improved in the area of classroom management and felt more inclined to share ideas and assist colleagues. Their knowledge of leadership and teaching increased, and their classroom instruction improved. Abbey (all names are pseudonyms), a high school teacher, explained, "I was comfortable in my subject area—always comfortable but now more comfortable." In reply to a question about how instructional practice improved, a Rosemont elementary school teacher explained, "During a math lesson I realized sooner that manipulatives needed to be supplied."

A majority of the teachers acknowledged that peer- and self-reflections were the most effective tool in self-mentoring. Rachel, an elementary teacher, was reassigned from being a music class instructor to teaching band. Unlike her principal, she considered teaching music and teaching band to be two different professions. She explained that while she could teach music, she was uncomfortable teaching students how to play band instruments. At first, she felt that she had failed before she began. The situation was more of an obstacle than an actual challenge. However, during the seminars she began to write almost daily about her interactions with the students. When she was asked to re-read the original entries, she realized that she was making progress and felt that success was obtainable. She explained, "Reflection makes you more aware of what you are doing so you can correct it."

School Leadership

The self-mentoring teacher leaders' experiences gave them courage to be more assertive and to speak up in meetings when their opinions were sought. They confidently took leadership roles and reached out as leaders to assist others when necessary. They gained confidence as leaders through a variety of self-selected activities that guided their efforts. In short, they were empowered to make decisions that provided growth as leaders.

Again, a majority of teachers acknowledged that peer- and self-reflections were the most effective tool in self-mentoring. Connie, an elementary school teacher, noted, "Reflection makes you more aware of what you are doing so you can correct it." Ruth, a middle school teacher, shared, "Reflection provided confidence to be able to support other colleagues. . . . I believe I will continue to gain confidence as a leader." As the teacher leaders began working through strategies, Amanda, a high school teacher, felt uncomfortable taking a risk as a member of a professional learning community (PLC). She worried that if she failed, her peers would not hold her in high regard. To her, this would be worse than not trying at all. During the self-mentoring seminars, Amanda sought help from one of the participants, a faculty member whom she trusted, for feedback as well as guidance. Amanda needed to take the lead in the organization of the PLC meetings. Personality conflicts and member complaints sabotaged task completion. The team could not even agree on a meeting time or place, so few if any goals were ever realized. Eventually Amanda realized that taking the risk was necessary for her own development. Between the seminars, she sent an email and shared her success:

> I made a decision about our PLC at [school]. Three of the four teachers can meet together. Number 4 cannot because of students, lunch, or homebound

responsibilities. So, I decided to meet with the majority. The last meeting was in Number 4's room because she could not leave her students. We met in there.

Teacher leaders emerge when they have the confidence to make decisions and plan for their success. Lucy, a high school teacher, shared, "Reflection provided [me] confidence to be able to support other colleagues. . . . I believe I will continue to gain confidence as a leader."

An interesting revelation resulted in the final review of the data. All teachers completed an evaluation of the school system before and after the self-mentoring program. During the first seminar, the teachers were asked to talk about their school system's work culture, specifically with regard to how it supported and empowered teachers. All viewed the system as a stronger organization prior to self-mentoring; however, they were more critical of it and ranked it lower after self-mentoring. As the teachers became more confident in leadership roles, they became more critical of the organization. During the time since the study was completed, there has been no opportunity to conduct follow-up interviews with the teachers to gain additional insights. In future studies, however, interview questions about the systems' culture will become an essential part of the data collection.

School system officials reported observing increased confidence in the participating teachers during the program. One official sent a memo to the superintendent after the first seminar and said, "The self-mentoring session . . . was exceptionally powerful. [I] am pleased with how productive this session was. The [teachers] stated this was one of the best professional development sessions that they have ever been a part of." When future studies are planned, these findings will guide the data collection in order to deepen the knowledge of leadership and self-mentoring.

The Impact and Importance of Self-Mentoring of Teacher Leaders

Self-mentoring impacts classrooms, schools, and communities on multiple levels. All three areas are considered equally important from the perspective of self-mentoring. This study shows that the classroom impact was primarily on teacher leader's self-efficacy, a term that refers to how confident an individual feels about handling particular tasks, challenges, and contexts. The field of self-efficacy is derived from Bandura's social cognitive theory (1986). According to the theory, teachers' self-efficacy is linked to student outcomes and behavior. In a more recent study, Tschannen-Moran and Hoy (2001) found that teachers' efficacy beliefs were related to students' sense of efficacy, achievement, and motivation. Future studies will examine the direct impact of self-mentoring on classrooms and students. Teaching efficacy, personal efficacy, social efficacy, and low-achiever efficacy will also be studied in detail (Henson, Kogan, & Vacha-Hasse, 2001).

A greater level of confidence is described in conjunction with taking risks and trying out new ways of teaching (Sadler, 2009). Teachers reported that self-mentoring increased their confidence in the classroom and the school setting. The findings show that confident teachers assume leadership roles in their schools by participating actively on teams, serving as role models for peers, and building school and community relationships. In short, the impact of teacher leaders enhances the school environment and community engagement.

Conclusion

Leadership is a framework for school improvement and a tenant of self-mentoring. The basic assumption is that everyone learns and everyone leads (Lambert, 2003). Self-mentoring views each learner as a potential leader. The ultimate goal of self-mentoring is to develop a high leadership capacity, which is characterized by teachers working together for a common goal and viewing the school's overall performance as their combined success.

For it to be effective, self-mentoring has to be an ongoing practice. According to Lambert (2003), "The integration of new teachers into the school is a critical aspect of leadership development and sustainability" (p. 428). The arrival of new teachers into an existing school culture can either support the existing structure or tear at the seams if assumptions shift or tenets are differentiated. Thus, supporting new teachers as future leaders becomes a basic tenet.

Self-mentoring programs provide opportunity to new teachers, struggling teachers, and seasoned teachers who are ready to move into leadership roles. It also identifies teachers for future administrative roles. Self-mentoring supports newcomers through self-directed learning opportunities (Carr, 2011) and provides opportunities for new staff to take the lead in their own professional growth. These individuals become responsible for developing a plan that includes observations, professional networking, and self-reflection. It can be difficult for newcomers to interpret the culture of an organization upon arrival, but they can do so through a self-mentoring program that identifies core values and beliefs early in the process.

Self-mentoring not only adds value to new teacher leaders, but also strengthens the existing culture in a system. Lambert (2003) explained,

> Leading is everyone's work and . . . we grow into those understandings when we engage with others to make sense of our world, reach out to bring new teachers into full membership in the community, commit to shared outcomes and develop our identities as owners, not tenants, of our schools.
> (p. 428)

While leadership is viewed as key to sustainability (Datnow & Springfield, 2000; Fullan, 2001), commitment is viewed as equally important. Unless those involved commit, the prevailing behaviors will return. Sustainability refers to actions of a teacher in applying leadership skills learned during self-mentoring to continue growth over the years in the absence of a formalized structure. Fullan (2001) recommended four areas that relate to commitment and passion. These areas are active initiation and participation, pressure and support, changes in behavior and beliefs, and ownership. Each is equally significant, and together they create an atmosphere or environment for sustainability. Self-mentors are more motivated and passionate in sustaining the success achieved through individual effort. They maintain control over their destiny. This sense of accomplishment is motivating so that teachers strive to sustain these skills for empowerment and self-efficacy.

Self-mentoring is not a cure-all, but it can become a practice to promote teacher leaders in any professional setting. It is only through continued study in this area that the importance of advocating for continued practices in self-mentoring will be discovered. As the approach grows nationwide, continued efforts to gather data through additional studies will yield more about its value. Self-mentoring is the act of accepting responsibility for one's own growth and success—you are the best leader in your own life. *Your life—You lead!*

Note

1. Self-mentoring is trademarked by the author.

References

Allen, T. D., Eby, L. T., O'Brien, K. E., & Lentz. E. (2008). The state of mentoring research: A qualitative review of current research methods and future research implications. *Journal of Vocational Behavior, 73*(3), 343–357.

Bandura, A. (1986). *Social foundations of thought and action: A social cognitive theory.* Englewood Cliffs, NJ: Prentice Hall.

Burk, H. G., & Eby, L. T. (2010). What keeps people in mentoring relationships when bad things happen? A field study from the protégé's perspective. *Journal of Vocational Behavior, 77*(3), 437–446. doi: 10.1016/j.jvb.2010.05.011

Carr, M. (2011). *The invisible teacher: A self-mentoring sustainability model.* Wilmington: University of North Carolina Wilmington, Watson College of Education.

Carr, M. (2012). *The invisible leader: A self-mentoring guide for higher education faculty.* Wilmington: University of North Carolina Wilmington, Watson College of Education.

Datnow, A., & Springfield, S. (2000). Working together for reliable school reform. *Journal of Education for Students Placed at Risk, 5*(1–2), 183–204.

Duke, D. L., Carr, M., & Sterrett, W. (2013). *The school improvement planning handbook: Getting focused for turnaround and transition.* Landham, MD: Rowan & Littlefield.

Eby, L. T., Durley, J. R., Evans, S. C., & Ragins, B. R. (2008). Mentors' perceptions of negative mentoring experiences: Scale development and nomological validation. *Journal of Applied Psychology, 93*(2), 358–373. doi: 10.1037/0021-9010.93.2.358

Fullan, M. G. (2001). *The new meaning of educational change* (3rd ed.). New York, NY: Teachers College Press.

Hansman, C. A. (2003). Reluctant mentors and resistant protégés: Welcome to the "real" world of mentoring. *Adult Learning, 14*(1), 14–16. doi: 10.1177/104515950301400103

Harré, R., & Van Langenhove, L. (Eds.). (1999). *Positioning theory: Moral contexts of intentional action.* Malden, MA: Blackwell.

Henson, R. K., Kogan, L. R., & Vacha-Hasse, T. (2001). A reliability generalization study of the Teacher Efficacy Scale and related instruments. *Educational and Psychological Measurement, 61*(3), 404–420. doi: 10.1177/00131640121971284

Lambert, L. (2003). Leadership redefined: An evocative context for teacher leadership. *School Leadership and Management, 23*(4), 421–430.

Lezotte, L. W., & McKee, K. M. (2002). *Assembly required: A continuous school improvement system.* Okemos, MI: Effective Schools Products.

Marshall, C., & Rossman, G. B. (1999). *Designing qualitative research* (3rd ed.). Thousand Oaks, CA: Sage.

Patterson, K., Grenny, J, McMillan, R., & Switzler, A. (2012). *Crucial conversations: Tools for talking when stakes are high* (2nd ed.). New York, NY: McGraw-Hill.

Sadler, I. (2009, August). *Emotions in higher education teacher development: The role of confidence upon the approach to teaching.* Paper presented at the biannual international meeting for the European Association for Learning and Instruction (EARLI), Amsterdam, The Netherlands.

Saldaña, J. (2009). *The coding manual for qualitative researchers.* Thousand Oaks, CA: Sage.

Scandura, T. A. (1998). Dysfunctional mentoring relationships and outcomes. *Journal of Management, 24*(3), 449–467.

Thomas, N., & Saslow, S. (2007). Improving productivity through coaching and mentoring. *Chief Learning Officer, 6*(5), 22–26. Retrieved from http://clomedia.com/articles/view/improving_productivity_through_coaching_and_mentoring

Tschannen-Moran, M., & Hoy, A. W. (2001). Teacher efficacy: Capturing an elusive construct. *Teaching and Teacher Education, 17*(7), 783–805. doi: 10.1016/S0742-051X(01)00036-1

Yarger, S. J., & Lee, O. (1994). The development and sustenance of instructional leadership. In D. R. Walling (Ed.), *Teachers as leaders: Perspectives on the professional development of teachers* (pp. 223–237). Bloomington, IN: Phi Delta Kappa Educational Foundation.

4

MAXIMIZING TEACHER LEADERSHIP

The Principal as Facilitator

William Sterrett

In an age where the job description for the principalship continues to grow, so does the need for authentic teacher leadership. The principal is uniquely and solely poised to cultivate and encourage the power and potential of teacher leaders. The ground is continually shifting in terms of economics, demographics, mandates, and innovations, yet the major challenge for schools is ensuring that "all students attain the skills, knowledge, and disposition they will need to be successful in the world that awaits them" (Lieberman & Miller, 2004, p. 6). The principal is positioned, in effect, to develop and facilitate reservoirs of insights, energies, and ideals by striving to maximize the leadership capacity within the school organization.

The concept of effectively maximizing teacher leadership remains a challenge for many principals. As with many confounding gaps in education, there is a continued disconnect between the ideal and the reality in many schools when it comes to teacher leadership. Birky, Shelton, and Headley (2006) noted, "Even though the concept of teacher leadership now seems to be common knowledge, the actual practice in many schools does not seem to be all that common" (p. 88). However, it is clear that the principal is positioned to foster teacher leadership. For the purposes of this chapter, *teacher leadership* is defined as collaborative involvement, initiative, and guiding direction from the teaching faculty to help realize the school goals, mission, and vision in a reflective manner.

The principal's role is typically anchored on state-specific guidelines, many of which are based on what is known as the "ISLLC Standards," which were developed originally by the Interstate School Leaders Licensure Consortium (Mitgang, 2013, pp. 8–9). Revised in 2008, these standards include the following: "Standard 1: Setting a widely shared vision for learning," and "Standard 2: Developing a school culture and instructional program conducive to student learning and staff professional growth" (Council of Chief State School Officers [CCSSO], 2008, p. 6).

In 2013, the Wallace Foundation issued a report titled *The School Principal as Leader,* which outlines five key practices for principals to employ to improve teaching and learning, including the following two components: "Cultivating leadership in others," and "Standard 4: Improving instruction" (p. 4). Thus, it is clear that policy, mandates, and the job description of the principal call for developing teachers to lead in order to ultimately further student instruction and achievement (Leithwood, Louis, Anderson, & Wahlstrom, 2004). Principals are the catalyst for cultivating teacher leadership in the school, a practice that can result in improved learning for students.

Building a Culture of Teacher Leadership

Teachers are not finished products when they exit their student teaching experience, complete their credentialing requirements, or successfully finish their probationary period as novices. Educators must continue to learn and grow and adapt to the changing realities of the field. This lifelong learning will not be maximized without sufficient planning, time, and follow-up in place. Of course, many teachers manage to prioritize learning and growing despite time constraints.

In seeking to build a culture of teacher leadership, the principal should continually strive to facilitate adult learning, collaboration, and reflection. The school community—including students, staff members, parents, and community members—stands to gain much from enhanced teacher leadership. York-Barr and Duke (2004) identified four reasons for enhanced teacher leadership: benefits of employee participation; expertise about teaching and learning; acknowledgment, opportunities, and rewards for accomplished teachers; and benefits to students (pp. 258–259). These reasons may seem obvious to those in the "trenches" of teaching and learning; yet the environment, in the absence of reflective and intentional leadership, may not necessarily be predisposed toward such teacher leadership and participation.

The principal must set forth the conditions for effective teacher leadership. York-Barr and Duke (2004) offered the following three categories of conditions that influence teacher leadership:

- School culture and context: providing faculty with ongoing opportunities to have a voice in leadership facets;
- Roles and relationships: establishing high levels of trust among faculty and principals and supporting both formal and informal structures and reflective feedback; and
- Structures: offering professional development (PD), considering time and space, facilitating site-based decision making. (pp. 269–271)

Simply put, these conditions cannot be sustained without principal leadership. Successful teacher leadership helps the school realize greater success. Lieberman and Miller (2004) suggested that teacher leaders have a "unique position to make change happen" as they "are close to the ground and have the knowledge and ability to control the conditions for teaching and learning in schools and classrooms" (p. 12). It is imperative that the principal engage teachers in key leadership areas.

Principals play a key role in fostering key teacher leadership areas that have been defined by research and framed in leadership standards (CCSSO, 2008; North Carolina State Board of Education [NCSBoE], 2013; Owings & Kaplan, 2012; York-Barr & Duke, 2004). York-Barr and Duke (2004) closely examined conditions that influence teacher leadership in terms of category, facilitators, and challenges (pp. 270–271). Specifically, the teacher leadership areas of school culture leadership, collaborative learning leadership, and school management leadership are identified for the purposes of this chapter in Table 4.1. By first understanding

TABLE 4.1 Practical Applications and Guiding Questions of Teacher Leadership

Key Areas of Teacher Leadership	Practical Applications	Guiding Questions
School culture leadership (Council of Chief State School Officers [CCSSO], 2008; Matthews & Crow, 2010; North Carolina State Board of Education [NCSBoE], 2013; York-Barr & Duke, 2004)	• School improvement team planning and implementation (Duke, Carr, & Sterrett, 2013; Lambert, 2003) • Collaborative faculty meetings (Sterrett, 2011) • Feedback exit slips (Sterrett, 2011) • Fostering traditions, norms, and symbols (Duke et al., 2013)	1. What is most important at our school? 2. What are our mission, vision, and school improvement goals? 3. How can we celebrate and affirm successes in our school?
Collaborative learning leadership (CCSSO, 2008; DuFour, 2004; Matthews & Crow, 2010; NCSBoE, 2013; Wallace Foundation, 2013; York-Barr & Duke, 2004)	• Professional learning communities (PLCs) (DuFour, 2004) • Cognitive coaching (Costa & Garmston, 2002) • Instructional rounds (City, 2011) • Peer observations (Kachur, Stout, & Edwards, 2013; Reeves, 2008; Sterrett, Williams, & Catlett, 2010)	1. How are our students learning, and what are our next steps? 2. How can we reflect and grow as learners, teachers, and leaders? 3. How can we learn from one another? 4. How can we share teaching and learning successes from within?
School management leadership (CCSSO, 2008; Glatthorn, Boschee, Whitehead, & Boschee, 2012; Matthews & Crow, 2010; NCSBoE, 2013; Owings & Kaplan, 2012)	• Principal facilitation of collaborative schedule workshop (Sterrett, 2011) • Student placement, extracurricular activities, budget priorities • Quality oversight committees, such as the Baldrige model (Walpole & Noeth, 2002)	1. How can we ensure that our school management structures are efficient and effective for the entire school community? 2. How can we prioritize our resources in a way that furthers our successes for all stakeholders? 3. Are our processes transparent and fair?

these key areas, focusing on related practical applications, and reflecting on guiding questions, principals foster an atmosphere of teacher leadership in their schools and strive for greater success for students and faculty alike.

Practical Applications and Guiding Questions for Teacher Leadership

Understanding each respective key area of teacher leadership is important. School leaders might then envision practical applications (see the middle column of Table 4.1). Guiding questions promote continual reflection in evaluating progress in these leadership areas (see the third column of Table 4.1). These key areas of teacher leadership, along with their practical applications and reflective questions, serve to strengthen efforts in realizing organizational success in a school.

School Culture Leadership

A Key Area of Leadership. Understanding and building on the school culture is paramount for the school leader. As noted earlier, Standard 2 in the ISLLC 2008 standards calls for "developing a school culture and instructional program conducive to student learning and staff professional growth" (CCSSO, 2008, p. 6). The NCSBoE (2013) described the cultural leadership standard, stating that it "implies understanding the school as the people in it each day, how they came to their current state, and how to connect with traditions in order to move them forward to support the school's efforts to achieve individual and collective goals" (p. 5). In summarizing two decades of scholarship on teacher leadership, York-Barr and Duke (2004) stated, "School culture is widely recognized as a dominant influence on the success of improvement initiatives in schools, and certainly it is regarded as influencing teacher leadership" (p. 269).

In fact, the school culture makes or breaks learning for students and staff alike. Owings and Kaplan (2012) observed, "The culture and environment either facilitate or inhibit learning" (p. 105). The question becomes, "In what ways can school leaders leverage school culture to promote teacher leadership?" Principals play an integral part in prioritizing the actual action steps to be taken (Sterrett, 2011). Often, a principal inherits a school with an unhealthy culture; rebuilding a culture of trust and teamwork takes years (Duke, Carr, & Sterrett, 2013). Matthews and Crow (2010) advised that a principal should carefully consider the culture that is in place prior to seeking to reform a school, noting, "After you understand the culture, you may then want to decide what parts of the culture need to change and what parts need to be enhanced" (p. 96). Changing the culture, however, requires time and teamwork.

Practical Applications of School Culture Leadership. Teacher leadership involvement with the school improvement process is important (Duke et al., 2013; Lambert, 2003). Teachers have an authentic perspective that must be cultivated in understanding, shaping, and communicating the school's vision in order to maximize success (Lieberman & Miller, 2004). A wise principal seeks to understand multiple teachers' perspectives at all times. As Matthews and Crow (2010) explained, "Listening to a respected teacher's criticism regarding the vision, often, will stave off serious criticism later and will help in building a stronger commitment to the vision" (p. 166). The teacher's perspective must be valued and understood.

Principals should evaluate how best to maximize teacher participation to better develop, monitor, and enact the School Improvement Team. Other school-based decision groups, such as a schoolwide curriculum team, a budget committee, or a school policy and procedure review team, also provide avenues for staff members to align their interests and engagement with the work of the school (Duke et al., 2013). The consideration of time is crucial. Muijs and Harris (2003) observed, "Time needs to be set aside for teachers to meet to plan and discuss issues such as curriculum matters, developing school-wide plans . . . and collaborating with colleagues" (p. 443). The principal, more than anyone else, facilitates this process through scheduling, prioritizing, and allocating time, and by providing coverage when needed.

Collaborative faculty meetings in which a two-way avenue of dialogue is expected as a meeting norm strengthen the culture of the school (Sterrett, 2011). Finding a way for teachers to recognize one another's work starts the meeting in an affirmative manner. Sharing teaching tips from within the school empowers teachers to lead discussions about best practices. Allowing the School Improvement Team to craft the agenda of the faculty meetings creates shared ownership.

Another practical application of taking the pulse of the teachers is to routinely use exit slips or feedback comments to better understand what is working and what is not working and to allow for open comments or suggestions (Sterrett, 2011). These exit slips are given at the end of each faculty meeting, or quarterly, to gain an ongoing perspective from teachers. With the advent of online survey apps, the innovative principal is able to solicit anonymous, ongoing feedback. Of course, it is up to the principal to reflect and act on these comments. While it is unrealistic for a principal to attend all professional learning community meetings, she or he can work with staff to use a system of meeting notes, minutes, and feedback slips that allow teams to follow a consistent format and share feedback.

Finally, creating and fostering traditions, norms, and symbols can have value. From a mascot for a varsity sports program to a school song for an elementary school, from naming an annex of a school to helping design a school logo, symbolism is an opportunity for shared leadership (Duke et al., 2013). Routine celebrations, pep rallies, and celebratory events foster a sense of community, consistency, and school pride. Teachers can take ownership for creating, enacting, and maintaining these traditions in order to promote buy-in.

Guiding Questions for School Culture Leadership. Asking the right questions aligns school culture leadership in a shared capacity. As the school leader, the principal works with leadership teams such as the school improvement committee or instructional design team. She or he might continue asking, at the beginning of framing the meeting, "What is most important at our school?" and "How will our work align with what is most important?" Kowalski (2012) cautioned that shared decision making "is neither simple nor problem-free," as "social unity" or "groupthink" can distract from the core work (p. 36; also Janis, 1982). Considering efforts and initiatives as they regard the school mission, vision, and school improvement goals may preserve unnecessary work, effort, and/or cost. Reeves (2006) famously encourages school leaders to "pull the weeds before you plant the flowers," to carefully weigh new initiatives in light of existing efforts (p. 89). Leaders should examine their initiatives with their teams and prioritize some while discontinuing others.

Finally, leaders should work to find ways to celebrate successes in the school for students and staff alike. All too often, leaders and teams work to solve problems rather than share successes. Possibilities include recognizing "Students of the Week" during the Friday televised announcements and sharing weekly bulletins full of innovative ideas and awards from within the school. Leadership teams should always ask, "What's *right* with our school that can be shared, cultivated, and continued?"

Collaborative Learning Leadership

A Key Area of Leadership. Trust is essential in a successful organization. Birky et al. (2006) reflected that trust results as effective collaboration emerges over time among school administrators and teachers. Principals must support the leading role that the adult learner plays as a teacher leader; as Ozuah (2005) explained, teacher leaders need "an opportunity to practice and apply what they have learned" (p. 86). Barth (2001) observed that teacher leaders can become "owners and investors in the school, rather than mere tenants" (p. 443). North Carolina's human resource leadership standard emphasizes that the school executive "provides structures for the development of effective professional learning communities" and "models the importance of continued adult learning by engaging in activities to develop personal knowledge and skill along with expanded self-awareness" (NCSBoE, 2013, p. 6), thus prioritizing adult learning.

The principal's role with regard to the school's professional learning communities (PLCs) is increasingly important in a new context of technological innovations, global perspective, and knowledge-based learning. A middle school principal, for example, cannot realistically be the curriculum expert for math, reading, science, and social studies, but must be able to gather data and process and interpret them in order to "diagnose needs and develop customized responses" (Matthews & Crow, 2010, p. 11).

Practical Applications of Collaborative Learning Leadership. Sometimes teachers' learning stagnates because they do not emerge from their own silos of teaching. Peer observation provides a continual, collaborative new perspective.

Shorter, informal walkthrough observations provide information about classroom instruction and should be seen as an opportunity for "supporting the sharing of best practices across the school" (Glatthorn, Boschee, Whitehead, & Boschee, 2012, p. 282). Peer observation fosters shared collaboration and vertical conversation (Sterrett, Williams, & Catlett, 2010). Peer observations are also an opportunity for a teacher-led collaborative team to facilitate planning and coordination through identifying areas in which to learn from one other, sharing an *instructional rounds* format that resembles the structure of medical rounds (City, 2011). Kachur, Stout, & Edwards (2013) stated, "Involving teachers as observers in the walkthrough process can transform the entire school into a learning community and build a culture that values the engagement of teachers in continuous and sustained professional growth" (p. 4). Reeves (2008) suggested making faculty meetings "an announcement-free zone," allowing for professional sharing and focus on instructional best practices (p. 73). Teachers stand to gain much from learning from one another, and the principal plays a key role in helping collapse these silos.

Many schools and districts claim to engage in PLCs, but there is variance in execution. Teachers are integral in leading these collaborative teams and in answering the key PLC questions offered by DuFour (2004) that seek to ascertain what it is that students are supposed to learn, how it is determined that they have learned it, and what the next steps will be after it is determined that they have (or have not) learned the material. As the principal alone cannot lead PLC teams, there is inherent opportunity for teacher leadership to emerge. The principal plays a key role in fostering leadership. For instance, ensuring that the department head or team leader position is rotated in a way that allows for new leaders to emerge prevents burnout or disenfranchisement in the ranks.

Innovation is another area where a principal makes a profound difference in helping shape schoolwide perspectives on teaching and learning. Encouraging teachers to engage students in new technologies and highlighting relevant examples help the collaborative dialogue focus on innovation in learning. By engaging in regular social media outlets, such as Twitter or other online professional learning networks (PLNs), or by maintaining an active blog that illustrates samples of learning or synthesizes relevant trends or developments in education, the principal models staying abreast of current trends, challenges, and changes. Matthews and Crow (2010) observed, "The context in which your school is located, the technology of teaching and learning, and a host of other factors require constant learning" (p. 327). In a constantly evolving context of changing leadership standards, curricula, and accountability mandates, such innovation is all but required for the school to succeed.

Finally, the practice of cognitive coaching holds promise as teachers seek to be reflective learners (Costa & Garmston, 2002). Focusing on making observations nonevaluative, collaborative, and reflective allows teachers to build trust and to view their own teaching with a new perspective. Principals equip teachers to engage in peer coaching cycles by providing relevant staff development and release time so teachers can have a preconference discussion, full observation in the classroom, and then a postconference.

Guiding Questions for Collaborative Learning Leadership. At the crux of the educator's work is the guiding question, "How are our students learning?" Focusing on next steps in light of student achievement refocuses priorities in terms of collaborative learning leadership. Seeking to learn and reflect as a learner, better understanding one's own growth, and being willing to learn from colleagues helps the leadership team to answer, "How can we learn from one another?" While there is certainly much to learn from "outside" sources, being willing to engage in learning from and with colleagues strengthens the learning community and, again, affirms the successes that are occurring with students and staff members alike.

School Management Leadership

A Key Area of Leadership. Without effective school management, all else in the school will fall apart. Even the greatest instructional leader cannot abdicate the responsibilities of budgeting, managing facilities, scheduling, and supervising extracurricular activities. As the CCSSO (2008) noted in ISLLC Standard 3, the "education leader promotes the success of every student by ensuring management of the organization, operation, and resources for a safe, efficient, and effective learning environment" (p. 14). Taking into consideration management and operational systems along with "human, fiscal, and technological resources," while also focusing on safety and efficient use of time and scheduling, indeed requires the leader to "develop the capacity for distributed leadership" (p. 14). Of course, one person cannot do it all alone, nor should anyone even if she or he could. North Carolina's managerial leadership emphasizes that the school executive "creates process to identify and solve . . . school-based problems/conflicts in a fair, democratic way" and "collaboratively develops and enforces clear expectations, structures, rules and procedures" (NCSBoE, 2013, p. 7).

Indeed, the role of the principal continues to shift in this managerial context. Glatthorn et al. (2012) explained, "The role of the principal has grown from that of a manager to that of a change agent, an administrative-organizational specialist" (p. 280). For a principal to truly "specialize" in managing the myriad expected and unexpected challenges and situations, she or he must put effective support structures in place. Owings and Kaplan (2012) commented, "Successful leaders are insightful and flexible" and permit "participative freedom when involving group members in decision making" (p. 335). This flexibility is key, as each school's needs are unique (Matthews & Crow, 2010). What works in one school may not always easily transfer to the next.

Practical Applications of School Management Leadership. This participative freedom in shared decision making manifests itself in numerous practical applications. Instructional scheduling is a challenge that must be taken into account when considering goals, resources, and leadership decisions. Taking steps to build a "collaborative schedule" that empowers teachers to craft the priorities of the schedule, emphasize equity (to avoid the perception of "winners and losers"), and emphasize common planning time in a shared manner ensures staff buy-in (Sterrett, 2011, pp. 28–29). Time is a valuable resource that, though limited, should be maximized in a collaborative approach (Sterrett, 2013).

Shared leadership also plays an important role in shaping student placements. Rather than relying solely on numbers or formulas to fill classes, organizing planning sessions that focus on student achievement, relationships, and equity shows a deliberate focus on realizing the school's mission and vision. Similarly, the school leader should consider priorities for addressing extracurricular activities such as sports, clubs, and trips. For schools striving to have a systemic, long-term impact on organization, an approach such as the Baldrige model, which focuses on quality in organizational operations, provides emphasis on working in "diverse and dedicated teams" (Walpole & Noeth, 2002, p. 20). Again, ensuring that stakeholders have a voice in the operational matters of a school improves the perception of shared leadership and ownership.

A principal promotes teacher leadership in hiring and retention efforts as well. When a principal approaches recruitment and hiring as a team decision, from interview to induction, team members are more likely to support the new hires. New teacher mentoring has much potential, but the mentoring process must be deliberately cultivated. Bowman (2004) observed that with "teachers as leaders, the mentors are committed to creating success for the new teachers" (p. 188). Matthews and Crow (2010) cautioned that the principal should "not assume that good or even outstanding teachers will be successful mentors without special training and support" (p. 199). Responsibilities and expectations must be made clear; and supports, such as extended planning time or release time, as well as stipends, should be prioritized to ensure that effective mentoring is sustained.

Guiding Questions for School Management Leadership. Enhanced teacher leadership leads to more questions regarding managerial items. Why does a particular grade level always take a field trip to "X" destination, which is more costly and time-intensive than the field trips of other grade levels? Why does one subject area always get the ideal time slot right before the lunch schedule? How are classrooms and parking spaces allocated? How should we spend this unexpected windfall of additional technology support? If one leader makes these decisions unilaterally, mistrust or disappointment can result. Striving to answer the question "How can we prioritize our resources in a way that furthers success for all stakeholders?" promotes leadership within the teaching ranks that fosters a perspective on managerial and structural support and equitable allocation. While this transparent approach will not necessarily result in the disappearing of perceived "winners and losers," it can instill a sense of democratic adherence to school priorities aligned with the organization's mission, vision, and goals.

Reflecting on the Nature of Teacher Leadership

Teacher leadership is greatly enhanced by effective principal leadership. From establishing effective PLCs and school improvement teams to engaging teachers in crafting a school schedule or facilitating a collaborative discussion in a faculty meeting, principals can rely on, and cultivate trust in, ongoing teacher leadership. Of course, teacher leadership is not solely dependent on effective principal leadership. As Danielson (2007) stated, "Sometimes on their own initiative and sometimes within a more formal structure, these professionals find a variety of ways to exercise teacher leadership" (p. 14).

The engaged administrator serves as a catalyst agent in crafting and maintaining these important structures, thus exponentially transforming the school culture from one of status quo and stagnation to one of vibrant engagement and growth. Teacher leadership may lie dormant if the conditions for this collaborative approach do not exist; it is up to the principal to make a key difference by facilitating this cooperation.

Collaborative school leaders will look for ways to involve new or novice teachers. Research indicates that these teachers are given less opportunity than they would prefer despite the fact that they feel capable and ready to assist in school leadership functions (Nolan & Palazzolo, 2011, p. 314). Principals, take a moment and reflectively ask yourself, "If I were a teacher in this school, would I feel supported? Would I feel encouraged to take healthy risks in terms of teaching strategies and professional growth? Would I feel that I have an open line of communication to the school leadership?" Teachers, ask yourself, "How might I engage more in my team or department structure to enhance teaching and learning? How might I share best practices and also learn from my colleagues? How might I support the school's vision? In what practical ways can I help lead in my school?"

Each school varies in its existing structures, leadership, history, and school community. There is no single magic formula or guaranteed approach, yet there is powerful potential in ongoing and continual striving toward greater collaboration, inquiry, reflection, and innovation. Realizing that leadership is not just for principals may help the principal lead more effectively. Fostering a greater reliance on shared expertise, ongoing growth, and collaborative dialogue offers potential for greater success and growth for students *and* staff alike.

References

Barth, R. S. (2001). Teacher leader. *Phi Delta Kappan, 82*(6), 443–449.
Birky, V. D., Shelton, M., & Headley, S. (2006). An administrator's challenge: Encouraging teachers to be leaders. *NASSP Bulletin, 90*(2), 87–101.
Bowman, R. F. (2004). Teachers as leaders. *The Clearing House, 77*(5), 187–189.
City, E. A. (2011). Learning from instructional rounds. *Educational Leadership, 69*(2), 36–41.
Costa, A. L., & Garmston, R. J. (2002). *Cognitive coaching: A foundation for renaissance schools* (2nd ed.). Norwood, MA: Christopher-Gordon.

Council of Chief State School Officers. (2008). *Educational leadership policy standards: ISLLC 2008*. Washington, DC: Author. Retrieved from http://www.wallacefoundation.org/knowledge-center/school-leadership/principal-evaluation/Documents/Educational-Leadership-Policy-Standards-ISLLC-2008.pdf

Danielson, C. (2007). The many faces of leadership. *Educational Leadership, 65*(1), 14–19.

DuFour, R. (2004). What is a professional learning community? *Educational Leadership, 61*(8), 6–11.

Duke, D. L., Carr, M., & Sterrett, W. (2013). *The school improvement planning handbook: Getting focused for turnaround and transition*. Lanham, MD: Rowman & Littlefield.

Glatthorn, A. A., Boschee, F., Whitehead, B. M., & Boschee, B. F. (2012). *Curriculum leadership: Strategies for development and implementation* (3rd ed.). Thousand Oaks, CA: Sage.

Janis, I. L. (1982). *Groupthink* (2nd ed.). Boston, MA: Wadsworth, Cengage Learning.

Kachur, D. S., Stout, J. A., & Edwards, C. L. (2013). *Engaging teachers in classroom walkthroughs*. Alexandria, VA: ASCD.

Kowalski, T. J. (2012). *Case studies on educational administration* (6th ed.). Upper Saddle River, NJ: Pearson.

Lambert, L. (2003). Leadership redefined: An evocative context for teacher leadership. *School Leadership & Management, 23*(4), 421–430.

Leithwood, K., Louis, K. S., Anderson, S., & Wahlstrom, K. (2004). *How leadership influences student learning: Review of research*. Minneapolis: Center for Applied Research and Educational Improvement, University of Minnesota. Retrieved from http://www.wallacefoundation.org/knowledge-center/school-leadership/key-research/Documents/How-Leadership-Influences-Student-Learning.pdf

Lieberman, A., & Miller, L. (2004). *Teacher leadership*. San Francisco, CA: Jossey-Bass.

Matthews, L. J., & Crow, G. M. (2010). *The principalship: New roles in a professional learning community*. Boston, MA: Allyn & Bacon.

Mitgang, L. (Ed.). (2013). *Districts matter: Cultivating the principals urban schools need*. New York, NY: The Wallace Foundation. Retrieved from http://www.wallacefoundation.org/knowledge-center/school-leadership/district-policy-and-practice/Documents/Districts-Matter-Cultivating-the-Principals-Urban-Schools-Need.pdf

Muijs, D., & Harris, A. (2003). Teacher leadership—Improvement through empowerment? An overview of the literature. *Educational Management & Administration, 31*(4), 437–448.

Nolan, B., & Palazzolo, L. (2011). New teacher perceptions of the "teacher leader" movement. *NASSP Bulletin, 95*(4), 302–318.

North Carolina State Board of Education. (2013). *North Carolina standards for school administrators*. Raleigh: North Carolina Department of Public Instruction.

Owings, W. A., & Kaplan, L. S. (2012). *Leadership and organizational behavior in education: Theory into practice*. Upper Saddle River, NJ: Pearson.

Ozuah, P. O. (2005). First, there was pedagogy and then came andragogy. *Einstein Journal of Biology and Medicine, 21*(2), 83–87.

Reeves, D. (2006). Pull the weeds before you plant the flowers. *Educational Leadership, 64*(1), 89–90.

Reeves, D. B. (2008). *Reframing teacher leadership to improve your school*. Alexandria, VA: ASCD.

Sterrett, W. (2011). *Insights into action: Successful school leaders share what works*. Alexandria, VA: ASCD.

Sterrett, W. (2013). *Short on time: How do I make time to lead and learn as a principal?* Alexandria, VA: Association for Supervision and Curriculum Development.

Sterrett, W., Williams, B., & Catlett, J. (2010). Using technology and teamwork to enhance peer observations. *Virginia Educational Leadership, 7*(1), 65–71.

Wallace Foundation. (2013). *The school principal as leader: Guiding schools to better teaching and learning.* New York, NY: Author. Retrieved from http://www.wallacefoundation.org/knowledge-center/school-leadership/effective-principal-leadership/Documents/The-School-Principal-as-Leader-Guiding-Schools-to-Better-Teaching-and-Learning-2nd-Ed.pdf

Walpole, M., & Noeth, R. J. (2002). *The promise of Baldrige for K–12 education: An ACT policy report.* Iowa City, IA: ACT. Retrieved from http://www.act.org/research/policymakers/pdf/baldrige.pdf

York-Barr, J., & Duke, K. (2004). What do we know about teacher leadership? Findings from two decades of scholarship. *Review of Educational Research, 74*(3), 255–316.

PART II

Roles of Teacher Leaders

5

TEACHER LEADERS AS PROFESSIONAL DEVELOPERS

Nathan Bond

Providing professional development for colleagues is an ideal role for teacher leaders (Killion & Harrison, 2006; York-Barr & Duke, 2004). The responsibility has traditionally belonged to the principal; however, in recent times, administrative positions have become more complex, making the leadership of a school challenging for one person (Ballek, O'Rourke, Provenzano, & Bellamy, 2005). Principals can be more effective when they share responsibilities with teacher leaders and follow a distributed leadership model (Hargreaves & Fink, 2006; Spillane, 2006).

Another reason for delegating professional development to teacher leaders is because they possess an insider's knowledge of the local school conditions, unlike an outside consultant would (Hargreaves, 1996; Webb, Neumann, & Jones, 2004). They know their colleagues, the curriculum, and the culture of the school and are able to plan relevant and responsive professional development. As Goode, Quartz, Barraza-Lyons, and Thomas (2004) stated, "Highly effective educators do not need to leave the classroom in order to build leadership skills and take on more professional roles at their school site. Schools employing built-in professional development tend to elicit greater teacher commitment" (p. 420). Moreover, teachers enjoy professional development experiences led by colleagues (Hickey & Harris, 2005).

Furthermore, teachers have a vested interest in the success of not only the students in their classrooms, but also of those in the entire school (Donaldson, 2006). Teachers are already leading in classrooms through their instruction. They "lead within their schools, whether implicitly or explicitly, for good or for bad, proactively or reactively" (Neumann, Jones, & Webb, 2012, p. 5). If schools are going to become places where all children are learning, then teachers have a moral obligation to step outside their classrooms and lead (Barth, 2001).

This chapter highlights six elementary school teacher leaders in the Eanes Independent School District (ISD) in Austin, Texas, who facilitated professional development on their campuses. Although there are many models of professional development teacher leaders can use, such as workshops, peer coaching, mentoring, and action research (Kennedy, 2005), these teachers were asked by the district to each individually lead a professional learning community (PLC). The scholarly literature defines a PLC as a group of people who share and critically examine their practice in an ongoing, reflective, collaborative, inclusive, learning-oriented, and growth-promoting way (Stoll, Bolam, McMahon, Wallace, & Thomas, 2006). The teachers developed the PLCs during the summer and implemented them during the following academic year. The author of this chapter, who was also the researcher and the teachers' professor, performed an analysis of the materials used in the PLCs, conducted interviews, and collected data for the case studies presented here. Permission was obtained from the teacher leaders and the district to use their real names.

Preparing to Lead PLCs

Eanes ISD is a high-performing school district with approximately 8,000 students in six elementary schools, two middle schools, and one high school. The U.S. Department of Education has named six of these schools Blue Ribbon Schools. The district regularly receives exemplary ratings from the state's education agency because of its high student scores on standardized tests and other required accountability measures. Ninety-eight percent of the students pursue a post-secondary education upon graduation.

In 2006, district administrators (Dr. Nola Wellman, Superintendent; Bill Bechtol, Deputy Superintendent for Curriculum, Instruction, and Assessment; and Lester Wolff, Assistant Director for Human Resources) approached the administrators at Texas State University (Dr. Rosalinda Barrera, Dean of the College of Education; and Dr. Patrice Werner, Chair of Curriculum and Instruction) about co-developing a master's degree program that would help the district's teachers to become teacher leaders. Eanes ISD wanted a cadre of teacher leaders to facilitate professional development for colleagues in their schools using the most current research-based information about pedagogy (Bond, Goodwin, & Summers, 2013). The program was established and, over the years, it has thrived under the district's and university's respective program coordinators, Julia Fortman and Dr. Marilyn Goodwin.

Each year since 2006, a new cohort of teachers from Eanes ISD has entered the program. To prepare for their leadership roles, the teachers completed a summer graduate course on teacher leadership taught by the author of this chapter. The curriculum focused on teacher leadership; leadership theory; and models of professional development, including PLCs, peer coaching, teacher study groups, mentoring, and action research. For the final course project, the teachers developed the materials for a PLC to implement with colleagues in the upcoming academic year.

The administrators in Eanes ISD embraced PLCs as a meaningful form of professional development. They worked collaboratively with the teachers to select the focus of their work in the PLCs and gave the teachers latitude in designing the PLCs. As a sign of support, the district set aside specific mornings throughout the year for the PLCs to meet and allowed the teachers to schedule additional meetings at their convenience.

Teachers Leading PLCs

A PLC is a type of professional development that brings teachers together to accomplish a task. For example, teachers may study a topic in-depth, share lesson plans, or analyze student data. Regardless of the focus, PLCs are characterized by six attributes: supportive leadership, common vision, intentional collective learning, physical and structural conditions, collegial relationships, and shared practice (Hord & Tobia, 2012). As a way to organize the case studies and present their richness, the researcher aligned each teacher and her PLC to one of the six attributes. In reality, each PLC included all six.

Janet: Share Leadership

PLC Attribute 1: "Supportive and shared leadership that expresses the school campus and district administrators' sharing of power and authority through sharing decision-making with the staff" (Hord & Tobia, 2012, p. 38).

Janet Couvillion taught third grade at Forest Trail Elementary School. During the summer, while taking the graduate course on teacher leadership, Janet planned her PLC. At the same time, she also dreamed of having multiple PLCs, rather than one, operating simultaneously throughout the school year. She and other teacher leaders in the school would host their own PLCs and make them available to everyone at Forest Trail. She shared her idea with the other teacher leaders from Forest Trail who were taking the graduate course, and they liked it. Working together, they brainstormed four PLC topics: experiential learning, nurturing the whole child, customizing learning, and future trends in teaching. Janet explained, "I wanted it to be a community of teachers coming together on a schoolwide basis to implement the PLCs as opposed to one teacher just getting like-minded colleagues together."

Next, Janet presented her plan to her principal and assistant principal, and both wholeheartedly supported it. Over the next few weeks, Janet reported, she and the administrators "met two or three times and bounced ideas back and forth." During these meetings, they decided that teachers who attended the PLCs and documented their learning in a portfolio would be exempt from attending one of the required schoolwide professional development days. In addition, experienced teachers who met certain eligibility requirements could use the PLC time as part of their annual performance evaluation. In Eanes ISD, experienced teachers for their annual performance evaluation could choose to either have an administrator observe them teach a lesson or investigate a topic in-depth. Studying in a PLC fit well with the second option.

Janet and the administrators decided that Janet and the teacher leaders who volunteered to facilitate the PLCs would introduce the idea to the other faculty during a staff development day before the school year began. On that day, they provided a general overview of the four topics, the benefits of participation, and the expectations for attendance and documentation. Janet clarified, "I wasn't going to tell teachers that they had to do it. And if they chose to participate, then I wasn't going to tell them what to do. I wanted the teachers to have lots of choice." They then asked interested teachers to sign up for a specific PLC and provide additional subtopics to explore in smaller inquiry groups within each PLC. These smaller groups would allow participants to study related issues more in-depth. Janet explained, "We wanted more than just the teachers' interest. We wanted them to give us their ideas and take ownership of the PLCs."

Janet noticed that during the faculty presentation, both administrators sat quietly and observed. She said,

> [The assistant principal] didn't stand up with us when we presented. She has been very helpful during the planning process showing us how to do these things. She has been very positive and hasn't said no to anything. She trusts us. The principal was also quiet because he's "letting it be our thing." There's so much respect for our administrators on our campus. What they're doing is very powerful.

When asked about the impact of the PLC, Janet replied, "It has, quite simply, been great! PLCs are now recognized at Forest Trail, and we are allowed to count them toward our staff development days. It has been hard work on me, but it has been worth it." As a teacher leader, Janet worked collaboratively with her administrators to make joint decisions about the PLCs on their campus.

In his research on teacher leadership, Lindahl (2008) stated, "Though it is clearly crucial that the formal leader prominently articulate and model the vision for a wide range of stakeholders, teacher leaders can, and should, have a strong voice in formulating the vision" (p. 304). Janet's vision of multiple PLCs became a reality because of her determination and the administrative support she received. Webb et al. (2004) asserted that teacher leaders succeed when administrators believe in the leadership abilities of their faculty members and give them sufficient resources and time to address issues related to student learning and instructional practice.

Sandy: Develop a Common Vision

PLC Attribute 2: "Shared beliefs, values, and vision that are grounded in the community's unrelenting commitment to student learning" (Hord & Tobia, 2012, p. 38).

Sandy Crump taught third grade at Cedar Creek Elementary School and served as the grade-level leader. She and three other teachers comprised the grade-level team. For her PLC, Sandy decided to collaborate with her colleagues to examine student data and use the findings to make instructional improvements. The ultimate goals were to identify students who needed extra support and differentiate the instruction to meet those students' academic needs. Her ideal was for teachers to closely monitor students' performance, ensuring that all students learn.

Before the school year began, Sandy invited her grade-level team to her home where she introduced the PLC project to them and invited them to participate. She spent time developing rapport with the teachers and getting to know them. She explained, "Relationships are vital to PLCs, so I tried to be their friend first. I wanted them to know that, as their grade-level leader, I would 'have their backs.' I wanted them to realize that we are a team." In this environment of trust and safety, her colleagues agreed to participate in the PLC.

Early in the school year, the teachers administered diagnostic standardized tests in math and reading. The district scored the tests and posted the data on an online assessment management system accessible by the teachers. During the first PLC meeting, Sandy guided her colleagues to analyze the data from the test results, and some teachers were initially embarrassed by the scores of their low-performing students. Relying on the rapport she had developed during the initial meeting at her home, she gently pressed the teachers to stay focused on the beneficiaries of their work. She asked, "Why are you here? What can we do for the children? How can we help them to learn?"

As the teacher leader in charge of the PLC, Sandy deliberately spent time in the beginning building positive collegial relationships. By carefully laying the groundwork of a shared goal for the PLC and then maintaining an undeviating focus on student learning during challenging times (Hord, 2004), Sandy and her PLC succeeded. When asked about the impact of the PLC, she concluded, "I was impressed with what our team did. We were able to study information and bring ideas back to the classroom that helped the children."

Research supports this approach of building trust and a shared vision or ideal. In a study of successful schools with active teacher leaders, Beachum and Dentith (2004) found that "trust and caring for others, along with a strong sense of self-efficacy and high regard for the mission of the school, surfaced repeatedly among those teacher leaders interviewed" (p. 281). Other teacher leadership studies, such as the one conducted by Searby and Shaddix (2008) in a high-performing district in Alabama, have affirmed the importance of cultivating a positive work environment based on trust, caring, and a focus on student learning.

Sherrie: Learn as a Group

PLC Attribute 3: "Intentional collective learning by the community that is applied in classrooms to benefit student learning" (Hord & Tobia, 2012, p. 38).

Sherrie Johnson taught fifth-grade science at Forest Trail Elementary. During instruction time, she noticed that her students were fascinated with technology-based activities, especially playing computer games. Student engagement and motivation increased when she used technology in her lessons. Although she was knowledgeable about computers, she wanted to learn more. Sherrie was already a participant in a PLC called Tech Mondays, and she began to notice comments from colleagues in the group about their desire for more professional development on integrating technology into instruction. To meet her students' and colleagues' needs, she designed a multi-week PLC called Video Games in the Classroom. For several Monday afternoons during the fall semester, faculty met voluntarily and studied strategies for using computers as a teaching and student learning tool.

During the first PLC meeting, Sherrie and the teachers spent time getting to know one another, sharing their prior knowledge and beliefs about technology integration, and identifying questions to investigate as a group. They discussed their insights from the scholarly articles they had read in preparation for the first PLC meeting. What emerged from the first gathering was, as she noted, "a positive feeling and a lot of good conversation." During subsequent meetings, she showed videos of teachers in other districts who had successfully integrated technology into their teaching. As the teachers discussed the ideas, they raised interesting points and posed thought-provoking questions. As the conversations moved in different directions, Sherrie modified the agendas several times. She commented, "It was important for me to remain flexible with the plan and let it develop organically because I was trying to address other teachers' needs."

According to Sherrie, the PLC provided valuable knowledge to teachers who were eager to learn about video games and their potential educational benefits. She added:

> The teachers were enlightened on their students' current interests, which in turn allowed them to communicate better on a personal interest level with their students. The PLC was also a place where teachers could branch out and connect with faculty members who have common interests and goals.

Sherrie and the PLC members succeeded in learning some strategies for integrating technology, and their success was realized because the PLC was voluntary, focused on a common and immediate instructional need, rich in information and conversation, and natural in the way the agenda unfolded over time. In their study of PLCs in elementary schools, Maloney and Konza (2011) found that "Professional learning had a better chance of succeeding if teachers contributed as equals to setting the agenda, bringing about change, and ultimately improving their own practice" (p. 85). If teachers are going to learn as a group, then they need opportunities to have input in what is studied.

Betty: Use Resources

PLC Attribute 4: "Physical or structural conditions, and provision of resources, that support the community in meeting to do their learning work" (Hord & Tobia, 2012, p. 38).

Betty Patterson taught physical education to children of all grade levels at Forest Trail Elementary. She decided to create a PLC that would involve the physical education teachers at the district's other elementary schools because they generally teach on campuses by themselves and have few opportunities to "meet as a group and bounce ideas off each other." Betty added, "It's hard for physical education teachers to find content-specific professional development."

Betty initially proposed the idea to two close colleagues in physical education. They responded, "We're excited! Let's do it!" Betty then sought assistance from the technology coordinator on campus who helped her to create a wiki on the district's protected website. Betty explained, "The wiki was intended to be a great sharing space." Soon thereafter, Betty emailed the other physical education teachers in the district, explained the idea of an online PLC, and worked with them to hone the PLC's focus. Betty recounted, "We decided to make the wiki a forum for us to share teaching ideas. We would answer questions, such as 'What is your favorite activity, how do you plan, and what does your class look like?'"

The wiki allowed the teachers to organize the information in useful ways. They created a calendar for posting each day's instructional activities and sorted the information according to students' ages. Because teaching physical education to younger and older children requires different pedagogical approaches, the teachers set up pages and links on the wiki for the various age ranges.

Betty explained the PLC's impact by stating, "Reading and discussing the activities caused me to reflect on my teaching in light of best practices in physical education. For example, I wondered if there were better ways to play a game or administer the fitness assessments." Betty's PLC showed that teacher leaders can use the district's technological resources to overcome barriers of time and space. This finding is also confirmed in the research literature. Stoll et al. (2006) noted that PLCs excel when teachers have time and either a physical or virtual place to come together and talk about their work.

Helene: Build Rapport

PLC Attribute 5: "Collegial or relational conditions that encourage and build the atmosphere for collective learning" (Hord & Tobia, 2012, p. 39).

After completing the teacher leadership course in the summer, Helene Houlihan began her first year as a life skills teacher in the special education department at Eanes Elementary School. Planning a PLC had been difficult because she, as a new teacher on the campus, did not know the school's faculty or culture well. She was forced to rely on her observations of the interactions between general education and special education teachers at the previous school where she had taught. Based on those insights, she believed that all teachers should spend more time discussing special education students and planning lessons that best addressed those learners' needs. In her opinion, a PLC would be an ideal vehicle for bringing together both groups of teachers.

When the school year began, Helene had the sensitivity and courage to delay the implementation of the PLC rather than forging ahead. She wisely understood that she needed time to establish herself at the school. She explained her reasoning,

> The biggest challenge was that I was new to the campus. As a life skills teacher, I had to know everybody, so I took the steps to feel more connected. I wrote down people's names when I met them and drew sketches so that I could remember them.

She made a point to get acquainted with the principal, the teachers in all grade levels, and the various support staff members. She stated, "I had to discover who these people were and how they were there to help me." She also immersed herself in the school's culture. She stated, "I didn't know the expectations and the kinds of responsibilities and freedoms that we had."

After reflecting on her decision to delay implementation of the PLC, Helene summarized,

> I had to understand the context and establish the relationships first. This past year has been more about building relationships, being more visible in the general education classrooms, advocating to others in the school on behalf of my special education students, and getting them out there with the other students.

She knew that establishing professional relationships with colleagues was laying the foundation for her future PLC work as a teacher leader. Teaching and leading are about making connections with people and building relationships with them (Crippen, 2010). In Helene's case, it was critical for her to get acquainted with colleagues first before initiating the PLC. Because her colleagues were already comfortable and trusting with one another when Helene convened the PLC, the group was able to realize early successes.

Leann: Share Practices

PLC Attribute 6: "Shared practice in which teachers invite and are invited to visit, observe, take notes, and consult with one another about their classroom practice, in the spirit of individual and community improvement, so students learn more successfully" (Hord & Tobia, 2012, p. 39).

Leann Brookshire taught English language arts to third graders at Forest Trail Elementary School. For her PLC project, she decided to explore with colleagues a commercial program that emphasizes the use of focused mini-lessons, small cooperative learning activities, and individual teacher-student conferences to teach reading and writing to children. The idea for the PLC came from another teacher leader at the school who had already administered a campuswide survey to identify teachers' professional development needs and interests.

After selecting the PLC topic, Leann championed it on campus. She invited colleagues to join the group, asked the principal to purchase the accompanying book for each participant, and subscribed to the program's website to learn more about its uses. She recruited several teachers on campus who were already familiar with the program to facilitate some of the meetings. By tapping into her colleagues' expertise, she made sure the teachers in the PLC heard multiple perspectives on the program.

After listening to and reading and talking about the program, the teachers tried it with their students. Leann explained, "Some people tried parts of the program, some never tried any, and some put the complete program into action." A few teachers observed their colleagues in the classroom teaching with the program. When the PLC participants attended their next meeting, all were able to discuss what they had experienced or witnessed. Leann exclaimed, "This diverse group had many great discussions!" The varying degrees of implementation gave them insights into the many ways that the program could be used while still adhering to the basic model of mini-lessons, cooperative learning, and conferencing. Besides gaining insights from the discussion, the PLC participants were able to troubleshoot problems they encountered and refine their understanding of the program.

Leann assessed the PLC's impact by saying,

> We became a more cohesive group. By engaging in professional development in a trusting environment, we had a chance to learn from others, share our perspectives, socialize, and visit other classrooms in the building. Teachers are now conferencing more with their students, differentiating instruction in more innovative ways, and giving students a say in their education.

Research affirms these benefits. In a study of PLCs in science courses, Richmond and Manokore (2011) learned that "the PLC participants leveraged each other's expertise and experiences in ways that suggested a kind of interdependence. The teachers had a common aim of sharing and learning, the ultimate goal of which was to enable their students to learn" (p. 559). Studying teacher leaders, Beachum and Dentith (2004) also found that teachers benefited when they "spent time in an organized and sustained fashion to plan curriculum together, talk generally about their teaching, relate student successes, and work on problems or new initiatives in the school" (p. 280).

Discussion of the Teacher Leaders and Their PLCs

These six case studies offer insights for others who want teacher leaders to facilitate professional development through PLCs, current teacher leaders, and those who aspire to serve as teacher leaders. The findings indicate positive effects on students, colleagues, the school district, and the teacher leaders themselves.

Students

Students in the schools benefited from the teacher leaders and PLCs. As Stoll et al. (2006) pointed out, "[A] key purpose of PLCs is to enhance teacher effectiveness and professionalism for students' ultimate benefit" (p. 229). The students in these case studies had teachers who were more attuned to their individual academic needs. The teachers were taking active measures to examine students' work and acquire teaching techniques that would improve learning. The students also had teacher leaders advocating to other teachers in the school on their behalf. Lieberman and Miller (2004) noted that teacher leaders are ideal advocates for student learning because of their keen ability to frame and reframe issues so that students and learning remain the central focus of what teachers do.

Colleagues

The teachers who participated in the PLCs reaped rewards from the teacher leaders and from the other PLC participants. They learned new pedagogical information specific to their subject areas, grade levels, and school context. Moreover, they felt a sense of camaraderie with other faculty members because of the time spent focused on common goals. The teachers reached out beyond their normal collegial circles and became acquainted with teachers of other grade levels and support staff members. In short, a sense of cohesiveness and unity developed over time; the teachers felt more at home in the school.

Researchers have noted similar effects on school climate. In a study of an elementary school in Georgia, Kelehear and Davison (2005) found that "teacher leadership directly translated into quality instruction and collegiality, leading to an atmosphere of high expectations" (p. 59). Likewise, Searby and Shaddix (2008) in their investigation of a high-performing district found that teachers in PLCs felt more confident and committed to teaching and learning.

Schools and District

The schools and district benefited from the teacher leaders and PLCs. They decentralized and differentiated the professional development by asking teacher leaders to offer a wide range of PLCs. Usually schools provide a limited number of professional development experiences to teachers, and teachers participate in these experiences as a group. The PLCs opened up the process, involved more teachers in sharing their expertise, and offered more choice to teachers in the schools. Furthermore, this approach encouraged teachers to become more self-directed and to take more responsibility for their professional growth and their schools' successes. As the teachers shared in the PLCs and found it acceptable to experiment and make mistakes, they were able to take instructional risks as educators, and such risk taking is a fundamental disposition of teacher leadership (Danielson, 2006). Finally, the teacher leaders shared the decision making with their administrators to select and host the PLCs. By collaborating and sharing the power, it was a win–win situation for the district and the teachers.

The district accomplished some of its goals, such as asking teachers to coordinate the professional development and focusing teachers' attention even more so on individual student's academic performance. Likewise, the teachers accomplished some of their goals, such as pursuing topics of interest and cultivating stronger collegial relationships. In their study of PLCs, Richmond and Manokore (2011) discovered that "the participants created hybrid spaces that enabled them to achieve their group goals and at the same time meet the demands of their school district" (p. 563).

Teacher Leaders Themselves

As PLC facilitators the teacher leaders reaped personal rewards. They enhanced their pedagogical skills by exploring relevant issues. They also strengthened their leadership skills by envisioning ideal teaching and learning on their campuses and then collaborating with administrators and colleagues to bring their visions to fruition. The daily management of the PLCs provided opportunities for reflection on teaching and on the PLCs in general. As Ackerman and Mackenzie (2006) found in their teacher leadership study, "Leadership is not just voicing beliefs but staying the course and looking for ways to deepen others' understanding on thorny issues" (p. 67). Finally, the experience gave the teacher leaders opportunities to advance their careers and contribute to the overall quality of the school while remaining in the classroom.

Conclusion

By assuming various leadership roles in the school, such as professional developer, teacher leaders help their school function at its highest level. As in the cases described in the previous sections, teacher leaders who work with administrators and colleagues to develop and implement PLCs foster positive working relationships with colleagues, focus on issues important to the teachers, and promote greater student learning. When teachers lead as professional developers, they themselves as well as students, colleagues, and the school and district all benefit.

References

Ackerman, R., & Mackenzie, S. V. (2006). Uncovering teacher leadership. *Educational Leadership, 63*(8), 66–70.

Ballek, K., O'Rourke, A., Provenzano, J., & Bellamy, T. (2005). Seven keys in cultivating principals and teacher leaders. *Journal of Staff Development, 26*(2), 42–48.

Barth, R. S. (2001). Teacher leader. *Phi Delta Kappan, 82*(6), 443–449.

Beachum, F., & Dentith, A. M. (2004). Teacher leaders creating cultures of school renewal and transformation. *The Educational Forum, 68*(3), 276–286. doi: 10.1080/00131720408984639

Bond, N., Goodwin, M., & Summers, E. (2013). The Partnership in Teacher Excellence Program: A district-university collaboration to create teacher leaders. *Journal of Curriculum and Teaching, 2*(1), 91–100.

Crippen, C. (2010). Serve, teach, and lead: It's all about relationships. *InSight: A Journal of Scholarly Teaching, 5,* 27–36.

Danielson, C. (2006). *Teacher leadership that strengthens professional practice.* Alexandria, VA: Association for Supervision and Curriculum Development.

Donaldson, G. A., Jr. (2006). *Cultivating leadership in schools: Connecting people, purpose, and practice* (2nd ed.). New York, NY: Teachers College Press.

Goode, J., Quartz, K. H., Barraza-Lyons, K., & Thomas, A. (2004). Developing teacher leaders: Exploring the multiple roles of beginning urban educators. *Teacher Education and Practice, 17*(4), 417–431.

Hargreaves, A. (1996). Transforming knowledge: Blurring the boundaries between research, policy, and practice. *Educational Evaluation and Policy Analysis, 18*(2), 105–122. doi: 10.2307/1164551

Hargreaves, A., & Fink, D. (2006). *Sustainable leadership.* San Francisco, CA: Jossey-Bass.

Hickey, W. D., & Harris, S. (2005). Improved professional development through teacher leadership. *The Rural Educator, 26*(2), 12–16.

Hord, S. M. (2004). Professional learning communities: An overview. In S. M. Hord (Ed.), *Learning together, leading together: Changing schools through professional learning communities* (pp. 5–14). New York, NY: Teachers College Press.

Hord, S. M., & Tobia, E. F. (2012). *Reclaiming our teaching profession: The power of educators learning in community.* New York, NY: Teachers College Press.

Kelehear, Z., & Davison, G. (2005). Teacher teams step up to leadership. *Journal of Staff Development, 26*(3), 54–59.

Kennedy, A. (2005). Models of continuing professional development: A framework for analysis. *Journal of In-service Education, 31*(2), 235–250.

Killion, J., & Harrison, C. (2006). *Taking the lead: New roles for teachers and school-based coaches.* Oxford, OH: National Staff Development Council.

Lieberman, A., & Miller, L. (2004). *Teacher leadership.* San Francisco, CA: Jossey-Bass.

Lindahl, R. (2008). Shared leadership: Can it work in schools? *The Educational Forum, 72*(4), 298–307.

Maloney, C., & Konza, D. (2011). A case study of teachers' professional learning: Becoming a community of professional learning or not? *Issues in Educational Research, 21*(1), 75–87.

Neumann, M. D., Jones, L. C. S., & Webb, P. T. (2012). Claiming the political: The forgotten terrain of teacher leadership knowledge. *Action in Teacher Education, 34*(1), 2–13. doi: 10.1080/01626620.2012.642279

Richmond, G., & Manokore, V. (2011). Identifying elements critical for functional and sustainable professional learning communities. *Science Education, 95*(3), 543–570. doi: 10.1002sce.20430

Searby, L., & Shaddix, L. (2008). Growing teacher leaders in a culture of excellence. *The Professional Educator, 32*(1), 1–9.

Spillane, J. P. (2006). *Distributed leadership.* San Francisco, CA: Jossey-Bass.

Stoll, L., Bolam, R., McMahon, A., Wallace, M., & Thomas, S. (2006). Professional learning communities: A review of the literature. *Journal of Educational Change, 7*(4), 221–258. doi: 10.1007/s10833-006-0001-8

Webb, P. T., Neumann, M., & Jones, L. C. (2004). Politics, school improvement, and social justice: A triadic model of teacher leadership. *The Educational Forum, 68*(3), 254–262.

York-Barr, J., & Duke, K. (2004). What do we know about teacher leadership? Findings from two decades of scholarship. *Review of Educational Research, 74*(3), 255–316. doi: 10.3102/00346543074003255

6

MENTORS AS TEACHER LEADERS IN SCHOOL/ UNIVERSITY INDUCTION PROGRAMS

Barbara H. Davis

Carol Gilles

Sheryl McGlamery

Saundra L. Shillingstad

Terri Cearley-Key

Yang Wang

Joanne Smith

Jenny Stegall

Since the 1980s, mentoring has become a key component of teacher induction programs (Odell & Huling, 2000). During this time, numerous studies have examined the benefits of a more experienced teacher (mentor) providing support and guidance to a beginning or less experienced teacher (mentee). The most frequently reported benefits for the mentee include staying in the profession, improving classroom practices, and increasing student achievement (Hobson, Ashby, Malderez, & Tomlinson, 2009; Ingersoll & Strong, 2011; Wang, Odell, & Schwille, 2008).

As university faculty who teach in mentoring/induction partnerships, we, too, have examined the effects of these programs on mentees (Davis & Higdon, 2008; Gilles, Cramer, & Hwang, 2001; McGlamery, Fluckinger, & Edick, 2006). Like others, we have found that mentoring provides positive benefits for the mentees. More recently, however, we have turned our attention to how mentors benefit from the mentoring process. In particular, we wondered how serving in the role of mentor fosters teacher leadership in the mentor.

Teacher leadership, though not a new concept, is currently garnering a lot of interest in educational literature. Numerous educators espouse the practice of teacher leadership as a method to promote effective teaching practices that can lead to improved student learning (Barth, 2001; Danielson, 2006; Teacher

Leadership Exploratory Consortium, 2011). Little has been written, however, on how the process of mentoring develops teacher leadership (Gilles & Wilson, 2004; Huling & Resta, 2001; Moir & Bloom, 2003) or how mentors as teacher leaders influence mentees' classroom practices. Moreover, few studies include mentors' own voices in how they learn to lead. Therefore, we decided to examine the following questions:

1. How does serving in the role of mentor develop teacher leadership?
2. In what ways do mentors as teacher leaders influence beginning teachers' practices?

Teacher Leadership

Teacher leadership, like mentoring, is a practice that evolved from the educational reform movement of the 1980s (York-Barr & Duke, 2004). In recent years, a new understanding about how leadership capacity develops has emerged. Current notions of leadership view it as active involvement by individuals at all levels within an organization rather than being situated in only formal authority roles (Lambert, 2003; Spillane, Halverson, & Diamond, 2004; York-Barr & Duke, 2004). For example, Lambert (2003) suggested leadership be redefined as "the reciprocal processes that enable participants in an educational community to construct meanings that lead toward a shared purpose of schooling" (p. 423). Similarly, Spillane et al. (2004) described leadership as a collaborative process. They defined it as "the interaction of leaders, followers, and their situation in the execution of particular leadership tasks" (p. 10). In other words, these authors viewed leadership as more than the function of one individual and his or her skills. They contended that leadership is stretched over, or distributed, among various participants in a social context.

These newer, more broad-based theories of leadership provide a theoretical framework for the concept of teacher leadership. Within this framework, teachers are encouraged to serve as leaders, both within and beyond their classrooms. Barth (2001) stated, "All teachers have the capacity to lead their schools down a more positive path, to enlist their abundant experience, and [to] craft knowledge in the service of school improvement" (p. 444). He emphasized, "All teachers can lead" (p. 444).

The concept of teacher leadership implies that teachers are key to improving teaching and learning in schools. According to York-Barr and Duke (2004), "Educational improvement at the level of instruction, for example, necessarily involves leadership by teachers in classrooms and with peers" (p. 255). As the concept of teacher leadership has evolved, so have the various roles for teacher leaders (Danielson, 2007; Katzenmeyer & Moller, 2009). Some roles emerge informally as teachers interact with their colleagues; others are more formal with designated responsibilities. Harrison and Killion (2007) listed ten possible roles in which teachers can contribute to a school's success (e.g., instructional specialist, learning facilitator, mentor, data coach). Frequently, these roles overlap within the school community. In this study, we focus specifically on how serving in the role of mentor develops leadership capacity.

Mentors as Teacher Leaders

In recent years, numerous researchers and educators have challenged the belief that beginning teachers are in "survival mode" and simply need emotional and technical support (Achinstein & Athanases, 2006; Feiman-Nemser, 2001; Moir, Barlin, Gless, & Miles, 2009; Odell & Huling, 2000; Strong, 2009). Current literature views beginning teachers as more than just "survivors." They are viewed as learners who are capable of reflecting on their practice, collaborating with others to solve classroom problems, and focusing on student learning. Such an approach calls for a new conception of mentoring—one that views a mentor as a leader. Feiman-Nemser (2001) called this approach to support "educative mentoring" (p. 18).

This vision calls for reform-minded mentors who not only provide emotional support but also help beginning teachers transform their thinking and classroom practice. In effect, these mentors are teachers of teachers. Moreover, in recent years Feiman-Nemser (2012) has espoused an expanded view of induction that encompasses school context as well as educative mentoring. She described this induction model as one that "situates new teacher's development within a professional learning community and school culture that supports the ongoing learning of all teachers" (p. 14). This collaborative model supports the development of teacher leadership for both beginning and experienced teachers alike. Each of the programs in the present study assumes this collaborative, transformational model of induction support.

Our Study of Mentors as Teacher Leaders

This qualitative study utilized a multiple case study approach (Merriam, 2009; Stake, 2006; Yin, 2009). For the purpose of this study, a "case" was defined as a school/university induction program for new teachers. Consistent with the case study approach, multiple perspectives and data sources established trustworthiness and credibility (Merriam, 2009).

Members of the Comprehensive Induction Consortium (CIC) conducted the study. The CIC, a national organization formed in 2006, comprises a group of public school/state university induction programs that have successfully utilized a similar model for the past 20 years. The consortium currently has three programs actively participating: University of Missouri, University of Nebraska at Omaha, and Texas State University. All three programs are based on the Albuquerque

Public Schools/University of New Mexico Elementary Teacher Induction Program model established in 1984 (Odell, 1992).

The CIC encourages collaboration among similar programs so they can share ideas and research opportunities. Each of the CIC programs has these components: (a) a full year of mentored support for first-year, already certified teachers by full-time experienced teachers who have been released from their classroom duties; (b) ongoing support for mentors in the form of weekly or monthly seminars; (c) coursework leading to a master's degree, which new teachers complete in 15 months; (d) a cohort group of beginning teachers (the mentees); and (e) job-embedded professional development (e.g., teacher research, peer coaching, videotaped teaching). Thus, the beginning teachers (hereafter referred to as *mentees*) exit the program in 15 months with a year of mentored teaching, courses that coincide with first-year teacher needs, and an advanced degree in education (Gilles, Davis, & McGlamery, 2009). Smith and Ingersoll (2004) defined induction programs that incorporate these various types of support as "comprehensive" (p. 704).

In this study, research teams consisting of two or more individuals from each program purposefully selected participants from their respective sites. The study participants were experienced mentors, former mentees, and school administrators. The mentors were chosen based on years of experience, effectiveness in mentoring, and availability. The mentees included participants who had successfully completed the program in the past 5 to 7 years. Each site also surveyed a sample of school administrators who had worked with the programs.

The procedures for data collection and analysis were conducted similarly across all three cases (programs). The data sources included: (a) transcripts of mentor semi-structured interviews conducted by researchers, (b) electronic mentee surveys, and (c) administrator questionnaires. The semi-structured interviews consisted of 11 questions that asked mentors in face-to-face interviews with the researchers to share their perceptions of teacher leadership and their influence on helping mentees develop leadership skills. The electronic surveys contained 10 questions that asked mentees to describe their perceptions of teacher leadership and ways their mentors influenced them to become leaders. The school administrator questionnaires, which were either mailed or sent electronically, included five questions related to teacher leadership in general and how the induction programs fostered leadership skills in particular.

Using the constant-comparative method (Strauss & Corbin, 1998), data analysis occurred in two phases. First, the researchers from each program analyzed their data independently and then met to discuss their findings and come to agreement. The within-case data analysis consisted of these steps: (a) reading and jotting marginal notes on the transcripts, surveys, and questionnaires; (b) identifying patterns and labeling concepts; (c) organizing labeled concepts into matrices; and (d) identifying themes.

During the second phase of analysis, research teams from each program met face-to-face to review the within-case findings and conduct a cross-case analysis. Using Miles and Huberman's (1994) method of cross-case comparison, the researchers shared data displays from the individual cases. The displays of the three cases were then assembled into meta-matrices, which enabled the systematic comparison of themes across the three cases. Through this process, we identified three major themes that appear to be associated with fostering teacher leadership through mentoring beginning teachers.

Fostering Teacher Leadership Through Mentoring Beginning Teachers

The themes are as follows: (a) building relationships through communication and collaboration, (b) modeling effective teaching practices, and (c) seeing the bigger picture. Each is described more fully in the next section.

Building Relationships Through Communication and Collaboration

The first theme focused on how mentors sought to build positive relationships with their mentees. In this study, mentors, mentees, and administrators mentioned numerous ways that positive relationships played a role in helping teachers become leaders within and beyond their classrooms. They described the interactions between mentors and mentees as being compassionate, encouraging, respectful, patient, caring, and open. Several administrators characterized mentors as patient teachers who helped novices reflect on practice in a caring and nonjudgmental way.

Nelda (all names are pseudonyms), an elementary mentor in a large suburban district, shared the importance of communicating effectively in leading others:

> In order to be a leader, you have to build relationships. . . . Leaders need to work with others and be able to listen to what others have to say. . . . They must listen skillfully and communicate effectively. They use effective questioning skills and understand the importance of the reflection process.

Active listening, an effective communication skill, was frequently mentioned as a tool that helped mentors build positive relationships with their mentees. Mindy, a mentor teacher, stated, "I think the ability to listen is really important and not with the intent to respond. . . . just the ability to try to listen and really hear what people are saying or what they're thinking."

Another mentor, Mike, responded, "Sometimes as a mentor and as a leader, [I find that] people just need to talk. They just need to feel like they've been heard and be validated for what concerns they are feeling."

Mentees from each of the programs shared how much it meant to have someone to talk to about their concerns during their first year of teaching. Mentors brought fresh ideas to solving problems in the classroom and served as sounding boards as the mentees talked through their struggles. Frequently, these mentor–mentee dialogues became opportunities to reflect on practice. As one mentor put it:

> Because the role forces you to offer opinions and insight, it forces you to have "difficult conversations" if necessary. It forces you to search yourself and see what you have done in the past and whether that is the proper direction for your mentee or whether you need to research and find new avenues for them. . . . Any role that causes you to examine yourself and others for positive strategies helps you be a leader.

Often, these conversations were based on data the mentors collected while informally observing in the mentees' classrooms. Mentees frequently noted that being observed and given specific feedback was what helped them improve their teaching the most. Feedback based on actual classroom practice and student data promotes an environment of collegiality, where teachers talk about practice with the goal of improving student performance. According to Katzenmeyer and Moller (2009), collegiality is a dimension of teacher leadership that can transform school culture from isolation to collaboration.

Collaborating with others was another category related to building relationships. As they worked together, mentors and mentees learned how to value differing opinions and ways of doing things. Frequently, mentors commented that working with different personality types was a challenging and yet valuable learning experience. Mentors also encouraged the mentees to collaborate with each other by sharing effective practices they were learning in their graduate programs, such as cooperative learning and positive discipline procedures.

This nudging by mentors led to mentees continuing to collaborate with others in the school environment after graduating from the induction programs. In the follow-up survey, many program graduates mentioned that they considered themselves to be teacher leaders because they were willing to help others and share ideas.

Modeling Effective Teaching Practices

The second theme describes what can happen once a trusting relationship has been established between the mentor and mentee. One mentor stated it like this:

> In order for the mentoring relationship to be valuable, the beginning teacher must feel comfortable and safe. This is in place after the mentor has taken time to build/maintain the relationship. The beginning teacher must also

see the mentor as a knowledgeable resource and one that can model effective instructional practices in the classroom. I feel these are both vital qualities of an effective teacher leader.

A majority of the mentors found that modeling lessons for their mentees was an effective way to teach the knowledge and skills necessary to succeed in the classroom. Moreover, modeling, also described by mentors as "leading by example," fostered collaboration and enhanced leadership skills. Effective modeling involves knowledge of practice and the ability to share that knowledge with colleagues.

Another component of modeling effective instruction relates to demonstrating differentiated teaching strategies in the mentees' classrooms. Beginning teachers often struggle with differentiation and seeing the individual needs of students in their classes. Kathy, a mentor, described the complex nature of modeling differentiation for other teachers:

> You have to be very aware of how you facilitate learning in the classroom. . . . They [mentees] will ask, "How did you get them to do that?" You have to be able to say, "Well I intentionally asked this question to this student at this time and then I intentionally gave wait time for this amount of time and then I intentionally looked at . . . the energy of the classroom and decided that they needed to talk and move and then come back to discuss it further." You have to really zero in on your own practice in order to be able to describe it to someone else.

Numerous mentees expressed the importance of seeing their mentors model lessons for them in their classrooms. In addition, they noted that taking time to debrief afterwards helped them talk through how they could implement the teaching strategies on their own. Demonstrating the lasting influence of modeling, several mentees mentioned that they have continued to use the strategies (e.g., literacy centers, guided reading instruction, management procedures) they learned from their mentors in their first year of teaching.

Most novices begin their careers with a knowledge base for teaching. It is when they assume full responsibility for their own classrooms, however, that assistance from a more experienced teacher (e.g., a mentor) can be critical in supporting and guiding them as they develop pedagogical knowledge. As the mentees in this study attest, having a mentor available to come alongside and model effective strategies can help beginning teachers increase their teaching expertise. One administrator observed, "They [mentors] model the pedagogical skills needed to be a great teacher." In *Cultivating High-Quality Teaching Through Induction and Mentoring,* Bartell (2005) supported this contention. She wrote, "Beginning teachers need to see models of expert teaching and be given opportunities to develop in ways that will encourage expertness as an eventual, long-term goal" (p. 28). Becoming effective teachers in their classrooms from the start builds capacity for beginning teachers to eventually become leaders in their schools.

Seeing the Bigger Picture

While the first two themes focused on the relationship between the mentor and mentee, the final theme centered on ways mentors expanded their own roles as teacher leaders. As mentors step out of their classrooms, they begin to gain a broader perspective on the school and the district. Outside of the isolation of the classroom where the focus is on the students and teaching, mentors begin to see the systemic nature of the schools. Mentors referred to this in various ways. Mike, who was an elementary mentor in a rural setting, explained:

> When you are in the classroom from day to day, you are so focused on what is needed . . . that you don't really get to step back. And afterwards you go home and you have family and you have all these other obligations, so you don't really ever have the time or the energy to sit back and think about bigger issues, like . . . what are we doing as a grade level team, or as a building or as a district or as a state or as a nation?

Moving into a mentor position gave Mike the time and the experiences to broaden his perspective.

Hanna, who was a mentor in a junior high, described understanding the broader perspective more as a sudden realization, "When I became a mentor, my classroom window expanded and I could see the eighth and ninth grade and every content area and I could see all these opportunities. That realization and perspective changed in a heartbeat for me."

This ability to see the big picture is closely tied to the mentors' vision. As one administrator put it, "Leaders have a vision for the future. They have the ability to help others see that vision and [to] want to be a part of it." The data identified several actions that mentors took because they had this broader perspective or vision for the future and they were able to communicate it. First, they encouraged current and especially former mentees to take leadership positions in the school or district. Hanna described it as asking others to be "instruments of change." Mentees indicated these leadership positions might involve serving as a grade-level leader, a professional learning community team member, a data team leader, a committee chair, a member of the leadership team, or a district committee member. Many mentors noted that they were more likely to encourage former mentees than current mentees into leadership positions because current mentees were still learning how to be effective teachers. They also often nudged former mentees into sharing instructional ideas or resources with other teachers, for example, volunteering for exemplar teaching opportunities (such as being videotaped or observed by visitors), submitting a proposal for a conference, or offering professional development for their school or district. These experiences helped former mentees move quickly into leadership roles themselves in their schools or districts.

Mentors often support other new teachers and not just their mentees, as part of their school responsibility. Working with other new teachers also offers them a larger, more systemic picture of the school. Instead of thoroughly understanding the one or two grade levels that their mentees taught, they garnered a larger view of multiple grade levels. This knowledge often makes the mentors more willing to, as one administrator put it, "speak up, ask questions, challenge the status quo, and agree to disagree." Another administrator suggested that these leaders have "the ability to look at the school from the balcony level rather than the dance floor, make connections to all staff and departments, not just their own, and have the time to be a part of district and university initiatives." Having this broader perspective and having influence in their schools oftentimes makes the opinions of these mentors especially critical to the principal. They might work with the principal to help a teacher who is struggling to learn new ideas in discipline and management or they might be able to "synthesize ideas (of teachers) into an appropriate plan and then present those ideas in a respectful way that includes everyone rather than antagonizes," as one former mentor suggested. Because they have a strong relationship with both the principal and fellow teachers, mentors are often sought out to organize and implement initiatives and projects for the good of the school.

Discussion and Recommendations

This study provides an example of how the process of being a mentor fosters teacher leadership skills for experienced teachers. Moreover, it demonstrates how mentors can help beginning teachers transform their thinking and classroom practices. In the role of mentor, these teachers serve as change agents who are involved in what others have called "transformational mentoring" (Achinstein & Athanases, 2006; Feiman-Nemser, 2012). As previously noted, the mentors in this study were members of comprehensive induction programs that provided release time for mentors to work alongside mentees in their classrooms and school communities. As classroom-based mentors, they were able to take time to build relationships, facilitate instructional conversations, and model effective teaching practices. Moreover, as part of the induction program, they interacted with others in the educational community, including mentees' grade-level team members, campus/district administrators, and university faculty, thus expanding their perspectives.

Yet, even in programs that provide release time and a supportive network, classroom-based mentoring can be challenging. Mentors in this study shared these challenges: (a) navigating the culture of different school sites; (b) learning about various grade-level and/or subject areas; (c) understanding adult learners and beginning teachers' needs; (d) knowing when to be directive and when to step back; and (e) initiating difficult conversations with mentees about teaching practices. We contend that working through these challenges within a collaborative network that consisted of other mentors and university faculty expanded the mentors' repertoire of leadership skills. As teacher leaders, they influenced the classroom practices of beginning teachers. Their positive impact on teaching led to improved school environments and novice teacher retention. Moreover, mentoring beginning teachers fostered teacher leadership not only for the mentors but for the mentees as well. Thus, these mentors were not only teachers of teachers, but also teachers of developing leaders.

Our hope is that this study will encourage others to form collaborative partnerships such as the ones described in this chapter. As the Teacher Leadership Exploratory Consortium (2011) recommended,

> We must consider how we can promote partnerships between schools and districts with [the] higher education community, state and national advocacy organizations, and organizations that support educational research and development. In order to be successful and productive, equal and reciprocal partnerships are needed among schools and external partners that focus on common goals and a mutual sharing of resources and expertise.
>
> (p. 25)

Such partnerships benefit all involved—novices, experienced teachers, and university faculty. Working together, we can foster teacher leadership across all levels of experience, with the result being school improvement and student success.

References

Achinstein, B., & Athanases, S. Z. (2006). *Mentors in the making: Developing new leaders for new teachers.* New York, NY: Teachers College Press.

Barth, R. S. (2001). Teacher leader. *Phi Delta Kappan, 82*(6), 443–449.

Bartell, C. A. (2005). *Cultivating high-quality teaching through induction and mentoring.* Thousand Oaks, CA: Corwin.

Danielson, C. (2006). *Teacher leadership that strengthens professional practice.* Alexandria, VA: Association for Supervision and Curriculum Development.

Danielson, C. (2007). The many faces of leadership. *Educational Leadership, 65*(1), 14–19.

Davis, B., & Higdon, K. (2008). The effects of mentoring/induction support on beginning teachers' practices in early elementary classrooms. *Journal of Research in Childhood Education, 22*(3), 261–274.

Feiman-Nemser, S. (2001). Helping novices learn to teach: Lessons from an exemplary support teacher. *Journal of Teacher Education, 52*(1), 17–30. doi: 10.1177/0022487101052001003

Feiman-Nemser, S. (2012). Beyond solo teaching. *Educational Leadership, 69*(8), 10–16.

Gilles, C., Cramer, M. M., & Hwang, S. K. (2001). Beginning teacher perceptions of concerns: A longitudinal look at teacher development. *Action in Teacher Education, 23*(3), 89–98.

Gilles, C., Davis, B., & McGlamery, S. (2009). Induction programs that work. *Phi Delta Kappan, 91*(2), 42–47.

Gilles, C., & Wilson, J. (2004). Receiving as well as giving: Mentors' perceptions of their professional development in one teacher induction program. *Mentoring and Tutoring, 12*(1), 87–106.

Harrison, C., & Killion, J. (2007). Ten roles for teacher leaders. *Educational Leadership, 65*(1), 74–77.

Hobson, A. J., Ashby, P., Malderez, A., & Tomlinson, P. D. (2009). Mentoring beginning teachers: What we know and what we don't. *Teaching and Teacher Education, 25*(1), 207–216.

Huling, L., & Resta, V. (2001). *Teacher mentoring as professional development.* Washington, DC: ERIC Clearinghouse on Teaching and Teacher Education. (ERIC ED 460 125).

Ingersoll, R. M., & Strong, M. (2011). The impact of induction and mentoring programs for beginning teachers: A critical review of the research. *Review of Educational Research, 81*(2), 201–233.

Katzenmeyer, M., & Moller, G. (2009). *Awakening the sleeping giant: Helping teachers develop as leaders* (3rd ed.). Thousand Oaks, CA: Corwin.

Lambert, L. (2003). Leadership redefined: An evocative context for teacher leadership. *School Leadership & Management, 23*(4), 421–430.

McGlamery, S., Fluckinger, J., & Edick, N. (2006). The CADRE project: Looking at the development of beginning teachers. *Educational Considerations, 33*(2), 42–50.

Merriam, S. B. (2009). *Qualitative research: A guide to design and implementation.* San Francisco, CA: Jossey-Bass.

Miles, M. B., & Huberman, A. M. (1994). *Qualitative data analysis: An expanded sourcebook* (2nd ed.). Thousand Oaks, CA: Sage.

Moir, E., Barlin, D., Gless, J., & Miles, J. (2009). *New teacher mentoring: Hopes and promise for improving teacher effectiveness.* Cambridge, MA: Harvard Education Press.

Moir, E., & Bloom, G. (2003). Fostering leadership through mentoring. *Educational Leadership, 60*(8), 58–60.

Odell, S. (1992). A collaborative approach to teacher induction that works. *Journal of Staff Development, 11*(4), 12–16.

Odell, S. J., & Huling, L. (Eds.). (2000). *Quality mentoring for novice teachers.* Washington, DC: Association of Teacher Educators. Indianapolis, IN: Kappa Delta Pi.

Smith, T. M., & Ingersoll, R. M. (2004). What are the effects of induction and mentoring on beginning teacher turnover? *American Educational Research Journal, 41*(3), 681–714.

Spillane, J. P., Halverson, R., & Diamond, J. (2004). Towards a theory of leadership practice: A distributed perspective. *Journal of Curriculum Studies, 36*(1), 3–34.

Stake, R. E. (2006). *Multiple case study analysis.* New York, NY: Guilford Press.

Strauss, A., & Corbin, J. (1998). *Basics of qualitative research: Techniques and procedures for developing grounded theory* (2nd ed.). Thousand Oaks, CA: Sage.

Strong, M. (2009). *Effective teacher induction and mentoring: Assessing the evidence.* New York, NY: Teachers College Press.

Teacher Leadership Exploratory Consortium. (2011). *Teacher leader model standards.* Retrieved from http://teacherleaderstandards.org/downloads/TLS_Brochure.pdf

Wang, J., Odell, S. J., & Schwille, S. A. (2008). Effects of teacher induction on beginning teachers' teaching: A critical review of the literature. *Journal of Teacher Education, 59*(2), 132–152.

Yin, R. K. (2009). *Case study research: Design and methods* (4th ed.). Thousand Oaks, CA: Sage.

York-Barr, J., & Duke, K. (2004). What do we know about teacher leadership? Findings from two decades of scholarship. *Review of Educational Research, 74*(3), 255–316.

7

THE SPECIAL EDUCATION TEACHER AS A SERVANT LEADER

Clinton Smith

Servant leaders possess attributes, qualities, and characteristics that distinguish them from other types of leaders. What makes servant leaders unique is their unwavering focus on people's needs. Servant leaders appear in many walks of life. Even classroom teachers who lead are sometimes referred to as servant leaders because of their focused attention to children's needs. The purpose of this chapter is to examine the ways in which special education teachers, a subset of the teaching population, embody the qualities of servant leadership. The chapter also explores the context, roles, and responsibilities of special education teachers, as well as the forces that act upon this group of educators.

A teacher leader is defined as "a person who leads by example, is a problem solver, and relates well to others" (Martin, 2007, p. 18). Not all teacher leaders are the same. In fact, there are two basic types: formal and informal (Ackerman & McKenzie, 2006; Martin, 2007). Formal teacher leaders possess specialized skills; assume voluntary or administratively assigned positions; and serve as department chairs, team leaders, or instructional coaches. By comparison, informal teacher leaders talk regularly with others about teaching and classroom practices and unofficially mentor colleagues who are new to the profession. When formal and informal teacher leaders act, their impact is felt throughout their schools (Barth, 2001).

Special education teacher leaders impact their schools by working closely with general education teachers to meet students' varying academic needs. Through powerful collaborations with colleagues, students, and parents, special education teachers foster a climate of inclusiveness. In fact, high-quality inclusive education cannot exist without special educators (York-Barr, Sommerness, Duke, & Ghere, 2005).

Recognizing the leadership of special education teachers and the ways they affect the quality of education for students with and without disabilities is important (York-Barr et al., 2005). For example, special education teachers are often the "go-to" people because of the instructional and behavioral strategies they provide to students with disabilities (Smith, 2009). Although special educators are generally held in high regard, they nonetheless face the same challenges and issues as their colleagues, including multiple responsibilities, time management, test accountability, and negative perceptions by coworkers and parents (Barth, 2001).

The Special Education Teacher

Special education teachers enter the profession because they want to contribute to society and improve the lives of students with disabilities. Special education teachers work as consultants, co-teachers, resource room teachers, or teachers in self-contained classrooms (Wasburn-Moses, 2005). Special educators at the high school level fulfill additional roles by providing vocational training and transition planning for their students (Edgar & Polloway, 1994). Scholars, such as York-Barr et al. (2005), suggested that special educators are teacher leaders because they lead through influence and relationships with students and parents. In many ways, special education teachers, regardless of the grade level, are simultaneously classroom teachers, co-teachers, colleagues, experts, relationship builders, and communicators. Besides being experts in matters relating to the instruction of students with disabilities, they must also be bridge builders who connect students with disabilities to their peers and to the community (York-Barr et al., 2005).

Forces Acting on the Special Education Teacher

Special educators face a multitude of responsibilities in meeting students' diverse needs. They develop individualized programming; personalize instruction through the implementation of adaptations, accommodations, and modifications; manage paraprofessionals; and manage student behavior (York-Barr et al., 2005). Furthermore, they interact with students early and often in the educational process in order to discover the students' cognitive, emotional, and social needs. Wasburn-Moses (2005) found that 67% of special education teachers provide adaptations or accommodations for their students daily. In the same study, this researcher found that 89.5% of special education teachers said they deal with behavior problems regularly. Special educators balance their students' basic needs while providing as much access to the general education curriculum as possible (Jatala & Seevers, 2006). Adding to these pressures is the accountability for student achievement through standardized testing and the implementation of standards-based instruction.

Special educators consult with parents and collaborate with colleagues. In these instances, clear communication is important and essential to providing inclusive instruction for students with disabilities. Friend and Cook (2006) claimed that successful collaboration occurs when two or more professionals work and plan together for the purpose of achieving common goals. When teachers collaborate, they share resources, make decisions, and accept joint responsibility for the decisions (Carter, Prater, Jackson, & Marchant, 2009). Building these collaborative relationships with teachers, as well as with students and parents, is an essential characteristic of effective teaching.

Effective time management is another challenge that special educators face. They find the time to plan instruction with general education colleagues. With the increasing number of educational reforms, special educators allocate time to attend professional development workshops as a way to hone their pedagogical skills. Furthermore, they manage an overload of paperwork, monitor student progress, and achieve a high level of performance on the annual teacher evaluation.

To balance these roles and responsibilities, special education teachers resemble air traffic controllers. They keep in mind the big picture while coordinating and communicating the smaller details of the implementation process (York-Barr et al., 2005). Special educators operate within a framework and philosophy that guide them as they work with a multitude of people. One such useful framework to guide special educators is that of servant leadership. This framework is ideal because special education teachers put other people's needs first.

Servant Leadership

Robert Greenleaf (1977) introduced the concept of servant leadership more than three decades ago. He explained the concept initially by writing:

> The servant leader is servant first. It begins with the natural feeling that one wants to serve. The conscious choice brings one to aspire to lead. The best test is: do those served grow as persons; do they, while being served, become healthier, wiser, freer, more autonomous, more likely themselves to become servants? And, what is the effect on the least privileged in society: will they benefit, or at least not be further deprived?
>
> (p. 27)

Although today's scholars have not reached consensus on the definition of servant leadership (Parris & Peachey, 2013), they view it as a lifetime of transforming oneself to become more trustworthy, humble, and responsible (Greenleaf, 2003). Servant leaders exhibit a strong character and an unwavering commitment to serving others and making others a high priority. As Frick and Spears (1996) stated, "Everything begins with the individual, leaders are chosen by followers, the only lead of a genuine leader is foresight, and a leader's impact is measured by his effect on followers" (p. 285). Servant leaders' vision to serve others and sacrifice personally motivates others to follow them (Green 2012; Greenleaf, 2003). A respected scholar in the field of leadership, Sergiovanni (1992), noted that these attributes are the "head, heart, and hand of leadership" (p. 6).

Special Education and Servant Leadership

The servant leadership theory is particularly applicable to special education teachers because, as mentioned earlier, servant leaders put the needs of others ahead of their own. Servant leadership provides a framework for special education teachers to use when attempting to be positive and proactive in dealing with students, parents, and colleagues; and also when trying to be effective teachers with multiple roles and responsibilities (Crippen, 2005a). As Hall (1991) stated, "A servant leader is one who invests himself or herself in enabling others, in helping them be and do their best. . . . At the very heart of servant leadership is the genuine desire to serve others for the common good" (p. 14).

Jennings and Stahl-Wert (2003) identified five principles of teachers acting as servant leaders in educational settings. Although these principles apply to any teacher acting as a servant leader, they pertain particularly well to special educators.

The first principle of servant leadership identified by Jennings and Stahl-Wert (2003) is that the teacher has a significant purpose in mind. The servant leader wants students to succeed in life. Like general education students, students with disabilities want to succeed in school and the community. Special education teachers work with students to help them dream dreams and achieve future goals. Through the process of developing Individual Education Plans (IEPs) for students and preparing them for life after school through transition planning, these educators guide students to achieve life goals.

The second principle is that teachers unleash the strengths, talents, and passions of those whom they serve (Jennings & Stahl-Wert, 2003). In his explanation of the concept, Greenleaf (1977) asked, "Do those served grow as persons; do they, while being served, become healthier, wiser, freer, more autonomous, more likely themselves to become servants?" (p. 27). Special education teachers teach students the knowledge, skills, and strategies for success in school and life. They help their students to grow as people and to become more independent now as young people and later as adults.

The third principle focuses on implementing high standards of performance (Jennings & Stahl-Wert, 2003). Expectations should be held high even though a student's ability may vary considerably. Special educators model the desirable skills and attitudes that the students must exhibit in order to meet these expectations.

The fourth principle is to address the weaknesses and enhance the strengths (Jennings & Stahl-Wert, 2003). Although special education teachers are aware of students' limitations, they help them to build on their individual strengths. Many students with disabilities excel in math, reading, art, music, or athletics. Speaking to educators, Buckingham and Coffman (1999) advised, "People don't change much. Don't waste time trying to fix what was left out. Try to draw out what was left in. That is hard enough" (p. 57). Special education teachers follow this advice and focus on students' strengths, while not completely ignoring the weaknesses.

The final principle is to "put oneself at the bottom of the pyramid so that one can focus on unleashing the energy, excitement, and talents of those being served" (Jennings & Stahl-Wert, 2003, p. 102). A major goal of special education teachers is to prepare students for transition into independent living and to teach them self-determination and self-advocacy skills. In order to do this, special education teachers foster the development of adaptive skills and age-appropriate behaviors (e.g., language and literacy skills, math skills, social skills, and practical living skills) in an effort to have students function as independently and safely as possible in life. They also assist and support students with disabilities by helping to remove numerous obstacles. The removal of these barriers helps students become more confident in their own abilities and prepares them for everyday life after graduation.

Greenleaf's Qualities of a Servant Leader and the Special Education Teacher

Larry Spears, who served as president and CEO of the Robert Greenleaf Center for Servant Leadership from 1990–2007, identified ten characteristic qualities of a servant leader based on the writings of Greenleaf. These qualities intertwine with the role and responsibilities of the special education teacher as a teacher leader. Each characteristic is explained in the following sections.

Listening

Effective servant leaders exhibit outstanding communication skills. An important aspect of effective communication is the ability to listen to others. A special education teacher learns the discipline of listening. Greenleaf (1977) believed that listening was an attitude that focused on other people and what they were trying to express. The goal is to hear what is said and what is unsaid when communicating with others (Spears, 2010).

Special education teachers exhibit the important skill of listening in the classroom when dealing with problematic students, during parent meetings, during telephone conversations, in IEP meetings, and with their colleagues. By listening carefully, these teacher leaders learn valuable information from parents and colleagues about students with disabilities as the information relates to the disability, medical issues, family issues, or related educational programs.

Empathy

Empathy is the skill of understanding the thoughts, feelings, and perspectives of others and caring about those others. Empathy goes hand in hand with the discipline of listening. Greenleaf (1977) and Spears (2010) posit that people must be accepted and recognized for their special and unique dispositions. Greenleaf (1970) stated, "The servant always accepts and never rejects" (p. 12).

When working with students with disabilities, the special education teacher leader focuses on students' strengths and abilities and helps them to strengthen the areas of need, whether academically or socially. This does not mean that inappropriate behaviors and unacceptable performance are accepted, but that the student will not be rejected when these occur. Empathetic special education teacher leaders put themselves in the shoes of students, parents, and colleagues. They understand, through listening and empathy, how to work effectively with students with disabilities and their parents. By being empathetic, special education teacher leaders provide colleagues and administrators with important information to assist students with disabilities.

Healing

The potential for healing one's self and one's relationships with others is another important characteristic of servant leadership (Greenleaf, 1977; Spears, 2010). Servant leaders care about the well-being of others, and they want to help those others to improve their circumstances (Hays, 2008). As Spears stated, "servant leaders recognize that they have an opportunity to help make whole those with whom they come in contact" (p. 27).

The parents of a student with disabilities face various emotional hurdles after learning of a diagnosis of a disability. They must cope with the child's medical and behavioral issues. Special education teacher leaders often comfort the parents of these children when the parents seek help in understanding the diagnosis of a disability and in sorting through the issues that arise from having a child with a disability. By practicing the skills of listening and empathy, the special education teacher leaders provide healing that comforts parents who are raising a child with a disability.

Awareness

The awareness of self and others is a strength of a true servant leader. By exhibiting awareness, one is able to listen to others, learn new things, reflect, and implement change. Servant leaders who cultivate awareness view situations from an integrated and holistic position (Spears, 2010).

Special education teacher leaders' awareness assists them in understanding issues that involve ethics and values (Spears, 2010). By stepping back and observing the advantages and disadvantages of a particular educational program or intervention, special education teacher leaders help parents and team members see the big picture and develop a more responsive IEP for the student.

Persuasion

The characteristic of persuasion is important to the decision-making process. Servant leaders seek to convince by drawing upon personal relationships to influence others and achieve goals rather than by trying to coerce compliance (Spears, 2010). Servant leaders build consensus within groups and act in fair, transparent, and consistent ways in order to persuade and influence (Crippen, 2005b).

Special education teacher leaders exhibit the attribute of persuasion when working with students, parents, administrators, and colleagues. Parents must often be counseled and mentored to place their child in special education programs, to implement a behavioral intervention, or to decide the plan for the child upon graduation from high school. Acting as experts in the field, special education teacher leaders use their expertise to guide parents and members of the IEP team through the decision-making process and help the group to make the best educational decisions for the child.

Conceptualization

Conceptualization requires one to dream big and broaden one's focus from the day-to-day realities outward. This means that servant leaders "stretch their thinking to encompass broader-based conceptual thinking" (Spears, 2010, p. 28). Many times they see the whole in perspective, visualize a concept, and develop a plan for the future.

More often than not, teachers and administrators focus on the day-to-day operations at the school. Likewise, students and parents struggle to make it through the day. When planning an educational program for students with disabilities, special education teacher leaders must think conceptually and long-term in order to guide parents and students to dream big and to prepare carefully and strategically for life after graduation. Special education teacher leaders strike a balance between conceptual thinking and practical implementation of the day-to-day program.

Foresight

The characteristic of foresight links closely to conceptualization. Greenleaf (1970) stated that a servant leader "needs to have a sense for the unknowable and be able to foresee the unforeseeable" (p. 11). Servant leaders foresee possible outcomes of various situations based on previous experiences, the actual realities of the present, and the consequences of future decisions (Spears, 2010). As Spears (2010) noted, foresight is the characteristic of servant leadership that may be innate instead of nurtured. He advised future researchers to study this area.

Special education teacher leaders help parents, students, and the IEP teams to make decisions based on previous experiences with the student. Many times, special education teachers have experienced similar situations with former students and parents who have made the same types of decisions, such as placement for special education services, the educational plan for high school, or the student's transition into the community after graduation. These previous experiences inform parents who are facing similar decisions. By knowing students' strengths and weaknesses, special education teacher leaders foresee the realities of the present, avoid unnecessary negative consequences, and plan the best future.

Stewardship

Servant leadership assumes a commitment to serving the needs of others (Spears, 2010). Stewards are entrusted with the management of the activities and affairs of other people. Sergiovanni (1992) believed that stewardship "involves the leader's personal responsibility to manage her or his life and affairs with proper regard for the rights of other people and for the common welfare" (p. 139). Greenleaf suggested that servant leaders play a significant role in holding something in trust for someone else.

Special education teacher leaders exhibit the characteristic of stewardship by nurturing and maintaining parents' trust during the child's educational career. By doing so, these professionals provide students with the best possible educational preparation for college, career, and life.

Commitment to the Growth of People

Servant leaders are deeply committed to the personal, professional, and spiritual growth of every individual whom they lead (Spears, 2010). They demonstrate an appreciation for others and seek to build unity and positive professional relationships. As Greenleaf (1970) advised, "Weld a team of such people by lifting them up to grow taller than they otherwise might be" (p. 14).

Special education teacher leaders commit themselves to the intellectual and emotional growth of all students. This unwavering commitment is not limited only to students; it extends to parents and colleagues as well. Special education teacher leaders take a personal interest in the lives of their students' families and offer encouragement and emotional support. When families need direction, information, and guidance to cope with the implications of the child's disability diagnosis, special education teachers provide this support. Because special education teacher leaders possess unique knowledge and ability, they become the "go-to" people for parents.

Likewise, special education teacher leaders play an important role for the general education teacher who is working with a student with a disability. The general education teacher may not know how to teach this population of students successfully; therefore, the special education teacher leader mentors the general education teacher and provides ongoing professional development regarding current best teaching practices.

Building Community

The size and complexity of large institutions have eroded the sense of community that united individuals in the past. Servant leaders realize that community can be reestablished with those who work together in institutions (Spears, 2010). As Greenleaf (1970) stated,

> All that is needed to rebuild community as a viable life form for large numbers of people is for enough servant leaders to show the way, not by mass movements, but by each servant leader demonstrating his own unlimited liability for a quite specific community-related group.
>
> (p. 30)

Special education teacher leaders foster a sense of community in classrooms by treating students with disabilities as valuable, contributing members of the school. These students enrich the learning environment and help classmates to learn how to work and live with people who are different. Special education teachers also build community in schools by collaborating with colleagues and administrators and by providing a sound educational program for students.

Implications of the Special Educator as a Servant Leader in the Classroom

In the past, special education teachers and their students were separated and tucked away from the rest of the school population. This physical isolation prohibited special education teachers from interacting easily with general education colleagues. Likewise, students with disabilities were stigmatized and labeled as different. As a result of the changes to more inclusionary practices and educational reform of service delivery models, special education teacher leaders now have more opportunities to influence positively both general and special education students, a process that in turn creates a greater sense of diversity and inclusiveness.

By teaching across different settings and adapting instructional content on all levels, special education teacher leaders use their instructional expertise to assist students in meeting educational goals and to prepare these young people for life after high school. Special educator teacher leaders also share their knowledge of working with students with disabilities and managing the special education process with colleagues and with the parents of students with disabilities. Providing this assistance requires collaboration, communication, and a desire to put others first.

Sergiovanni (2005) asserted, "Leadership is about helping people understand the problems they face, helping them manage these problems, and even helping them to learn to live with them" (p. 122). This statement rings especially true of special education teacher leaders because a great deal of trust is placed in them. They assist students and parents through the path of having a disability; they show them ways to build upon students' strengths; and they guide families to academic, personal, and social success. Integrating the characteristics of servant leadership is enhanced through learning and practice (Spears, 2010). By incorporating these characteristics of servant leaders, special education teacher leaders impact the lives of students and help them to build self-advocacy skills, learn self-determination, and increase their autonomy. Consequently, the students are empowered to succeed and to become more confident.

Through effective collaboration and communication, special education teacher leaders provide instruction and knowledge to those with whom they interact. They build positive relationships and establish trust and respect. They exhibit a commitment to the growth of people by building a greater sense of citizenship and an appreciation for community. As servant leaders, they build stronger relationships with their students, the parents of their students, and their colleagues (Hays, 2008). When they exhibit the characteristics of servant leadership (i.e., listening, empathy, healing, awareness, persuasion, conceptualization, foresight, stewardship, a commitment to the growth of people, and building community) and incorporate the five principles of servant leadership, special education teacher leaders apply the best practices and become more effective leaders.

References

Ackerman, R., & McKenzie, S. V. (2006). Uncovering teacher leadership. *Educational Leadership, 63*(8), 66–70.

Barth, R. S. (2001). Teacher leader. *Phi Delta Kappan, 82*(6), 443–449.

Buckingham, M., & Coffman, C. (1999). *First, break all the rules: What the world's greatest managers do differently.* New York, NY: Simon & Schuster.

Carter, N., Prater, M., Jackson, A., & Marchant, M. (2009). Educators' perceptions of collaborative planning processes for students with disabilities. *Preventing School Failure, 54*(1), 60–70.

Crippen, C. (2005a). Inclusive education: A servant-leadership perspective. *Education Canada, 45*(4), 19–22.

Crippen, C. (2005b). The democratic school: First to serve, then to lead. *Canadian Journal of Educational Administration and Policy, 47,* 1–17.

Edgar, E., & Polloway, E. A. (1994). Education for adolescents with disabilities: Curriculum and placement issues. *Journal of Special Education, 27*(4), 438–452.

Frick, D. M., & Spears, L. C. (Eds.). (1996). *On becoming a servant leader: The private writings of Robert K. Greenleaf.* San Francisco, CA: Jossey Bass.

Friend, M., & Cook, L. (2006). *Interactions: Collaboration skills for school professionals* (5th ed.). Boston, MA: Allyn & Bacon.

Green, R. L. (2012). *Practicing the art of leadership: A problem-based approach to implementing the ISLLC standards.* Boston, MA: Pearson/Allyn & Bacon.

Greenleaf, R. K. (1970). *The servant as leader.* Westfield, IN: Robert K. Greenleaf Center for Servant Leadership.

Greenleaf, R. K. (1977). *Servant leadership: A journey into the nature of legitimate power and greatness.* Mahwah, NJ: Paulist Press.

Greenleaf, R. K. (2003). *The servant-leader within: A transformative path.* Mahwah, NJ: Paulist Press.

Hall, A. S. (1991). Why a great leader. In K. Hall (Ed.), *Living leadership: Biblical leadership speaks to our day* (p. 14). Anderson, IN: Warner Press.

Hays, J. M. (2008). Teacher as servant: Applications of Greenleaf's servant leadership in higher education. *Journal of Global Business Issues, 2*(1), 113–134.

Jatala, S. J., & Seevers, R. L. (2006). Nature and use of curriculum in special education. *Academic Exchange Quarterly, 10*(1), 192–196.

Jennings, K., & Stahl-Wert, J. (2003). *The serving leader: 5 powerful actions that will transform your team, your business, and your community.* San Francisco, CA: Berrett-Koehler Publishers.

Martin, B. (2007). Teacher leaders: Qualities and roles. *The Journal for Quality and Participation, 30*(4), 17–18.

Parris, D. L., & Peachey, J. W. (2013). A systematic literature review of servant leadership theory in organizational contexts. *Journal of Business Ethics, 113*(3), 377–393. doi: 10.1007/s10551-012-1322-6

Sergiovanni, T. J. (1992). *Moral leadership: Getting to the heart of school improvement.* San Francisco, CA: Jossey-Bass.

Sergiovanni, T. J. (2005). The virtues of leadership. *The Educational Forum, 69*(2), 112–123.

Smith, A. (2009). Enhance the image of the special education teacher. *Delta Kappa Gamma Bulletin, 75*(2), 27–29.

Spears, L. C. (2010). Character and servant leadership: Ten characteristics of effective, caring leaders. *The Journal of Virtues and Leadership, 1*(1), 25–30.

Wasburn-Moses, L. (2005). Roles and responsibilities of secondary special education teachers in an age of reform. *Remedial and Special Education, 26*(3), 151–158.

York-Barr, J., Sommerness, J., Duke, K., & Ghere, G. (2005). Special educators in inclusive education programmes: Reframing their work as teacher leadership. *International Journal of Inclusive Education, 9*(2), 193–215.

8

TEACHER LEADERS IN CURRICULUM REFORM

Integrating the Expressive Arts

Laurie J. DeRosa
Susan Trostle Brand

In the wake of the No Child Left Behind legislation, scripted teaching and an increased emphasis on standardized testing have become the norm in many public schools today (Armstrong, 2006). Once considered pillars of child-centered education, the arts have taken a back seat to literacy and math instruction. Despite this situation, research continues to find that all children do not learn and achieve in the same ways (Armstrong, 2009; Gardner, 1983). Arts instruction may provide a vital pathway to learning for some students who encounter difficulties with the verbal and quantitative skills assessed on standardized exams.

The potential for art to transform a student's academic career for the better is illustrated by the poignant story of Michele Sommer. As a result of her struggles with traditional academic subjects, Michele felt "dumb, humiliated, and worthless" throughout her school years. On graduation day, she was astonished to receive an award for her drawing of a geranium. During the ceremony, her art teacher commended Michele for her accomplishments and noted the happiness and satisfaction others felt from viewing the drawing. Michele claims that her art teacher saved her life that day. She recounted, "The feeling of success and the knowledge that I had a valuable skill that I could share with others did buoy me and set me on the path to my bright future" (Sommer, 2013, p. 41). Now an art teacher herself, Michele maintains that art education has the power to help every child experience success and joy in learning; indeed, art can powerfully transform children's perceptions of the world. As an educator, Michele recognizes and celebrates the creativity of her students who struggle with academics. Having a parent or teacher witness and nurture a learner's creative side is extremely valuable in working toward a deeper understanding of that student.

Forward thinking educational systems and schools accommodate diversity such as Michele's in the student population (United Nations Educational, Scientific and

Cultural Organization [UNESCO], 1994). In contrast, traditional curricula offer little diversity in teaching methods or opportunities for diverse learning and assessment styles. Teacher leaders, working with other teachers, administrators, parents, and the community, play a major role in transforming the traditional curriculum and infusing it with the arts (Bond, 2011; Danielson, 2006; Katzenmeyer & Moller, 2009). Given the paramount role of the arts in student motivation and learning (Ashbury & Rich, 2008; Eisner, 2002), some model teacher training programs are now preparing candidates to become change agents for arts integration in schools, addressing the needs of all students. Unless these beginning teachers lead the way, school reform will not progress substantially or significantly, especially because curriculum leadership is not part of most teacher training programs in the United States today. Even inservice teachers reluctantly view themselves as leaders. Too frequently, a major role of teacher leaders is to pass information from the principal to the teachers and from the teachers back to the principals. The extent of their "leadership" responsibilities is relatively mundane, including such tasks as ordering supplies and textbooks and recommending teaching assignments.

However, when student teachers and inservice teachers hold conversations about the arts, work in collegial relationships with other teachers, realize that they can influence other teachers' practice in arts integration, and begin to recognize their much grander roles of affecting students' futures, they glean confidence about their leadership abilities (Rosenholtz, 1991). Accompanying this awakened sense of confidence, preservice and inservice teachers develop a sense of efficacy (Katzenmeyer & Moller, 2009). Efficacy enables them to assume a new teacher leader role—that of taking responsibility for the learning and well-being of all students in a smoothly functioning school environment that values the arts. In essence, teacher leaders can affect major curriculum changes, including promoting arts integration into the curriculum in significant and meaningful ways through drama, storytelling, visual arts, music, and dance.

Stages of Teacher Leaders in the Arts

As teachers become leaders and change agents, they proceed through four stages. Admittedly, teacher leaders in all stages continually evolve and may demonstrate qualities that represent more than one stage at any given time in their careers. The four states are the following: Stage One: *Self-Protective;* Stage Two: *Conformist;* Stage Three: *Conscientious;* and Stage Four: *Autonomous* (Katzenmeyer & Moller, 2009). Teachers move through these four stages in their own unique ways, depending upon their prior experience, dispositions, availability of mentoring, and degree of comfort with their environments and positions. During the Self-Protective Stage, teachers seek one "right" answer to a question and blame others or the system when they struggle. At the Conformist Stage, the teacher leaders rarely vary from the established rules and existing ways of behaving and performing, although they begin to accept more responsibility for the challenges they encounter. The

Conscientious Stage involves teacher leaders' exploring possibilities and remaining flexible about the future. Finally, when the teacher leaders reach the highest stage of Autonomous functioning, they recognize the interdependent nature of teaching and learning and welcome others' contributions and points of view while simultaneously functioning independently.

An examination of the teacher leader stages and behaviors elicits recognition of the importance of professional growth throughout the career in effecting positive changes in the school climate and curriculum. When infusing arts-integrated programs into the school, it is prudent for teacher leaders who are functioning at the Conscientious or Autonomous Stages to lead and scaffold other teachers who are in the Self-Protective Stage. Identifying a mutual goal that is shared by Self-Protective new teachers and Autonomous teachers may enhance beginning teachers' "comfort levels" and enable them to embrace change that leads to their attainment of valued and identified goals.

The autonomous teacher leader employs several strategies in eliciting positive change in the novice or self-protective teacher's autonomy and, ultimately, in the curriculum. Effective strategies of teacher leaders in the arts include meetings; co-teaching; demonstrations; visitations to exemplary arts-infused classrooms; tutoring; mentoring; and sharing of resources, workshops, and conversations about the importance of arts integration with colleagues and administrators.

The autonomous teacher leader may agree to meet weekly with a novice fourth-grade teacher to discuss and plan the arts-infused curriculum. The teacher leader may co-teach lessons with the novice, demonstrating how to write arts-infused lessons, activities, and units of study. High-quality and consistent preservice teacher leadership experiences and training often provide the necessary scaffolding to assist the beginning teachers in more readily embracing roles as teacher leaders early in their careers (Bond, 2011). Likewise, the practice of assigning mentors and scheduling visitation appointments and workshops with self-protective teachers, both in the school and the district, provides newer teachers with a source of inspiration as well as a plan of action to follow. Finally, scheduling meetings with a supportive principal or curriculum leader, facilitated by the autonomous teacher leader/mentor, conveys a critical sense of support and security to self-protective teachers as they begin to vary from the scripted textbook and explore new and creative horizons for teaching and learning.

Melissa Marino (real name, used with permission), the principal at the Wawaloam Elementary School in Exeter, Rhode Island, oversees teacher evaluation at her school. Important components of the teacher evaluation rubric are student engagement and creativity. Principal Marino promotes creativity and student engagement by encouraging teachers, both novice and expert, to share how they are meeting the highest level of student engagement in their classrooms by posting ideas in the faculty room that they have seen in their colleagues' classrooms or have implemented on their own. Teachers in this K–2 level school also visit one another's classes to exchange ideas and learn new approaches.

These teachers realize the value of working collaboratively as a community of lifelong learners. An atmosphere of trust and mutual respect characterizes this dynamic elementary school. As teachers share ideas and lend support, they pave the way for motivation, arts-infused curriculum improvement, and teacher leadership among the entire faculty. Arts-infused, student-centered teaching in today's schools is standards related, interdisciplinary, and attainable for novice and expert teachers. When autonomous educators lead novices to teach student-centered, multidimensional, arts-integrated lessons, such as those shown in Table 8.1, learners and teachers alike reap the benefits (Kostelnik, Soderman, & Whiren, 2011). As attested by a parent of a student at Wawaloam Elementary, "I witnessed my child transform from being depressed, unhappy, unmotivated, with no self-esteem, into a confident, spirited, determined, successful young man."

Need for Arts-Integrated Curriculum: Theory and Research

For decades, educational researchers have investigated the effects of learning through the arts and student achievement (Burnaford, Brown, Doherty, & McLaughlin, 2007; Deasy, 2002; Fiske, 1999; Ruppert, 2006). Additional research has supported arts integration as a means of increasing comprehension (Catterall, 2009; Catterall, Dumais, & Hampden-Thompson, 2012; Shanahan et al., 2010; Weiss & Lichtenstein, 2008). A teacher leader who is aware of the theories and research that support the arts also acknowledges the various levels of arts integration throughout the curriculum. Arts integration levels include *learning with the arts, learning in the arts,* and *learning through the arts* (Burnaford et al., 2007; Cornett, 2011). An investigation of these levels reveals ways that teacher leaders can positively affect students, schools, and the community.

In the first level of arts integration, *learning with the arts,* arts experiences are not directly connected to the curriculum. For example, a teacher might sing a song to begin the day, and during transitions or while students are working on projects, soft music is played in the background. The arts-infused classroom may include a learning center where arts materials are available for use during free time. These arts experiences are engaging, but are not assessed nor aligned with curriculum standards.

The next level of integration, *learning in the arts,* implies that the teacher leader consciously designs arts experiences that are tied to the general curriculum. Art elements, principles, and techniques are incorporated and assessed along with the content and skills in curriculum areas. For example, if students explore the historical timeline of the United States using music, they not only learn the historical, political, geographical, and political context of the songs, but simultaneously appreciate the melody, composition, and tonality of instruments.

The final level of integration is *learning through the arts.* Here, the arts are the focus, and the entire classroom environment becomes an aesthetic experience (Cornett, 2011). When students prepare a musical play depicting a specific time period, such as "Slavery in the 1800s," they role play living in that time period

TABLE 8.1 Common Core and Content Areas in Teacher-Centered versus Arts-Infused Classrooms Using the New National Core Arts Standards

Content Area	Teacher-Centered	Arts-Infused	Teacher Leader Role
Reading CCSS.ELA-Literacy.RL.3.3 (Grade 3) Describe characters in a story (e.g., their traits, motivations, or feelings) and explain how their actions contribute to the sequence of events.	Teacher follows scripted lesson from basal reading series teacher's manual, which may not include children's ideas or insights.	Teacher and students refer to story illustrations and text to retell stories sequentially and depict characters, using a variety of storytelling methods, including shadow, white board, balloon, computer apps, draw-talk, pantomime, puppetry, role play, and chant. NCAS, VA: Cr2.1.3a	Teacher leaders meet frequently with other teachers to discuss Common Core Standards and schoolwide curriculum reform related to infusing the arts. The teacher leader values all suggestions and is open-minded, respectful, and flexible in working with the teachers and students to promote the use of creative retelling methods and props.
Social Studies CCSS.ELA-Literacy.RL.3.2 (Grade 3) Determine the meaning of words and phrases as they are used in a text, including figurative and connotative meanings; analyze the impact of specific word choices on meaning and tone, including analogies or allusions to other texts.	Teacher assigns selected, sequential text chapters to read each week. Chapter tests monitor vocabulary words and comprehension.	Donning historical costumes and wigs, students create living timelines depicting historical characters and events. They consult texts, movies, letters, books, and video clips to locate relevant information and historical versus contemporary figures of speech. NCAS, TH: Cr1.1.3a,b,c	Teacher leaders collaborate with the librarian to identify and distribute appropriate historical fiction containing figurative language; they model how to identify figurative language and its meaning using a variety of sources.
Mathematics CCSS.Math.2.G.A.1 (Grade 2) Recognize and draw shapes having specified attributes, such as a given number of angles or a given number of equal faces. Identify triangles, quadrilaterals, pentagons, hexagons, and cubes.	Teacher assigns math pages with 20 geometric shape identification problems to solve in 15 minutes. Teachers use red pens to mark incorrect answers on students' papers.	Students take field trips outdoors around the school to collect objects and data about shapes, colors, sizes, patterns, and quantities. Working in groups, students create eye-catching "shape data" displays and retrieval charts as they identify and label each of their shapes. NCAS, VA: Cr2.1.2a	Teacher leaders work with math, technology, and art specialists and assist students as they discover and use various types of data displays, both technological and three-dimensional.

(Continued)

TABLE 8.1 (Continued)

Content Area	Teacher-Centered	Arts-Infused	Teacher Leader Role
Science CCSS.ELA-Literacy.RST.6-8.2 (Grade 6) Determine the central ideas or conclusions of a text; provide an accurate summary of the text distinct from prior knowledge or opinions.	Teacher holds a lecture, accompanied by a set of flashcards. Students take notes and memorize the cards for a test.	Working with others, students engage in discovery activities using related science texts. Students create illustrated brochures and newsletters using technology. NCAS, MA: Cr2.1.6	Teacher leaders collaborate with local science centers to develop arts-infused activities. Teacher leaders conduct research and present professional development sessions addressing science processes and Common Core integration.
Health/Physical Education National Health Education Standards 8.12.3; 8.12.4 (Grades 9–12) Work cooperatively as an advocate for improving personal, family, and community health.	Teacher lectures and shows a slide show of healthy/unhealthy bones of the human or animal body. Students fill in the blanks on a related worksheet.	Students examine human x-rays to research and record facts about human bones and effects of good nutrition. Students compose a song and dance about healthy eating, nutrition, and bone health. NCAS, MU: Cr2.1.8 NCAS, DA: Cr1.1.II	Teacher leaders serve on curriculum and grant committees; they order appropriate programs and materials including health kits, medical x-rays, and music and art supplies.
Art NCAS, VA: Cr1.2.8a Understanding and applying media, techniques, and processes	Teacher informs students that they have 45 minutes to use colored pencils to draw their homes and neighborhoods on 8" × 11" white paper.	Students select a variety of materials to create their own neighborhood representations with different textures and colors. CCSS.ELA-Literacy.SL.5.5	Teacher leaders collect recycled materials from a variety of community sources. With help from other teachers, the leader establishes a supply of arts materials for creative, interactive teaching and learning.
Music NCAS, MU: Pr5.1.7 Singing alone and with others. Reading and notating music. Composing and arranging music within specified guidelines	Teacher plays the piano or a CD while the students, using a photocopy of the words, sing along until they have memorized the song, musical notes, and arrangement.	Students create their own musical instruments using recycled materials. They then compose and play their own songs. Students write a reflection to describe the meaning of the song and process of making the instrument. CCSS.ELA-Literacy.W.6.4	Teacher leaders encourage students to explore a variety of music genres. The teacher leader arranges a music night for the school, inviting parents, teachers, and administrators to attend and view the displays of student-created, recycled musical instruments.

and experience dramatic elements, such as using movement and voice to express the story. The entire experience activates multiple areas in the brain, including the limbic, or emotional, system that helps to encode memory for future recall of content (Gazzaniga, 1988). By providing rich, multisensory learning, the teacher leader exerts a positive and lasting effect on students, schools, and the community. Karen Kapp, a teacher at Ashley River Creative Arts School, reported (in Cornett, 2011, p. 54), "The arts captured the children internally from the start by awakening their emotions and physical self. We now have kids with fire on the inside."

Integrating Standards Into an Arts-Infused Curriculum

State standards and the Common Core Standards now serve as the basis for curriculum development, instruction, and assessment strategies in the United States. These curricular documents divide knowledge into discrete areas such as math, literacy, science, and social studies. The Common Core Standards lay a foundation for educators and identify student expectations in literacy and math at each grade level. However, education of youth is not just about content knowledge; it is also about developing traits that contribute to well-being and society (President's Committee on the Arts and the Humanities [PCAH], 2011). A statistic cited since the establishment of standards, their implementation, and an increase in standardized testing is the distressing increase in the number of high school dropouts in the United States (PCAH, 2011, p. 27). It is imperative, therefore, that teachers find ways to engage learners in meaningful ways in standards-based curricula. The National Coalition for Core Arts Standards (NCCAS), formed in 2011, launched new National Core Arts Standards (NCAS) in June 2014. The new standards update the 1994 standards and support the 21st century needs of students and teachers (NCCAS, 2014).

Since teacher leaders possess in-depth knowledge of child development, they can influence the implementation of an effective standards-based and arts-based curriculum. Given the impetus for schools to adopt and implement the Common Core Standards, a relevant and timely stimulus for arts infusion into the curriculum might involve a close perusal of the intersections among the Common Core Standards, the new National Core Arts Standards, and the school's curriculum. At Genesee Community Charter School in Rochester, New York, which has a long-standing reputation for arts integration, teachers at all levels are finding natural ways to integrate the Common Core and art-infused lessons.

Principal Lisa Wing (in Robelen, 2012) claimed, "Using art as text, we're teaching children to look at art or movement or listen to music and derive meaning from it," whether a "famous painting or through watching 'Swan Lake' or singing Erie Canal [folk] songs" (p. 18). She further explained that the school also looks at "using the arts as a vehicle of expression, the communication side of the Common Core, and knowing how to create artwork that creates a message and that conveys details." Other schools across the country have also benefited from arts-infused curricula. The A+ Schools in North Carolina use the arts daily, and the teachers are mentored in arts-infused instruction by a statewide network of peer professionals. The Chicago Arts Partnerships in Education have established long-term partnerships with teachers, artists, and arts organizations to provide teaching artists for residencies. These model programs provide a motivating platform for arts-infused curriculum reform.

Designing and assessing an effective arts-integrated curriculum is dependent on the development of teacher leader skills and related knowledge about creating, performing, and responding within and through the arts. Developing personal creativity is critical so that teacher leaders can model techniques and utilize effective strategies in their classrooms. Effective teacher leaders foster the four elements of creativity, as defined by Guilford (1950), within themselves and with their students. The elements of creativity include *fluency, flexibility, elaboration,* and *originality.* Fluency involves creating as many ideas as possible. The goal is to brainstorm many strategies of integrating the arts; the more ideas, the better. Flexibility is developing variations of ideas, while elaboration is changing ideas by adding different dimensions, thus turning something simple into something complex. The final element of originality involves the teacher leader's ability to create something unique. In an ideal arts-infused school, teachers and students learn to develop originality and imagination. Albert Einstein (1931/2009) maintained, "Imagination is more important than knowledge. For knowledge is limited, whereas imagination embraces the entire world, stimulating progress, giving birth to evolution" (p. 97). The teacher leader recognizes the power of imagination and provides multiple arts integrated opportunities in the learning environment.

Teacher Preparation: A Three-Module Curriculum Approach to Arts Integration

Preparing teacher leaders with the knowledge and skills to meet the needs of the standards-based curriculum requires models that account for multiple ways of knowing, along with creative and critical thinking. Ideally, teacher preparation programs create opportunities for emerging teacher leaders to understand the elements and principles of the arts and to practice the skills for implementation (PCAH, 2011). Development in the field of arts integration is dependent on exemplary programs, preservice training, ongoing professional development, and stronger certification requirements to include training in the arts (PCAH, 2011). Given the demands of curriculum standards and the challenges of attaining national accreditation, many teacher preparation programs have eliminated arts method courses. As a result, untrained teachers too often design simple, ineffective "arts activities" rather than developing meaningful experiences connected to "arts education."

Fitchburg State University in Massachusetts requires all of its teacher candidates to graduate with an understanding of the theory, research, practice, and assessment of meaningful arts activities. The goal of the methodology courses is to provide teacher candidates with knowledge and skills to enhance developing arts-integrated curricula for their future classrooms. The Fitchburg model uses a three-module arts-integrated curricular approach, with students receiving one college credit after completing each module.

The first module, *The Arts I: Inspiration,* focuses on research-based theories of arts integration, understanding and developing creativity, examining the content knowledge base for the arts, and viewing the connection to historical and cultural contexts as defined in curriculum standards. The second module, *The Arts II: Imagination,* focuses on using and evaluating the content knowledge base for the arts and enhancing personal creative potential so that skills and knowledge can be modeled and integrated throughout core curriculum subjects. The third module, *The Arts III: Integration,* is an opportunity for teacher candidates to make connections across the curriculum while learning in, about, and through the arts in an authentic field-based experience. Teacher candidates are paired with elementary students from a local school for an experience called "Invitation to the Arts." In this collaborative setting, teacher candidates design, implement, assess, and reflect on developmentally appropriate arts activities including visual art, dance, music, and drama. The preservice teachers benefit from firsthand, authentic experiences in meaningful arts integration. In the words of Kara Mitton, a preservice teacher at Fitchburg State University, "As a future teacher, I believe the arts are extremely important to expand the imagination of our students and open their eyes to the world."

What Teacher Leaders Can Do: Future Directions

Learning is continuous and does not occur in isolation. Learning is cumulative and transpires over time. The paucity of time dampens creativity. Few administrators, teacher leaders, or teachers would disagree with these statements. However, many schools and teachers today experience challenges and roadblocks to arts integration because of the lack of time to teach in creative, learner-centered ways. Teacher leaders play a major role in working with the administrators and curriculum committees to ensure meaningful arts infusion into the curriculum and in training teachers in professional development, mentoring, and modeling as they learn creative ways of integrating arts into a standards-based curriculum. When teacher leaders collaborate to pursue the arts, they may change their school's existing curriculum or open an entirely new school with a curriculum that inspires optimal learning.

Well-prepared and inspiring teachers enter the teaching arena and prepare students for today's world of technology, innovation, and problem solving. These educators integrate the local, state, and national standards in creative ways so that learners' needs are continually addressed. Great teachers turn everyday lessons into active and memorable experiences that learners love (Partnership for 21st Century Schools, 2010). The teacher leader's role in arts-infused curriculum reform requires collaboration, partnerships, and staying informed through professional development and research. Arts-focused organizations offer a plethora of resources and networking opportunities for teacher leaders. Future directions for curricular reform include establishing mutually beneficial partnerships among teacher leaders and these organizations. Facilitating artist residencies and enlisting teaching artists are two strategies that bring meaningful arts integration into the classroom. Local and state arts councils and agencies often provide a rich supply of potential connections with artists. National organizations offer additional opportunities for teacher leaders to stay informed, and they provide resources and ideas for infusing the arts into the classroom.

Ultimately, research informs curriculum reform, and aspiring teacher leaders bring that research into practice. Arts integration research continues to demonstrate the positive effects of keeping students motivated, excited, and engaged in school so that they can succeed in the workforce throughout their lives (PCAH, 2011, pp. 57–59). Teacher leaders incorporate the 21st century skills of critical thinking, creative thinking, problem solving, good community and collaboration abilities, information and technological literacy, innovation and flexibility, and global competence (PCAH, 2011). Experiences in the arts build skills such as critical and creative thinking and problem solving (Partnership for 21st Century Schools, 2010). Likewise, recent and future jobs require that business people, engineers, and other professionals possess the skills of inventiveness, resourcefulness, and imagination. Teacher leaders realize and impress upon others that the arts are a gateway to a higher degree of understanding and expression and that the arts are the seeds of promise and innovation for a brighter future.

Conclusion

Since student achievement and good citizenship are the primary focal areas of schools, all teachers are responsible for serving as teacher leaders and improving learning at their schools. According to Bond (2011), rather than postponing leadership roles until they have gained classroom experience, teachers can begin acquiring the knowledge, skills, and dispositions of teacher leaders during their preservice programs. As preservice educators reflect on current practices in the arts and on ways to improve teaching, as they engage in arts-infused service learning, and as they become involved in arts-related university student professional organizations, they prepare to enter the teaching arena as agents of change for arts integration across the curriculum.

References

Armstrong, T. (2006). *The best schools: How human development research should inform educational practice.* Alexandria, VA: Association for Supervision and Curriculum Development.
Armstrong, T. (2009). *Multiple intelligences in the classroom.* Alexandria, VA: ASCD.

Ashbury, C. A., & Rich, B. (Eds.). (2008). *Learning, arts, and the brain: The Dana Consortium report on arts and cognition.* New York, NY: Dana Press.

Bond, N. (2011). Preparing preservice teachers to become teacher leaders. *The Educational Forum, 75*(4), 280–297.

Burnaford, G., Brown, S., Doherty, J., & McLaughlin, H. J. (2007). *Arts integration frameworks, research & practice: A literature review.* Washington, DC: Arts Education Partnership.

Catterall, J. S. (2009). *Doing well and doing good by doing art: A 12-year national study of education in the visual and performing arts; Effects on the achievements and values of young adults.* Los Angeles, CA: Imagination Group/I-Group Books.

Catterall, J. S., Dumais, S. A., & Hampden-Thompson, G. (2012). *The arts and achievement in at-risk youth: Findings from four longitudinal studies.* Washington, DC: National Endowment for the Arts.

Cornett, C. E. (2011). *Creating meaning through literature and the arts: Arts integration for classroom teachers* (4th ed.). Boston, MA: Pearson.

Danielson, C. (2006). *Teacher leadership that strengthens professional practice.* Alexandria, VA: Association for Supervision and Curriculum Development.

Deasy, R. J. (Ed.). (2002). *Critical links: Learning in the arts and student academic and social development.* Washington, DC: Arts Education Partnership.

Einstein, A. (2009). *Einstein on cosmic religion and other opinions and aphorisms.* New York, NY: Dover. (Original work published 1931)

Eisner, E. W. (2002). *The arts and the creation of mind.* New Haven, CT: Yale University Press.

Fiske, E. B. (Ed.). (1999). *Champions of change: The impact of the arts on learning.* Washington, DC: Arts Education Partnership and President's Committee on the Arts and the Humanities.

Gardner, H. (1983). *Frames of mind: The theory of multiple intelligences.* New York, NY: Basic Books.

Gazzaniga, M. S. (1988). *Mind matters: How mind and brain interact to create our conscious lives.* Boston, MA: Houghton Mifflin.

Guilford, J. P. (1950). Creativity. *American Psychologist, 5*(9), 444–454.

Katzenmeyer, M. H., & Moller, G. V. (2009). *Awakening the sleeping giant: Helping teachers develop as leaders* (3rd ed.). Thousand Oaks, CA: Corwin.

Kostelnik, M. J., Soderman, A. K., & Whiren, A. P. (2011). *Developmentally appropriate curriculum: Best practices in early childhood education* (5th ed). Boston, MA: Pearson.

National Coalition for Core Arts Standards. (2014). *National core arts standards.* Retrieved from www.nationalartsstandards.org

Partnership for 21st Century Schools. (2010). *21st century skills map: The arts.* Tucson, AZ: Author.

President's Committee on the Arts and the Humanities. (2011). *Reinvesting in arts education: Winning America's future through creative schools.* Washington, DC: Author.

Robelen, E. W. (2012, December 12). Common core taught through the arts. *Education Week Online, 32*(14), 1, 18–19.

Rosenholtz, S. J. (1991). *Teachers' workplace: The social organization of schools.* New York, NY: Teachers College Press.

Ruppert, S. S. (2006). *Critical evidence: How the arts benefit student achievement.* Washington, DC: National Assembly of State Arts Agencies and the Arts Education Partnership.

Shanahan, T., Callison, K., Carriere, C., Duke, N. K., Pearson, P. D., Schatscheinder, C., & Torgeson, J. (2010). *Improving reading comprehension in kindergarten through 3rd grade: IES practice guide.* Washington, DC: National Center for Education Evaluation and Regional

Assistance, Institute of Education Sciences, U.S. Department of Education. Retrieved from http://ies.ed.gov/ncee/wwc/practiceguide.aspx?sid=14

Sommer, M. K. (2013). The cream does not always rise: The plight of visual-spatial learners and the power of art education. *Harvard Educational Review, 83*(1), 40–42.

United Nations Educational, Scientific and Cultural Organization. (1994, June). The Salamanca statement and framework for action on special needs education. Adopted by the World Conference on Special Needs Education: Access and Quality, Salamanca, Spain.

Weiss, C., & Lichtenstein, A. L. (Eds.). (2008). *AIMprint: New relationships in the arts and learning.* Chicago, IL: Columbia College.

9

TEACHER LEADERS AS SCHOOL REFORMERS

Shawn Christopher Boone

> Never doubt that a small group of thoughtful, committed citizens can change the world; indeed, it's the only thing that ever has.
>
> —Margaret Mead

Throughout the late 20th and early 21st century, school reformers have observed a transformation in the role classroom teachers play within the school and within school reform. Who are teacher leaders? What roles do teacher leaders play in 21st century school reform? How essential are teacher leaders as transformational change agents? If given autonomy by the district, what would teacher leaders do to reform schools? These are some of the questions that have become important to answer in current school reform discussions.

The emergence of teacher leaders as school reformers developed out of the need for schools to become centers of sustained progress within present realities of teaching and learning. Over the last 30 years, teachers have witnessed constant changes in education reform, to wit, *A Nation at Risk* in 1983, the 1990s standards movement, the No Child Left Behind Act of 2001, the Race to the Top initiatives, the Common Core Standards, the Skills Framework for 21st Century Learning, and the Elementary and Secondary Education Act. These mandates have affected classroom realities by requiring teachers to focus more on policy than on effective instructional practices and closing the achievement gap. Furthermore, both public and private entities have taken vested interests in correcting the deficiencies in the teaching profession in hopes of closing the achievement gap and bolstering test scores across all content areas.

Equally critical is the public perception of teacher involvement in school leadership and the extent to which teachers are involved in comprehensive and total school decision making. As a result of local school reconstitutions and marginal student achievement, teachers have been prompted to engage the education agenda and to move beyond their classrooms into leadership positions to focus on greater student achievement and increased teacher professional learning and development.

A longstanding debate has existed within school reform discussions as to whether or not schools should move from principal leadership to teacher leadership. Principal leadership (or classical leadership) has consisted of top-down decision making. Teacher leadership (or reform reality) has consisted of bottom-up decision making (Donaldson, 2006; Murphy, 2005).

Implementation of teacher leadership as a reform model has been difficult. It has long been the view of teachers that principal leaders receive their marching orders from district-level mandates, and teachers have been skeptical of the relevance of such mandates because of classroom realities (Donaldson, 2006; Urbanski, 2003). On the other hand, districts perceive teacher leadership with skepticism because of the underlying motives of teacher unions. Presently, the two perspectives have come into conflict as teachers seek to gain professional autonomy within school-wide decision making on governance, curriculum and assessment, and professional learning, while districts maintain control over decision making, curriculum and assessment, and professional learning practices (Darling-Hammond, Wei, Andree, Richardson, & Orphanos, 2009). Although teachers have rarely viewed their work roles as extending outside of classrooms, and although school reform scarcely has involved teachers as true transformational leaders (Barth, 2001), the impetus to see teachers' roles as leaders outside of classrooms provides a paradigm shift in a long-awaited attempt to create meaningful and sustainable school reform. One such reform movement that provided teachers with the opportunity to lead school reform efforts was in the nation's second largest school district, the Los Angeles Unified School District (LAUSD).

Context of Teacher-Initiated School Reform

In 2009, the LAUSD initiated local school reform called the Public School Choice Initiative (PSCi). Although many opponents viewed the initiative as an attempt to give newly constructed schools away to private and charter school organizations, the initiative was opened to bids from both internal teacher and administrative groups in addition to community groups. All groups submitting a proposal to operate schools had to provide a complete school operation plan focused on elevating student achievement.

PSCi was an opportunity for teachers to demonstrate school reform capacity never before permitted. School proposals focused on school autonomy in curriculum and assessment, professional development, teacher performance expectations, student discipline, and selection of teachers and administrators. From the PSCi, teacher leaders were given a voice in reforming teaching and learning to improve student achievement. One group of LAUSD teachers, the South Area Teacher Collaborative (SATC), stepped forward to demonstrate transformational teacher leadership not heretofore experienced in the LAUSD. Teacher Shawn Boone, founder of SATC, led this teacher team through the writing of the extensive school development plan. SATC teachers who wrote the PSCi proposal immersed themselves in extensive research on leadership and school effectiveness literature. Teachers who agreed to teach at the school became innovators for change and embarked on a rigorous journey to become school reformers. This indelible experience demanded extensive time in collaborating, learning, and evaluating processes that increase student achievement and teacher self-awareness as leaders.

Although much work has been done on the theoretical design of school reform, practical presentations and results indicating teachers' experiences and progress are often lacking. Throughout this chapter, both theoretical implications and practical applications and results of building and sustaining teacher-led school reform are presented. Teacher-led school reform is a model of professional learning communities of practice (DuFour & Eaker, 1998; Hord, 2009). The model is interconnected by six major tenets (see Figure 9.1) that define teacher leaders as school reformers. The six tenets are shared vision, shared leadership, re-culture of staff, effective professional development, ongoing evaluation, and sustainability of the PSCi plan. The application of theoretical research moves teacher-led communities of practice forward by providing teacher leaders with a framework for change within school reform. School reform requires a transformational and behavioral change in organizational processes and goals consisting of vision and mission, professional development and teacher learning, continuous evaluation for improvement, and reflective practice.

FIGURE 9.1 New Paradigm of Teacher Leaders as School Reformers: Six Tenets for Success

Tenet 1: Shared Vision

Theoretical Implications. Shared vision is the collective process by which successful schools create focus and purpose for elevating student achievement (Murphy, 2005) and take ownership for daily tasks and operation of the school (Boone, 2010). Current school reform focuses on the school's ability to implement effective instruction and strategies, evaluate student assessment and data, and make decisions that move the community closer to achieving shared goals (DuFour, 1999). As a prerequisite to school reform and change, teachers in schools must agree to create a shared vision focused on their collective participation in academic achievement and school operations.

The paradigm shift moves schools from a conventional model of involvement, where principals and districts unilaterally make decisions, toward a collegial model of leadership, where schools establish decisions and learning goals through non-hierarchical relationships and collaborative practices (Barth, 2001). However, one challenge in this new model of involvement pertains to teachers' willingness to work together. In classical school paradigms, teachers have customarily worked in isolation. A second challenge deals with lack of collegial trust, which prevents teachers from sharing their professional opinions and experiences. To create a shared vision, school reformers must create processes that overcome these challenges and influence all teachers to become leaders inside and outside the classroom.

Practical Applications and Results. One of the first activities at the PSCi school focused on creating a shared vision by merging the shared vision described by plan writers in the PSCi plan with the vision of the school staff. This required plan writers and teacher leaders to influence the newly recruited staff members, create a culture of collaboration and trust, and open discussions on purpose and focus for the school among all staff members. Teacher leaders, in concert with all teachers and the principal, organized 2 weeks of professional development activities focused on establishing shared vision, team and trust building, and the PSCi school plan's five categories: (a) Curriculum and Instruction, (b) Pupil Services, (c) Community and Family Involvement, (d) Professional Learning, and (e) School Culture and Climate. All teachers worked in teams to create and implement 4 hours of professional learning activities for the entire staff. This practice embraced teachers' development of a shared vision and allowed teachers to share professional expertise.

During the 2 weeks of professional development, teachers participated in revision of the school's vision to incorporate all the teachers' philosophical and pedagogical perspectives (Blankstein, 2004). Teachers went through each plan category and discussed how they interpreted and would implement elements. Teachers further built consensus around plan items that needed revision. This practice emphasized teachers' ownership for the school's success. As a result, teachers collaboratively agreed to a shared vision that incorporated four fundamental principles focused on student achievement and school reform: Purpose, Collaboration, Foundation, and Ownership. Anecdotally, the shared vision has guided the school in goal setting and student learning focus, resulting in a 55-point increase on the state's academic achievement test in the school's second year.

Tenet 2: Shared Leadership

Theoretical Implications. Shared leadership shifts complete control from having the principal make all the decisions to having teachers and administrators collectively share in decision-making processes (Kelehear & Davison, 2005). Current leadership systems hinder progressive schooling because principals and districts are not always aware of teachers' and students' needs (Urbanski, 2003). Building shared leadership means that effective leaders develop and move teaching staff from the tendency of having problems solved for them to solving problems as a collective in order to build team responsibility (Donaldson, 2006; Kelehear & Davison, 2005). Once district leadership initiates the "change process and the corresponding capacity-building" (Fullan, 2005, p. 213), teachers and administrators in the school will develop a greater awareness of what needs to be accomplished.

Effective leaders develop and maintain collaboration to sustain teachers' capacities for growth inside and outside the classroom. When a school is being reformed, organizational structures and roles should focus on staff members "learn[ing] from each other (lateral capacity-building)" (Glickman, Gordon, & Ross-Gordon, 2007, p. 213). Current school reform approaches to shared leadership foster the purpose of having all staff members learn from each other to break practices of isolation (Fullan, 2001). Three challenges associated with constructs of shared leadership are role avoidance by teachers who do not want to engage in leadership, while other teachers who are eager to become involved become controlling and possessive, a situation that creates resentment coming from still others in the school (Darling-Hammond et al., 2009). Establishing shared leadership roles does not mean that one teacher is at the helm, but rather that all teachers are engaged in decision-making processes.

Practical Applications and Results. The PSCi provided the school with many opportunities for leadership paradigm shifts. Collaborative, shared leadership teams focused on fulfilling PSCi goals in instruction, professional development, safety, discipline, community relationships, and school culture throughout the year. The PSCi writing team wrote a governance structure known as Extended School-Based Management Model (ESBMM) into the PSCi plan. ESBMM is a teacher-created governance that provides the school with complete autonomy over hiring, budget, curriculum, assessment, and professional development. The ESBMM structure immediately moved decision making toward a collegial process with the creation of a council composed of four elected teachers and the school principal. The role of the council was to facilitate the broader school operation discussions and decisions among all teachers, as well as to monitor leadership teams' progress and action plans. In addition, the council oversaw ongoing progress and evaluation discussions at the school. ESBMM provided the leadership philosophy embraced by the teachers on how students, teachers, and administrators would learn within the school, both collaboratively and collectively. Although ESBMM has historically been perceived as successful, it is always under threat of being taken over by district-imposed mandates because of the skepticism with which districts view complete local school autonomy.

For issues that surfaced during the school year, ESBMM facilitated discussions in the larger group to build consensus for resolving issues. To build consensus and sustain shared leadership, teachers created a consensus protocol that could be used in all committees and in schoolwide decision-making meetings. While consensus is not a requirement of teacher-led reform, consensus building is a way to develop teacher ownership in decision-making processes. A thumb protocol was agreed upon by teachers and used to create nonthreatening agreement and disagreement in decision making. Thumb up indicated absolute agreement; thumb in the middle indicated agreement with reservations, but a willingness to try; and thumb down indicated no agreement with the decision. When teachers indicated thumbs down, teachers' issues were addressed, a compromise was made to achieve agreement, and consensus was reached.

As part of the discussion on shared vision and shared leadership, teachers decided to participate in collaborative, shared leadership teams. All teachers participated in at least two teams that met during lunch, after school, or online to discuss goals and create action plans. Within leadership teams, teachers mapped out yearly goals and projects using a sequential planning sheet (see Figure 9.2), which included such items as persons responsible for tasks, deadlines, resources needed, and anticipated challenges. On a monthly basis, teams presented their progress to the entire group. An example of a collaborative team was the instructional rubric team. As a community of practice, teachers saw a need to use schoolwide rubrics to monitor and assess student learning and achievement. The rubric team was responsible for providing professional development for teacher-created, content-specific, holistic, and criterion rubrics. The rubric team further conducted technical assistance to support teachers' classroom practices. As a result of participation on these teams, teachers discovered that one challenge to shared leadership was self-imposed leadership roles taken on by some teachers, thereby creating a level of distrust among other teachers.

Tenet 3: Re-culture of Staff

Theoretical Implications. The re-culturing of staff is necessary to move successful, sustainable school reform forward. Increasing teachers' collaboration, relationships, and participation in schools has also become a major focus within 21st century school reform (Barth, 2006; Muijs & Harris, 2003). A review of the literature explicates the need for school districts to reinvent their organizational structures to accommodate teacher-led reform efforts. Additionally, there is a need to

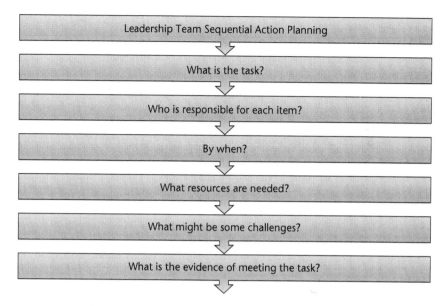

FIGURE 9.2 Leadership Team Sequential Action Planning Sheet

re-culture teachers in accepting 21st century school reform as a permanent reality rather than a passing fad (Giles & Hargreaves, 2006). To accomplish this goal, teachers must be provided with opportunities to learn, reflect, and experiment together with focus on organizational restructuring, peer observation, common planning, and sustainability of practices (King & Newmann, 2001; Spear, 1992).

Teachers' hesitation in participating in teacher-led reform draws attention to the challenges experienced by past collaborative experiences. A common challenge to collaboration is elevated hierarchy in teacher work groups, with some teachers taking charge of meetings while others experience retaliation for going against groupthink processes (Wells & Feun, 2007). In addition to interpersonal relationships, teachers have lacked sufficient autonomy in their roles, undermining the investment of time, expertise, and attention given to collaboration. Implementation of reform efforts often receives lukewarm response from teachers because of perceived underlying ulterior motives by administrators (Boone, 2010). Strategies such as decision-making autonomy, trust-first approaches, collaborative processes, and continued monitoring challenge old preconceptions and offer a process of continued support for teacher-led school reform.

Re-culturing the staff speaks to the necessity of teacher-led school reformers to create a culture of trust in the collective team (Zmuda, Kuklis, & Kline, 2004). Opportunities to re-culture the staff must occur throughout the school year through ongoing team- and trust-building activities (Boone, 2010). When teachers have absolute control over teaching quality, they can circumvent situations that prevent students from learning and prevent teachers from teaching.

Practical Applications and Results. The school focused on three practical, sustainable applications to emphasize collective re-culturing of the staff: examining behavior and communication, team building and trust building, and dispelling teacher isolation.

Re-culturing the way teachers engage in professional dialogue, communication, relationships, and teamwork was a critical task to encourage open and honest professional communication and evaluation of ideas (Little, 2007) and relationships among staff. As a collective, teachers first looked at their personal profile assessments, development tools used to determine how individuals communicate and behave in groups. For guidance, teachers completed the DISC® Dimensions of Behavior Map to reflect on their behaviors and strategies to develop successful collaborative teams. In addition, teachers were able to determine those behaviors that block and promote productive communication within teams. This exercise complemented teachers' roles in teams by making teachers aware of their communication and group behaviors. Furthermore, results reinforced collaborative teams by grouping teachers with like-minded individuals to prevent hierarchical structures from forming within teams.

Next, team building and trust building required purpose-driven attention to building trust capacities among staff. Activities requiring teachers to share professional and personal attributes helped to create trusting environments. Building trust required regular activities to bring staff together both within and outside of school. Inside school, trust exercises were conducted during weekly professional development activities. Group activities such as team scenarios, leadership exercises, and identifying hidden talents became weekly occurrences. Opportunities to socialize outside school hours further expanded a sense of collegiality. The social team focused on celebrating the team members' special occasions and taking time to be present during tragic events such as family deaths. Meet and greets at colleagues' homes and collective visits to hospitals became ubiquitous social calls in which all members participated.

Finally, building trust gave way to monthly teacher observations of one another's classrooms. Team learning walks became a monthly practice for teachers. Teachers practiced instructional strategies and agreed on a set of schoolwide, instructional strategies including rubrics, scaffolds, and specially designed academic instruction in English strategies to use in classrooms. During learning team walks, teachers observed implementation of these and other instructional activities to provide constructive feedback on classroom delivery and professional development needs.

Tenet 4: Effective Professional Learning

Theoretical Implications. Effective professional learning enhances teachers' skills and knowledge to produce student learning and achievement, including enhancement of teachers' content and pedagogic knowledge, collegiality and collaborative exchange, activity alignment with reform initiatives, and professional learning programs driven by vision for effective teaching and learning (Guskey, 2003). Teacher professional development has long been at the core of the discussion of school reform because of the relationship between teachers' knowledge and skills, and student achievement. With the emergence of the professional learning community (PLC) structure, schools latched onto constructs that teachers' discussion would be centered on application of three major strategies: focus on student learning, a culture of collaboration, and results-oriented goals (DuFour, Eaker, & DuFour, 2005; Hord, 2009).

Teachers enjoy the PLC structure because it parallels the 1990s *restructuring movement,* which promised to release teachers "from the shackles of top-down mandates and bureaucratic rules and regulations [so that] teachers and principals could respond creatively to the issues they faced" (DuFour & Eaker, 1998, p. 7). The restructuring movement failed as a result of "marginal changes" to teaching and learning structures (p. 8). The PLC would remedy the neglect of such structures and center attention on designing effective adult learning to elevate student achievement (DuFour & Eaker, 1998).

Practical Applications and Results. The entire school staff, which identified as a PLC, focused on student and teacher learning. The PSCi plan incorporated greater focus and freedom of the professional learning of teachers and encouraged staff members to become reflective and constructive practitioners.

The professional development team conducted a yearly teachers' needs assessment to identify areas in which teachers wanted growth. In conjunction with teachers and the principal, the team designed a professional development and learning plan that was coherent, job embedded, results oriented, collaborative, and evaluated regularly. The professional development cycle was based on a continuous 5-week structure. Teachers engaged in weekly professional learning community exercises focused on instructional practices and student data (see Table 9.1).

Teachers embraced autonomy in creating professional development that addressed their professional learning needs and school community identity. At the center of the school community identity were respect, collaboration, leadership, and learning advancement of the entire educational community. The school's focus on professional learning and development and teacher instructional quality supported the school's unprecedented 55-point increase on the state's academic achievement test in the school's second year.

Tenet 5: Evaluation and Progress Monitoring

Theoretical Implications. Theoretical implications for evaluation and progress monitoring of professional learning and school reform effectiveness are often absent from literature. Furthermore, review of the effectiveness of school reform is usually conducted by outside entities. Perennial evaluation of school processes allows schools to concretize PLC purposes from beginning to end (Boone, 2010), as well as to support focus and alignment to school reform goals (Lowden, 2005).

TABLE 9.1 Professional Learning Schedule

Week 1: 1 hour
Focus on team building, common schoolwide instructional strategies; classroom management strategies; Response to Intervention and Instruction (RtI²) strategies

Week 2: 2 hours
Focus on team building; teacher discussion about effectiveness of common strategies used; data analysis from weekly assessments or district assessments; creation of Formative and Common Summative Assessments (CSAs)

Week 3: 1 hour
Focus on department and content area needs; review of student data (such as grades, attendance, behavior, and parent conferences); instructional strategies or RtI²

Week 4: 2 hours
Focus on team presentations and action plan updates; student data analysis of Formative Assessments and CSAs; teacher discussions of areas of need and support; review of common instructional strategies used in classrooms

Week 5: 1 hour
Focus on sharing best practices (including student-led parent–teacher conferences, rubrics, and student-data analysis); project-based/oriented learning strategies

Professional development evaluation and school improvement evaluation need to be continuous (Zmuda et al., 2004) as they allow for making timely improvements to school reform efforts and professional development design (Gajda & Koliba, 2008). Similarly, continuous evaluation of PLCs allows organizational learning supports to be more responsive to teachers' professional and students' learning needs. Implementation of evaluation methods would allow schools to focus on teachers' professional learning and to progress toward the school's goals.

Practical Applications and Results. One of the major evaluation tools was the LAUSD's evaluation of the PSCi school, which was conducted by outside central and local district administrators. The teachers used this evaluation to conduct mock reviews of the school's progress throughout the year. As part of the PSCi mock reviews of the school, teachers observed one another's classrooms to assess instruction, student engagement and learning, classroom environment, and levels of differentiated instruction. Teachers also reviewed collaborative teams' action plan sheets to determine which tasks were completed.

Another evaluation tool used at the school was an ongoing PLC Progress Monitor Rubric (see Table 9.2). The rubric was implemented to foster assessment and accountability of professional learning, whereas the district's PSCi rubric assessed other aspects of the school's growth. The rubric consists of three performance indicators (although Table 9.2 presents only high-success indicators): (a) high success, (b) progressing, and (c) developing, which were reflective actions for teachers' assessment of their own learning and professional learning community experiences. Furthermore, the rubric reflected a component missing from current PLC literature: teachers' assessment of progress. Rubric categories focus on reflective

TABLE 9.2 Ongoing PLC Progress Monitor Rubric

Ongoing Professional Learning Community Progress Monitor Rubric
Implementation and Delivery of Professional Learning Community Meetings

Sustained, Coherent, Ongoing	Job Embedded	Incorporates Practitioners' Comments About Delivery and Results	Change in Classroom Practice	Feedback to Delivery
High-Success Indicators	High-Success Indicators	High-Success Indicators	High-Success Indicators	High-Success Indicators
• Delivery is directly responsive to professional learning needs identified by participants' presurvey information and the school's action plans. • Delivery builds on prior learning in a spiraling way. • Delivery offers ongoing support during classroom implementation.	• Delivery provides ongoing opportunities for teachers to practice new learning. • Ongoing learning is considered the norm; professional development is part of the school culture. • System supports are in place that provide teachers daily opportunities to collaborate with peers, including co-observations of teachers, team teaching, modeling and feedback, and mentoring.	• Delivery provides ongoing opportunities for teachers to practice new learning. • Ongoing learning is considered the norm; professional development is part of the school culture. • System supports are in place that provide teachers daily opportunities to collaborate with peers, including co-observations of teachers, team teaching, modeling and feedback, and mentoring.	• Use of new learning is demonstrated in lesson/instructional planning. • Evidence of revisions of instructional practice based on assessment of results. • Classroom application of new learning is documented. • Adjustments in teaching based on use of student data. • Teachers exhibit sharpened skills in use of student data for lesson design.	• Professional learning is evaluated in terms of impact on classroom and teacher satisfaction. • Feedback is given to refine/revise the professional learning community. • Adjustments are made in response to teacher comments, evaluation data, and impact.

Adapted from New York State Education Department's *A Framework for Professional Development* (2008, pp. 4–13). Public domain material used with permission.

data and include (a) teacher input and delivery feedback, (b) relevance and sustainability of the PLC, and (c) the PLC's influence on professional learning and classroom instructional practices.

In addition to PSCi mock reviews, teachers regularly evaluated professional development and their own practices using journaling and the monitoring progress rubric (see Table 9.2). Based on teachers' criticisms, plan goals and school activities were modified to reflect teachers' collaborative feedback. Offering continuous cycles of evaluation benefited the staff by allowing immediate focus on revisions to existing procedures and activities, preventing disconnect between the shared vision and goals of the teacher-led reform.

Tenet 6: Sustainability Plan

Theoretical Implications. Sustainability of school change is dependent on school leadership and district management (Scribner, Cockrell, Cockrell, & Valentine, 1999). Monitoring the implementation and assessing the impact of school change aids in sustainability and accountability needed to move schools forward, and by bringing PLC members together, schools could share innovation, context, and sustainability (Leverett, 2008). Equally important is that teacher-led school reform is supported and sustained regardless of district policy changes (Giles & Hargreaves, 2006). Schools are often entangled in the dichotomy of existing problems and dealing with the tensions of "caring for students, critical reflection, and collaboration on the one hand, and the bureaucratic necessities of hierarchy, accountability, rationality, and control [on the other]" (Scribner et al., 1999, p. 154).

Questions of sustainability are at the forefront of the PSCi school reform. How do teacher leaders and schools sustain autonomy? How much autonomy do districts allow teacher-led school reformers? How do reformed schools maintain shared vision and shared culture? Theoretical implications to sustain school reform require that all teachers are engaged in leadership and in collective solutions to student achievement, and committed to change. To sustain teacher-led school reform and change, school reform must be viewed as a means to transformative teaching and learning processes. Sustainability requires schools to reflect upon the continuity of practices; however, continuity does not imply that teachers lose individuality.

Practical Application and Results. Sustainability of teacher-led school reform requires the school to begin each year as though it is its first year. Prior to the start of the school year, teachers engage in professional development activities focused on shared vision, trust building, goal setting, and PSCi plan review. In addition, when new teachers join the school community, their innovative ideas are coalesced into the culture of the school.

A critical aspect to teacher-led school reform is creating a sustainability plan that incorporates cycles of review and change to determine both effective and ineffective practices (see Figure 9.3). Teachers develop processes to review whether or not the school is meeting its goals and to implement strategies to enhance practices

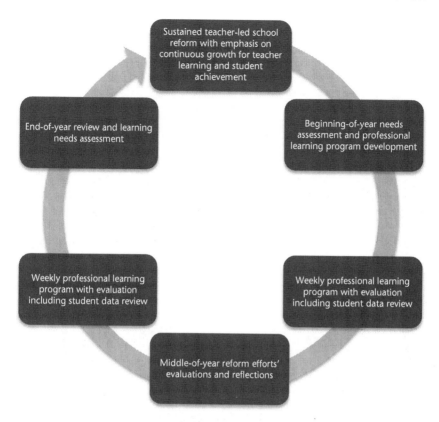

FIGURE 9.3 Sustained Teacher-Led School Reform With Emphasis on Continuous Growth for Teacher Learning and Student Achievement

that produce student gains. Teachers conduct mock and evaluative reviews of student performance data, teacher learning, and shared decision making. The school's cycle provides methods to measure policy, program, and progress effectiveness. In addition, teachers participate in needs assessments at the beginning, middle, and end of the year. Finally, professional learning activities are juxtaposed with student assessment data to determine instructional and student learning effectiveness.

Although the cycle of continuous growth has been successful in sustaining teacher-led reform, one of the challenges in sustaining the PSCi reform effort has been maintaining autonomy from the district's unilateral mandates. Following the school's 55-point increase on the state's academic achievement test in the school's second year, the district began to place unilateral goals and mandates on the school, such as setting the school's new API growth target and instructional focus. The reasons for why the district began to set targeted growth are unclear; however, district involvement contradicts the purpose of the PSCi, which provides autonomy in school reform. Within this teacher-led school reform initiative, teachers transformed the notion of teacher leadership, expanded the discussion on how to move learning communities forward, and demonstrated strategy on how to raise student achievement.

Conclusion

The PSCi provided an opportunity for unfettered access to the autonomy that teachers have long awaited and eagerly demanded from their district. The success of the teacher-led school reform at one school site resulted in the identification of six major tenets (see Figure 9.1) that move school reform forward: shared vision, shared leadership, re-culture of staff, effective professional development, ongoing evaluation, and sustainability of a teacher-created school reform plan. When districts provide teachers with opportunities to create reform plans, teachers should create plans that focus on elevating student achievement, professional learning, and decision-making processes. Teacher leaders need to continue to advocate for school autonomy and district collaboration, thereby demonstrating that a small group of teachers can change the world and, possibly, it is the only thing that will ever change the current state of schools.

References

Barth, R. S. (2001). Teacher leader. *Phi Delta Kappan, 82*(6), 443–449.

Barth, R. S. (2006). Improving relationships within the schoolhouse. *Educational Leadership, 63*(6), 8–13.

Blankstein, A. M. (2004). *Failure is not an option: Six principles that guide student achievement in high-performing schools.* Thousand Oaks, CA: Corwin.

Boone, S. C. (2010). *Professional learning communities' impact: A case study investigating teachers' perceptions and professional learning satisfaction at one urban middle school* (Doctoral dissertation), Walden University. Available from ProQuest Dissertations and Theses database. (UMI No. 3419559)

Darling-Hammond, L., Wei, R. C., Andree, A., Richardson, N., & Orphanos, S. (2009). *Professional learning in the learning profession: A status report on teacher development in the United States and abroad.* Dallas, TX: National Staff Development Council.

Donaldson, G. A., Jr. (2006). *Cultivating leadership in schools: Connecting people, purpose, and practice.* New York, NY: Teachers College Press.

DuFour, R. (1999). Autonomy: In the midst of community, there's room for the individual. *Journal of Staff Development, 20*(3), 69–70.

DuFour, R., & Eaker, R. (1998). *Professional learning communities at work: Best practices for enhancing student achievement.* Bloomington, IN: Solution Tree.

DuFour, R., Eaker, R., & DuFour, R. (Eds.). (2005). *On common ground: The power of professional learning communities.* Bloomington, IN: Solution Tree.

Fullan, M. (2001). *Leading in a culture of change.* San Francisco, CA: Jossey-Bass.

Fullan, M. (2005). Professional learning communities writ large. In R. DuFour, R. Eaker, & R. DuFour (Eds.), *On common ground: The power of professional learning communities* (pp. 209–224). Bloomington, IN: Solution Tree.

Gajda, R., & Koliba, C. J. (2008). Evaluating and improving the quality of teacher collaboration: A field-tested framework for secondary school leaders. *NASSP Bulletin, 92*(2), 133–153.

Giles, C., & Hargreaves, A. (2006). The sustainability of innovative schools as learning organizations and professional learning communities during standardized reform. *Educational Administration Quarterly, 42*(1), 124–156.

Glickman, C., Gordon, S. P., & Ross-Gordon, J. M. (2007). *SuperVision and instructional leadership: A developmental approach* (7th ed.). Boston, MA: Pearson/Allyn & Bacon.

Guskey, T. R. (2003). Analyzing lists of the characteristics of effective professional development to promote visionary leadership. *NASSP Bulletin, 87*(637), 4–20. doi: 10.1177/019263650308763702

Hord, S. M. (2009). Professional learning communities: Educators work together toward a shared purpose. *Journal of Staff Development, 30*(1), 40–43.

Kelehear, Z., & Davison, G. (2005). Teacher teams step up to leadership. *Journal of Staff Development, 26*(3), 54–59.

King, M. B., & Newmann, F. M. (2001). Building school capacity through professional development: Conceptual and empirical considerations. *International Journal of Educational Management, 15*(2), 86–93.

Leverett, L. (2008). Pursuit of sustainability. In A. M. Blankstein, P. D. Houston, & R. W. Cole (Eds.), *Sustaining professional learning communities* (pp. 121–142). Thousand Oaks, CA: Corwin.

Little, J. W. (2007). Professional communication and collaboration. In W. D. Hawley & D. L. Rollie (Eds.), *The keys to effective schools: Educational reform as continuous improvement* (2nd ed., pp. 55–56). Thousand Oaks, CA: Corwin.

Lowden, C. (2005). Evaluating the impact of professional development [Electronic version]. *The Journal of Research in Professional Learning, 84*(5), 1–22.

Muijs, D., & Harris, A. (2003). Teacher leadership—Improvement through empowerment? An overview of the literature. *Educational Management, Administration & Leadership, 31*(4), 437–448.

Murphy, J. (2005). *Connecting teacher leadership and school improvement.* Thousand Oaks, CA: Corwin.

New York State Education Department. (2008). *A framework for professional development.* Retrieved from http://www.p12.nysed.gov/ciai/tqpd/documents/PDFrameworkPDF.pdf

Scribner, J. P., Cockrell, K. S., Cockrell, D. H., & Valentine, J. W. (1999). Creating professional communities in schools through organizational learning: An evaluation of a school improvement process. *Educational Administration Quarterly, 35*(1), 130–160.

Spear, R. C. (1992). The process of change: Developing effective middle school programs. In J. L. Irvin (Ed.), *Transforming middle level education: Perspectives and possibilities* (pp. 102–138). Boston, MA: Allyn & Bacon.

Urbanski, A. (2003). Improving student achievement through labor-management collaboration in urban school districts. *Educational Policy, 17*(4), 503–518.

Wells, C., & Feun, L. (2007). Implementation of learning community principles: A study of six high schools. *NASSP Bulletin, 91*(2), 141–160. doi: 10.1177/0192636507302085

Zmuda, A., Kuklis, R., & Kline, E. (2004). *Transforming schools: Creating a culture of continuous improvement.* Alexandria, VA: Association for Supervision and Curriculum Development.

10

FIRST-YEAR TEACHERS

New and Ready to Lead!

Catherine Hagerman Pangan
Angela Lupton

Inexperienced. Novice. Green.

While all of these words may be true of a new teacher, they skew the perception of those already established in the school community toward thinking of a new teacher as someone who needs to assume a passive role in the leadership culture. Beginning teachers, outside their own classrooms, are often viewed through a myopic lens that causes the viewer to see them as "just a learner." This view creates an interesting dynamic between the seasoned teachers and induction-level teachers—one in which the roles of leader and learner take on the structure of hierarchy rather than reciprocity. While many educators purport to learn as much from their students as their students learn from them, the ways in which veteran teachers can learn from and with first-year teachers are often overlooked.

Energetic. Innovative. Unclouded.

There is strength when we view the role of learners and leaders differently.

> Learning and leading are deeply intertwined and we need to regard each other as worthy of attention, caring and involvement if we are to learn together. Indeed, leadership can be understood as reciprocal, purposeful learning in a community. Reciprocity helps us build relationships of mutual regard, thereby enabling us to become co-learners.
>
> (Lambert, 2003, p. 2)

What happens when we shift our view of new teachers and look through a different lens? By reframing the perception using a strength-based perspective, we can see a new professional who is energetic, innovative, and unclouded. Using this perspective is what Kathy Cramer refers to as Asset-Based Thinking. She writes,

"With Asset-Based Thinking you discover the possibilities, detect the strengths, mine the resources, and create positive momentum. It's at your disposal. With deficit-based thinking, opportunities loom on the horizon, but you deny yourself the opportunity to ever see them" (Cramer & Wasiak, 2006, p. 117).

These new colleagues have been hired because they have the capacity to be strong instructional leaders in their classrooms, yet we often relegate them to the backseat of enculturation as they start their careers. Of course those who join an existing staff need to have a sense of mission, vision, and history. Enculturation into a school community can provide this by "helping new teachers . . . to hit the road running, welcoming them to the staff from the very beginning, and encouraging them to become part of a strong learning community" (Lambert, 2003, p. 38). However, there is also the unique synergy that comes from having someone outside the established community bring a perspective that can begin to shift the existing culture and move it forward in a different direction. In fact, in many ways, it is this very potential for leadership that must become a cornerstone in the hiring process. As the average level of experience in the teaching profession continues to shift from the seasoned to the new (National Commission on Teaching and America's Future, 2013), we must cultivate an expanded vision for teacher leadership through the eyes of our beginning teachers.

In this chapter, these ideas are explored: the role of strong teacher preparation programs in training first-year teacher leaders, the new teacher's capacity to provide healthy disruption toward a culture of relational leadership, specific opportunities for new teacher leaders, and critical factors for supporting first-year teacher leaders.

Not All New Hires Are Created Equal

We must prepare our [education] students for schools as they should be, not simply perpetuating schools as they currently exist. We must be willing to explore with our students the difficult issues of inequities that exist in our schools and society and to help them to become agents of change.

(Butler University, 2006)

"New" teachers come in many forms—new to a district, new to a school, new to a grade level or subject. However, in exploring the topic of first-year teachers as leaders and agents of change, it is important to focus on what it means to be new to the profession; and the degree to which a teacher is truly new varies based upon his or her preparation. A beginning teacher coming from a program with limited time spent in thoughtful field and clinical experience or with no experience working alongside high-quality mentors may respond less confidently to the expectations of being a learner and leader than would a beginning teacher who has had those kinds of experiences. Clearly, if we are looking for first-year teachers to be transformative leaders in both the classroom and the larger school community, the foundation for success is in the preparation they receive. A 2013 report from the Center for Teacher Quality notes the importance of teacher training programs in creating teacher leaders:

> To attract and retain a talented workforce, the teaching profession must offer diverse opportunities for satisfying, impactful, and rewarding career growth—within and beyond the classroom. We must not only improve preparation programs but also build demand for the teacher leaders they must produce.
>
> (TeacherSolutions, 2013, p. 4)

If teacher preparation programs want to be intentional about developing the capacity for leadership, then the opportunities for experiences and mentorship need to foster the role of teacher leader. While the definition of a teacher leader varies, for our purposes, we most closely align with a definition that does not remove a teacher from the classroom in favor of an administrative or hierarchical leadership role, but rather emphasizes how teacher leadership can be part of the professional teacher spectrum. In defining the broader term of leader, "a leader is anyone who holds her- or himself accountable for finding potential in people and process" (Brown, 2012, p. 185); and, more specifically, in schools, "TL (teacher leadership) is an umbrella term for work that encompasses three developmental foci among practicing teachers: (a) individual development; (b) collaboration; and (c) organizational development" (Taylor, Goeke, Klein, Onore, & Geist, 2011, p. 921). In using these areas as the foundation, essential questions to explore when hiring new teachers can be framed thus:

1. Individual Development: What experiences has the candidate had that led him or her to reflect deeply on educational theory and put it into practice? Does the candidate have an ability to move beyond educational "buzzword bingo" and instead share cogent and integrated ideas around student learning and pedagogical structures? What is the established teacher identity of the candidate, and how has he or she put it into practice through field and clinical experiences?
2. Collaboration: What type of mentoring has the candidate received in field and clinical experiences? How many hours were spent co-teaching and learning from master teachers and fulltime faculty in school-based classrooms? What opportunities have there been for meaningful collaboration with peers and other professionals in research, professional learning communities, and school-based partnerships?
3. Organizational Development: How many different types of schools has the candidate been able to observe, learn, and work in during field and clinical experiences? What was the intensity and duration of the clinical experience? Was the candidate truly part of a school culture for a significant period of time during his or her preparation?

Teacher Deanna Schmidt (all names are real unless noted otherwise) acknowledges that in her first year of teaching, it was her principal who seemed to recognize her capacity as an instructional leader/model before she recognized it in herself. However, she also reflects that it was her preparation that allowed leadership qualities to come through in the hiring process and eventually led to her own recognition of her leadership ability. She stated:

> I was prepared to develop a strong sense of what I know as good teaching. We were, from the very first class, taught to have strong beliefs in what you are doing and if you don't believe strongly and are not passionate about it then you need to rethink it. . . . I am able to talk with confidence to others about what I think. Other teachers are starting to see that I'm not just that gung-ho first year teacher that needs to be knocked down a peg or two, but . . . that there is something to me deeper than that. It is not just that excitement or newness to the field that is making me make these decisions, it's because deep down it is about good teaching and what I believe.
>
> (D. Schmidt, personal communication, May 18, 2013)

First-year teacher Mary Ellen Estridge got her start in a new Reggio Emilia-inspired school in the city's largest urban district. In addition to her teaching talents, Mary Ellen believes she was hired for the position because of her understanding of strong relational aspects in learning and leading and her ability to connect to learners and the school community. As school started in the fall, Mary Ellen was also given the responsibility of mentoring junior preservice teacher education students. She stated, "I had four to five juniors in my classroom during the semester watching me. It was great for me." In addition to being relational, Mary Ellen defined leadership as "conversation," or the ability for all voices to be heard and honored. It is the same philosophy of leadership that undergirds her classroom. She also stated that for her, leadership "is the ability to find what makes people uniquely gifted and then find opportunities [for them] to use their gifts" (M. Estridge, personal communication, May 14, 2013). Mary Ellen's stance is similar to that in *The Constructivist Leader*. As Lambert (2002) reflected, "Authentic work must be experienced by adults as well as children, as must authentic relationships and possibilities" (p. xvi).

Mary Ellen's thoughts are also congruent with findings of research on relationships and teacher leadership. Donaldson (2007) wrote about the strength and identity of relational leadership. At the heart of relational leadership is the question: How do relationships influence the adults in this school to do good things for students? Leadership is a particular type of relationship—one that mobilizes other people to improve practice.

Relational leadership runs through the daily life of every school as educators attend to the quality of relationships, insist on commitment to the school's purposes and goals, and examine and improve instruction (Donaldson, 2006). Leadership is about how individuals together influence these three streams of school life to make learning better for all students. Although school administrators play a vital role in these efforts, teachers are uniquely positioned to contribute special assets to the school leadership mix.

The importance of including new teacher voices in the creation of Mary Ellen's school was driven by the focus on establishing a strong school culture. As Donaldson (2007) stated, "Teacher culture based on relationships is hugely influential in schools" (p. 27).

When we put good preparation for both teaching and leadership at the forefront of the hiring process, we increase the likelihood that our new hire will jump into action as part of the larger group of teacher leaders in a building. However, we must also prepare for the change and disruption in the culture of relationships that the new teacher may bring.

Healthy Disruption in School Culture

In careful selection of a new teacher leader, the stage is set for not only supporting the good work going on in the school, but also creating a climate for healthy disruption in the school culture. Schools are serious business, but "considering the staggering turnover of new teachers . . . it is in everyone's interest to help teachers find joy in their work" (Wolk, 2008, p. 14). Beginning teachers enter the profession unclouded and joyful about the potential for making a difference in the world, and this enthusiasm, if welcomed, can have a profound impact on school culture. Why is culture important? Tony Hsieh, CEO of Zappos, a company that has thrived in part because of a strong intention to build a healthy company culture, believed, "If you get the culture right, most of the other stuff will happen naturally on its own" (Hsieh, 2010, p. 152). However, in building culture, he also suggested that part of the core value of that culture must be to embrace and drive change. He wrote:

> We must all learn not only to not fear change, but to embrace it enthusiastically and, perhaps even more important, encourage and drive it. We must always plan for and be prepared for constant change. Although change can and will come from all directions, it's important that most of the changes . . . are driven from the bottom up.
>
> (Hsieh, 2010, p. 163)

As Lambert (2003) stated, "Leadership is about contributing to, learning from, and influencing the learning of others" (p. vii). New teachers may be the "new kids on the block" when entering a school community, but a first-year teacher can serve as a catalyst to other voices in the building who are ready to create change and, in turn, "influence the learning of others." The synergistic effect can produce results even if, historically, such change has not been the dominant discourse.

One of the ways in which the discourse can shift is through the intentional creation of social networks within the school community that value all voices at the table, including those of the newest colleagues. There is nothing new about creating social networks for "emotional, social, and financial support for people and communities" (Baker-Doyle, 2011, p. 14). Baker-Doyle (2011) posited that teacher networks, professional learning communities, and mentorship programs are all important for the support of new teachers. However, the new "millennial" teachers often bring in well-developed physical and virtual "Social Network Perspectives" (p. 2) that seasoned teachers may not have. This perspective can help bring colleagues and school communities together in powerful and intentional ways. Further, it can provide the new teacher with a sense of a targeted point of leadership within the school.

The theme of social networking and connecting with others is a common thread found in many areas of teacher leadership. Danielson (2007) described teacher leaders as "call[ing] others to action and energiz[ing] them with the aim of improving teaching and learning" (p. 14). Danielson also noted the work of Fullan, quoting him when writing, "The litmus test of all leadership is whether it mobilizes people's commitment to putting their energy into actions designed to improve things. It is individual commitment, but above all it is collective mobilization" (p. 14). Danielson (2007) also suggested that collaboration and the ability to connect colleagues to their own vision and build consensus with diverse groups is a "hallmark of leadership" (p. 15). Examples of new teachers taking leadership roles in the creation of social networks are more common than one might imagine.

> New teacher leader, Jennifer Brinn, started a class Twitter @MissBrinnsClass to keep connected with families and her new school community. She not only wanted to keep parents informed, but also to let the school community know what engaging experiences her first graders were having. Jennifer stated, "I [also] started @Jenn_TeachLearn . . . for more Professional Development purposes. I had a Parent Tweet Up earlier in the year to teach them how to use it and sign some up for accounts. . . . It was awesome! There are lots of possibilities with it."
>
> (J. Brinn, personal communication, May 19, 2013)

One college of education hosts "Collaboration Nights," where new teacher alumni are invited to come once a month as mentors for current student teachers. The new teachers learn and share with each other while providing "seasoned" ears for student teachers. As first-year teacher Kate Robinson reflected on these experiences, "I have really loved the opportunity to do this throughout the year. Every few Wednesdays it's so awesome to talk and problem solve with student teachers, and I always leave feeling so recharged and optimistic (even if the problems we talk about are frustrating and difficult)."

(K. Robison, personal communication, April 16, 2013)

The idea of supporting new teachers who have the ability to create social networks breaks the mold of traditional, hierarchical school leadership positions. Interestingly, Lord and Miller (2000) suggested that traditional roles, including department chairs, grade-level leaders, and mentors to some degree, are still principal-driven roles and do not lead to meaningful change. In contrast, "independent teacher networks have the potential to transform traditional concepts of teacher input and staff development" (Berry, Norton, & Byrd, 2007, p. 49). They went on to state, "Independent networks . . . make it possible for teachers to draw on external communities that promote divergent thinking. Such networks support the view that teachers have unique insights that can improve education and accelerate student achievement" (Berry et al., 2007, p. 49).

Opportunities + Potential = New Teacher Leaders

In addition to shifting the culture and leading the social networks, harnessing the impact of a first-year teacher leader within the school community is the first step in creating a climate for innovation. Brown (2012) stated, "No corporation or school can thrive in the absence of creativity, innovation, and learning, and the greatest threat to all three of these is disengagement" (p. 187). Administrators and colleagues need to highlight the opportunities available to new teachers. These potential experiences blend well with Harrison and Killion's (2007) statement, "The ways teachers can lead are as varied as teachers themselves" (p. 74). Two specific themes for new teacher leaders are noted under selected "Roles for Teacher Leaders," as articulated by Harrison and Killion (2007).

Resource Provider

It is not uncommon to think of the experienced teacher becoming the "resource provider" (Harrison & Killion, 2007, p. 74) for the new teacher; but what if the new teacher had the opportunity to become a resource provider for the team or school community? Well-trained new teachers come with several fresh ideas in their pedagogical toolboxes, and why not support their professional growth by helping them share their pedagogical strengths and ideas? Often the new teachers have come with a diverse set of teaching experiences that represent different contexts and communities. They have "tricks of the trade" of their own that can be used in powerful ways—both to inspire growth in others and to build confidence in the new teacher.

Emily Alaimo, a first-year special education teacher, stated that her principal encouraged her to share frequently with the staff and team members. "I DID know what I was doing and because I was given the opportunity to share those understandings, I felt good about my contributions in my school" (E. Alaimo, personal communication, May 13, 2013).

Human resource administrator Mike Whitman also sees the resources a new teacher can provide. He stated:

> I think the advantage of being an educator in 2013 is that we're all learners. Practice is changing at such a wicked rate that many times the beginning teacher has a knowledge base that is being infused into the existing culture. . . . [New teachers] coming out of school may have more experience with that and more current practice knowledge of that, and they can slowly begin to support teachers who are just now making those transitions.
>
> (M. Whitman, personal communication, May 24, 2013)

Learning Facilitator

In addition to sharing resources with her colleagues, Emily participated in the Positive Behavior Support team after being invited by her mentor. Through this team, Emily shared data with teachers in her building and learned and shared new behavior strategies with her colleagues from across the district. "It really opened up my eyes. . . . I learned about what other teachers do in the district and it was a great way to learn new things and then share those ideas in a professional manner with your own school" (E. Alaimo, personal communication, May 15, 2013). Emily agreed that her colleagues saw her as a leader after she participated in the support team.

In Deanna's school, her classroom was used as a provocation for other colleagues to explore both environments and the workshop approach as the building worked to shift its pedagogical structures.

Supporting First-Year Leaders

Besides the transformative energy that new teacher leaders can bring to a school community, there are other critical professional issues that can be addressed in supporting first-year teachers as leaders. At a time in our educational history where almost one out of every two new teachers has left the classroom by the end of the fifth year (Fulton, Yoon, & Lee, 2005), we must also recognize the value that a leadership role can play as a protective factor in professional resiliency. One way to address this idea of retention and longevity in the profession is to explore what it means to be a thriving professional. Lambert (2003) wrote:

> Teachers who exhibit vitality are energized by their own curiosities, their colleagues, and their students; they find joy and stimulation in the daily dilemmas of teaching and are intrigued by the challenge of improving adult learning communities. Teachers become fully alive when their schools and

districts provide them with opportunities for skillful participation, inquiry, dialogue, and reflection. Such environments foster leadership.

(p. 32)

When new teachers are valued for what they bring to a learning community, they regenerate their capacity to lead, their desire to teach, and their commitment to the profession as a whole.

However, it would be a mistake to believe that those who have already been working hard to establish a sense of identity and culture in a school are always ready to embrace the lens of the new teacher as leader. In fact, the insertion of an "outsider" can feel challenging and even threatening. Part of supporting new teachers in their multifaceted roles of teacher, learner, and leader must also come from an intentional community norm to provide the space and framework needed to have courageous conversations. Margaret Wheatley (2009) reminded us:

> Sometimes it takes faith to believe that others have as much concern and skill as we do. But in my experience, when the issue is important to others, they do not disappoint us. If you start a conversation, others will surprise you with their talent and generosity, with how their courage grows.
>
> (p. 31)

She further described one of the essential principles that must be present for these conversations. Wheatley (2009) wrote:

> Conversation is an opportunity to meet together as peers, not as roles. What makes us equal is that we're human beings. A second thing that makes us equal is that we need each other. Whatever we know, it is not sufficient. We can't see enough of the whole. We can't figure it out alone. Somebody sees something that the rest of us might need.
>
> (p. 34)

First-year teacher Deanna noted this need for "conversation as equals" in her own reflections on becoming a new teacher leader:

> We (grade level team) didn't meet regularly, and we were supposed to. Technically we were supposed to have an hour meeting every week within our team, and it wasn't happening. . . . I realized that I kind of needed to be upfront with what I want. This is as much my year as it is their year. It is not that I am becoming part of their team, but we are a team together. Kind of flipping that thinking: It is not me going into an already established community, but it is a community that we have to build together.
>
> (D. Schmidt, personal communication, May 18, 2013)

In modeling the capacity for teacher leadership, we would be remiss in not asking first-year teachers what they would offer to their future new teacher colleagues. What advice would first-year teacher leaders pass on to those who will soon follow in their footsteps?

1. TAKE opportunities for leadership.
2. Create time for reflection for continued learning, because this reflection can build confidence when challenges present themselves.
3. Surround yourself with people who also feel comfortable sharing experiences.
4. Take time to build culture in your classroom and in the school. "It was one of the most important experiences of my first year. I heard the words, but did not realize it would be my most important work" (M. Estridge, personal communication, May 14, 2013).
5. Ask for help.
6. Mistakes are a good thing if you learn from them.
7. Get to know others in your building in meaningful ways: Teach with them, and share ideas to show your leadership capacity.
8. Be confident in the fact that you DO bring different types of experiences to the table as well as a fresh perspective, and focus on what you DO know. It is substantial.

Mike Whitman also added advice that is true for all teachers:

> At the end of the day, you have to be a rock star in the classroom before you can be a rock star in your building. . . . Make sure you take care of your home-front before you take care of someone else's.
>
> (M. Whitman, personal communication, May 24, 2013)

In all, it is important to continually check our own leadership lens as we view the role of new teacher leaders. At the forefront of our thinking should always be seeing new teachers' abilities to provide healthy disruption to school cultures, seeing their ability to guide our community toward more relational leadership, and seeing the unique perspectives that they can provide when they come from strong preparation programs. It is when we move from mere enculturation, and instead embrace openness to change, that we truly capitalize on the capacity for transformation that new teachers bring.

Finally, perhaps the most poignant way to summarize the role of a new teacher is to embrace the charge of "daring greatly" (Brown, 2012). We feel the power of a beginning teacher's words with and through Brown's voice as stated in her Daring Greatly Leadership Manifesto:

> We want to show up, we want to learn, and we want to inspire.
> We are hardwired for connection, curiosity, and engagement.

We crave purpose, and we have a deep desire to create and contribute. We want to takes risks, embrace our vulnerabilities, and be courageous.

When learning and working are dehumanized—when you no longer see us and no longer encourage our daring, or when you only see what we produce or how we perform—we disengage and turn away from the very things that the world needs from us: our talent, our ideas, and our passion.

What we ask is that you engage with us, show up beside us, and learn from us.

Feedback is a function of respect; when you don't have honest conversations with us about our strengths and our opportunities for growth, we question our contributions and your commitment.

Above all else, we ask that you show up, let yourself be seen, and be courageous.

Dare Greatly with us (p. 212).

From DARING GREATLY: HOW THE COURAGE TO BE VULNERABLE TRANSFORMS THE WAY WE LIVE, LOVE, PARENT, AND LEAD by Brene Brown, copyright © 2012 by Brene Brown. Used by permission of Gotham Books, an imprint of Penguin Group (USA) LLC.

References

Baker-Doyle, K. J. (2011). *The networked teacher: How new teachers build social networks for professional support.* New York, NY: Teachers College Press.

Berry, B., Norton, J., & Byrd, A. (2007). Lessons from networking. *Educational Leadership, 65*(1), 48–52.

Brown, B. (2012). *Daring greatly: How the courage to be vulnerable transforms the way we live, love, parent, and lead.* New York, NY: Gotham Books.

Butler University. (2006). College of education vision statement [Web content]. Indianapolis, IN: Author. Retrieved from http://www.butler.edu/coe/student-resources/mission-vision

Cramer, K. D., & Wasiak, H. (2006). *Change the way you see everything through asset-based thinking.* Philadelphia, PA: Running Press.

Danielson, C. (2007). The many faces of leadership. *Educational Leadership, 65*(1), 14–19.

Donaldson, G. A., Jr. (2006). *Cultivating leadership in schools: Connecting people, purpose, and practice* (2nd ed.). New York, NY: Teachers College Press.

Donaldson, G. A., Jr. (2007). What do teachers bring to leadership? *Educational Leadership, 65*(1), 26–29.

Fulton, K., Yoon, I., & Lee, C. (2005). *Induction into learning communities.* Washington, DC: National Commission on Teaching and America's Future.

Harrison, C., & Killion, J. (2007). Ten roles for teacher leaders. *Educational Leadership, 65*(1), 74–77.

Hsieh, T. (2010). *Delivering happiness: A path to profits, passion, and purpose.* New York, NY: Business Plus.

Lambert, L. (2002). *The constructivist leader* (2nd ed.). New York, NY: Teachers College Press.

Lambert, L. (2003). *Leadership capacity for lasting school improvement.* Alexandria, VA: Association for Supervision and Curriculum Development.

Lord, B., & Miller, B. (2000, March). *Teacher leadership: An appealing and inescapable force in school reform?* Newton, MA: Educational Development Center.

National Commission on Teaching and America's Future. (2013). Evaluation [Web content]. Washington, DC: Author. Retrieved from http://nctaf.org/research/evaluation

Taylor, M., Goeke, J., Klein, E., Onore, C., & Geist, K. (2011). Changing leadership: Teachers lead the way for schools that learn. *Teaching and Teacher Education, 27*(5), 920–929. doi: 10.1016/j.tate.2011.03.003

TeacherSolutions. (2013, May). *Teaching 2030: Leveraging teacher preparation 2.0.* Carrboro, NC: Center for Teaching Quality. Retrieved from http://www.teachingquality.org/sites/default/files/TEACHING_2030_Leveraging_Teacher_Preparation.pdf

Wheatley, M. J. (2009). *Turning to one another: Simple conversations to restore hope to the future* (2nd ed.). San Francisco, CA: Berrett-Koehler Publishers.

Wolk, S. (2008). Joy in school. *Educational Leadership, 66*(1), 8–15.

11

CLASSROOM TEACHERS AS TEAM PLAYERS

Nancy P. Gallavan

Classroom teachers are required to fulfill a range of roles and responsibilities associated with being both followers and leaders; they are expected to serve as well-rounded faculty members and as well-honed educational coaches. In addition to completion of tasks for their school administrators, as followers, and facilitation of learning with their classroom students, as leaders, teachers also are assigned to participate on various teams or committees in their grade levels, subject areas, and school communities. Although it is presumed that teachers can serve effectively in these roles, teachers generally appear to be underprepared for collaborating professionally on teams and modeling leadership with colleagues. Teachers seem more comfortable working autonomously, tend to encounter interpersonal challenges when working on teams, and receive little or no continuing education to improve their teamwork participation.

The premise of this chapter asserts that teamwork offers opportunities for classroom teachers in three important ways. First, through teamwork, they can model and teach teamwork in their P–12 classes to increase achievement in their students, their schools, and themselves. Second, teamwork offers opportunities for teachers to model and teach team participation and team leadership to their P–12 students and to teacher candidates. Finally, through participation on and leadership of teams, teachers develop professionalism among colleagues and community members. To explore these three assertions, a study was conducted with three different focus groups that generated the four essential components of TEAMwork as Trust, Efficacy, Agency, and Mentorship.

Classroom Teacher Preparation and Practice

Across the United States, most university business students are taught the structures, functions, rigor, and benefits of effective teamwork. Through these lessons, students become intricately acquainted with various approaches for increasing individual achievement and team productivity, for realizing the advantages of developing and modeling leadership, and for applying the gains to growing personally and advancing professionally through a multitude of academic exercises. Quickly, these students discover that their course feedback and individual evaluations often depend upon their experiences and expertise with collaboration, contribution, constructiveness, and conflict resolution. Teamwork is touted highly in both business schools and today's workforce (Van den Bossche, Gijselaers, Segers, Woltjer, & Kirschner, 2011). Prospective employers seek business students and new hires who model comfort, competence, confidence, collaboration, and congeniality in a culture that values effective teamwork and leadership (Mutch, 1998; Rodriguez, 2009).

However, teacher candidates tend to be prepared differently (Main, 2010). More often, candidates are asked to organize (or are assigned to) groups, rather than teams, in order to complete specific projects. This approach indicates that teacher educators may be unclear on the differences between the purposes of groups and the purposes of teams. Groups tend to be short-term and outcome oriented. Teams tend to be long-term and process driven. Although all teams are groups, not all groups are teams. Eby, Meade, Parisi, and Douthitt (1999) reported that while groups attend primarily to task completion and social interactions, teams capitalize on positive intentions, productive communications, coordinated procedures, distributed tasks, available resources, and social support.

Compounding the challenge, most teachers do not see, experience, or learn teamwork either as P–12 students or as teacher candidates. As candidates, they pursue careers based on their own past memories of being P–12 students who enjoyed the social environment and academic engagement of school, and they expect to offer similar experiences to their own future students (Hellsten & Prytula, 2011) while working cohesively with their professional colleagues.

Too often, today's teachers find themselves isolated in individual classrooms, overwhelmed with burgeoning tasks, and unsupported in their work (Mawhinny, 2008), striving to prepare their students for the required standardized testing. Additionally, teachers are assigned by their administrators to serve on groups, frequently called committees, and given directives to complete specific tasks to benefit the school community. Although these groups or committees may be labeled *teams,* they tend to default to group status for two primary reasons: Teachers are not equipped for or supported in working as team players, and teachers tend not to be comfortable with or capable of working effectively as team players or teacher leaders (Main, 2007). As Barth (2001) noted, all teachers must lead in some way in order for education to improve. More teachers are being asked to fill leadership positions in their schools; thus, all educators need to become teacher leaders and must be prepared for these expanding expectations.

Understanding Two Special Conditions in Education

Two special conditions in education exist that deter teachers from developing as effective team players and teacher leaders. The first condition is the generational perpetuation of practice (Gallavan, 2007). Teachers learn to become teachers as: (a) P–12 students, (b) university students, (c) candidates in teacher education courses, (d) interns in clinical field experiences, and (e) professionals interacting with colleagues. Although teachers are provided mandated academic standards, they adopt practices for themselves based on these five sources, contributing to their own generational perpetuation of practice. Frequently the theories and practices featured in university teacher preparation programs are superseded by the self-selected techniques acquired by classroom teachers (Borko, 2004; Gallavan, 2007).

The second condition is the propinquity effect (Festinger, Schachter, & Back, 1950), the tendency for people to form friendships with and become more like the people they encounter most often, such as family and colleagues. The propinquity effect influences people's professional decision making. The more people are assigned to teams and asked to work together constructively, the more likely they are to get to know, understand, and appreciate one another. However, the propinquity effect can create two opposing outcomes. Teams that are led with and fueled by positive and productive members more likely will create positive and productive outcomes. Conversely, teams that are led with and/or fueled by negative and nonproductive members more likely will create negative and nonproductive outcomes. Such negative and nonproductive outcomes can be detrimental to the entire institution, including the classroom, school, school district, and other interested stakeholders.

Just as classroom teachers build upon content and pedagogical knowledge (Shulman, 1986) to guide and support their P–12 students, teachers need to receive guidance and support themselves to become effective team players, especially classroom teachers responsible for preparing candidates and mentoring novice teachers. Teachers must be provided information, access, and opportunities (Gallavan, 2002) to maximize their growth and development to benefit themselves and their students, schools, candidates, and communities just as business students prepare for the dynamics of their future careers.

Listening to Teachers

The study described in this chapter was organized to investigate the perspectives of three different focus groups: classroom teachers, teacher candidates, and teacher educators. Given that focus group discussions center on a particular topic or issue (Morgan, 1998), the participants were asked to reflect upon and respond to predetermined questions and to engage in continued interactive conversations (Patton, 1990). The four primary questions that guided the conversations were the following:

1. Why are teamwork and leadership important for teachers, P–12 students, candidates, and teacher educators?

2. How does a professional model teamwork and leadership with teachers, P–12 students, candidates, and teacher educators?
3. How do teaching and learning teamwork and leadership increase achievement?
4. How do teamwork and leadership advance your professionalism?

The focus group conversations provided more extensive and enriched perspectives than the feedback gathered from the individual interviews (Morgan, 1998). The participants in the focus group conversations added meanings, applications, examples pertinent to the issues, and information shared by other members of the focus group (Bloor, Frankland, Thomas, & Robson, 2001). Focus groups are considered a valid method for examining context (Edmunds, 1999), which was a major purpose of this study.

Specifically, teamwork and teacher leadership are built on Rueda's (1998) five sociocultural tenets:

> 1. Facilitate learning and development through joint productive activity among leaders and participants . . . 2. Promote learners' expertise in professionally relevant discourse . . . 3. Contextualize teaching, learning, and joint productive activity (schooling) in the experiences and skills of participants . . . 4. Challenge participants toward more complex solutions in addressing problems . . . and 5. Engage participants through dialogue, especially the instructional conversation. (pp. 1–2)

As the assorted members of each focus group engaged in their conversations, they provided evidence related to each tenet of teaching, learning, and schooling, and strengthened the purposes, processes, and productivity of the study.

The participants received a matrix (see Table 11.1) for recording individual responses before, during, and after the focus group conversations. The individual matrix allowed each participant to express her or his voice safely (Mitra, 2008) and feel equally empowered in the decision making (Chi Keung, 2008). Horizontally, the three columns of the matrix are labeled: Teaching, Learning, and Schooling—three essential aspects of education. Teaching embodies all of the thoughts, beliefs, words, actions, interactions, and documents associated with the teacher. Learning

TABLE 11.1 Blank Matrix for Focus Group Research About Teamwork and Teacher Leadership

	Teaching	Learning	Schooling
Success			
Satisfaction			
Significance			
Sustainability			

entails all of the thoughts, beliefs, words, actions, interactions, and documents associated with the learners. Schooling involves all of the thoughts, beliefs, words, actions, interactions, documents, and people associated with the institution, such as vision, mission, goals, theme, curriculum, instruction, assessment, and discipline.

The four vertical rows of the matrix are labeled: Success, Satisfaction, Significance, and Sustainability (Gallavan, 2013). Success describes achievement of expectations and tasks. Satisfaction portrays attainment of contentment and happiness. Significance represents identification of meaning and importance. Sustainability denotes continuation and encouragement.

Discovering and Identifying Outcomes

The analyzed data collected during the focus groups produced information presented here in four different ways: summarized quotes from participants, summary statements developed by the group, single words that capture the components of TEAM (Trust, Efficacy, Agency, and Mentorship), and single words that connect teaching, learning, and schooling. The following sections expand on these four forms of presentation.

Summarized Quotes

The first form of presenting outcomes manifested as three overarching outcomes emerging during the focus group conversations. The participants in all three groups strongly stated and wholeheartedly supported the beliefs that teaching and learning teamwork within the context of appropriate schooling effectively helps with (1) increasing achievement in P–12 students and classroom teachers, (2) modeling and teaching leadership with P–12 students and teacher candidates, and (3) advancing professionalism both individually and collectively among colleagues. The focus group participants shared the following comments.

Teamwork Increases Achievement. Teamwork increases achievement when every member of the team is encouraged to contribute honestly, freely, and equally. All members of the team must feel valued for their strengths to make meaningful personal connections. Team members hear other members' ideas and perspectives; P–12 students interact with peers rather than teachers; and teachers interact with colleagues rather than administrators. Team members are more likely to articulate their own ideas and are stimulated to build upon other members' ideas creatively. Teams are motivated to excel when competing with an established challenge/goal or another team. Every member of the team increases in achievement through shared critical thinking, resourcefulness, problem solving, and decision making.

Teamwork Models Leadership. Teamwork models leadership and is more highly valued when teams are engaged in and/or select authentic challenges that seem to make an important difference in their schools and communities and when it is evident that the leadership comes from within the team. During these experiences, P–12 students strengthen their approaches to learning and living; teacher candidates fortify their applications to their careers and living. Candidates also benefit greatly from experiences in schools and classrooms with effective team teaching where teachers plan, organize, facilitate, and reflect collaboratively. Opportunities to lead should be made available to all members of the team so each member can experience the responsibilities as both a leader and follower. The research participants admitted that too often they select the same students to lead, and teachers must be sure that all students can grow naturally from safe opportunities to lead.

Teamwork Advances Professionalism. Teamwork advances professionalism among classroom teachers and teacher candidates when each member of the team experiences a growing sense of safety and comfort with the other members of the team and is allowed to participate and be accepted. Concomitantly, professionalism advances when everyone contributes positively to the team processes and products as feelings of reliance on the team to fortify. Professionalism is demonstrated in the classroom, around the school, and within the district through improved confidence and competence. Classroom teachers and teacher candidates experience an enhanced sense of responsibility and accountability. Collaboration and mentorship intensify in ways that benefit teacher retention, career promotion, new experiences, and educational networking, yielding many new opportunities.

Summary Statements From Reaching Consensus

During the second form of presentation of outcomes, each group reflected on the key descriptors recorded by the participants in their focus groups, reached consensus, and wrote a single summary statement. Reaching consensus entailed crafting a statement that all participants in the focus group could accept. Four guidelines from Habermas (as cited in Gareis, 2010) framed the process for reaching consensus: (1) No one capable of making a contribution is excluded; (2) Participants have equal voice and equal chances to make arguments; (3) Participants are honest with each other and with themselves (i.e., they assert only what they truly believe); and (4) No coercion is allowed. If the conditions are met, arguments can be weighed purely on their own merit, and group decisions are optimized. Given the time limitations for each focus group and the opportunity to contribute to the conversations, the participants cooperated well with one another and completed the task quickly and enthusiastically. A sample of one consensus matrix is shown in Table 11.2.

Identifying the Components of TEAM

For the third form of presenting outcomes, the researcher selected one word to capture the meaning of the comments shared during the focus group conversations and the statements recorded on the three matrices by the teacher educators, classroom teachers, and teacher candidates (see Table 11.3). In the category of

TABLE 11.2 Matrix From Group B (Classroom Teachers) Related to Teamwork and Teacher Leadership

	Teaching	Learning	Schooling
Success	I meet my students' needs to learn the content through teamwork.	My students apply new learning appropriately to solve problems through teamwork.	All grade and department course objectives are unique yet comprehensive for developing teamwork.
Satisfaction	I keep my students engaged in the content.	My students appear to like new learning and the class.	Activities and assignments build upon one another logically and seamlessly.
Significance	I connect content that I have taught with the new content to be learned.	My students make valuable connections with prior learning, other courses, and the world.	Outcomes apply to learning and to living as well as to learning about living.
Sustainability	I can identify the main ideas and ways they are woven throughout the units and lessons.	My students work cooperatively and seek assistance from their peers.	Students co-construct new knowledge, help guide the class, and contribute to classroom management.

TABLE 11.3 Matrix With Consensus Data from Groups A, B, and C Related to Teamwork and Teacher Leadership

	Teaching	Learning	Schooling
Success	Efficacy	Self-Sufficiency	Productivity
Satisfaction	Agency	Pleasure	Likeability
Significance	Trust	Accomplishment	Accountability
Sustainability	Mentorship	Readiness	Nurturing
		Knowledge	
	TEAM	SPARK	PLAN

teaching, success was defined as efficacy, satisfaction was defined as agency, significance was defined as trust, and sustainability was defined as mentorship. The first letters of these four words, in slightly different order, spell TEAM.

Trust. Trust was the word selected to define the significance of teaching teamwork. Trust (Mangin & Stoelinga, 2011) comprises the process of internalizing and demonstrating beliefs of honesty and reliability. For each of the focus groups, the most important evidence of their teaching teamwork was embodied by the trust that the participants experienced with their students, colleagues, and system.

Dirks (1999) reported that when the level of trust is increased, the group tends to experience higher levels of cooperation and performance; when the level of trust is decreased, the group tends to experience lower levels of cooperation and performance. Trust among team players is the hallmark of effective teamwork.

Efficacy. Efficacy defined success in teaching teamwork. Efficacy (Bandura, 1997) involves accepting responsibility for one's actions. Although the focus group participants did not use the word *efficacy,* the participants in each of the three groups articulated words with similar meanings. The participants commented that they were successful only when they taught their students about teamwork in the best ways possible and with the best information available. Efficacy emanates from four sources: mastery experiences when people achieve success themselves; social modeling when people observe other people like themselves becoming successful; social persuasion when people are encouraged to believe they can be successful; and psychological responses when people convince themselves that they can be successful. All four sources of efficacy contribute to success in teaching and learning teamwork and participating as team players.

Agency. Satisfaction of teaching teamwork was defined as agency (Bandura, 2006) or the self-influence and ownership of one's responsibilities. Differing from efficacy, agency requires an individual to internalize outcomes as a charge or an obligation. Teachers must not only facilitate the best ways possible with the best information available, but they also must be accountable for the results, within reason. Agency is manifested in two dichotomous ways: inhibitive and proactive. When agency is inhibitive, it prevents an individual from behaving inappropriately. When agency is proactive, it propels an individual to behave appropriately. Agency includes intentionality; forethought; self-regulation through self-reactive influence; and self-reflectiveness related to purpose, quality, and capabilities (Bandura, 2006). Agency can be expressed through one's direct personal interactions, relying on others through proxy for personal interactions and relying on others through collective interactions (Bandura, 2006). Effective teamwork incorporates all aspects and expressions of agency.

Mentorship. Sustainability of teaching teamwork involves mentorship (Hellsten, Prytula, Ebanks, & Lai, 2009). Mentorship consists of establishing relationships that stimulate nurturing support, through the reciprocity of ideas and insights, for both mentor and novice in honing success and finding satisfaction. Effective mentorship allows both participants to identify their needs and interests so time and energy can be tailored to the participants. This form of differentiated instruction guides the mentor to attend to the diverse, complex, and ever-changing issues in the relationship and the process. However, mentorships offer the potential for constructive outcomes and not-so-constructive outcomes. Mentorship, like agency, is influenced by the generational perpetuation of practice theory (Gallavan, 2007) and the propinquity effect (Festinger et al., 1950).

Connecting the Categories of Learning and Schooling

The fourth form of presenting outcomes extended the focus group members' statements summarizing success, satisfaction, significance, and sustainability in the categories of learning and schooling from the category of teaching. In the category of learning, success was defined as self-sufficiency, satisfaction was defined as pleasure, significance was defined as accomplishment, and sustainability was defined as readiness. The category of learning seemed incomplete, so the word *knowledge* was added. The first letters of these five words—*self-sufficiency, pleasure, accomplishment, readiness, and knowledge*—spell *SPARK*. In the category of schooling, success was defined as productivity, satisfaction was defined as likeability, significance was defined as accountability, and sustainability was defined as nurturing. The first letters of these words—*productivity, likeability, accountability,* and *nurturing*—spell *PLAN*. Consequently, success, satisfaction, significance, and sustainability related to teamwork subdivided into the three categories of teaching, learning, and schooling can be viewed as *TEAM:* identification of actions; *SPARK:* motivation of the actions; and *PLAN:* direction of the actions.

TEAMwork and Teacher Leadership

Ideally, every member of every team participates effectively as both a follower and a leader fulfilling Main's (2010) five characteristics of effective team followers and leaders:

> (a) attitudes toward working on a team emphasizing both perceived benefits and disadvantages, (b) group processes while working on a team for making decisions, (c) facilitation of tasks and responsibilities to work cooperatively and constructively, (d) intrapersonal communication skills for building relationships, and (e) conflict management. (paraphrased, p. 83)

Teachers need to understand and participate as both follows and leaders in order to teach these same expectations to their own P–12 students (Danielson, 2007; Donaldson, 2007; Gordon, 2004); therefore, teacher preparation must include teamwork and leadership to transform professionals from technicians to teachers (Neumann, Jones, & Webb, 2012). Today's teachers must be cognizant of the power and authority that teachers gain as followers and leaders (Neumann et al., 2012). Becoming an effective team member calls for all teachers to advance their team leadership.

In 2011, the Model Teacher Leader Standards, developed by the Teacher Leadership Exploratory Consortium (TLEC, 2011), stated that the standards were

> intended to codify, promote, and support teacher leadership as a vehicle for transforming schools to meet the needs of 21st-century learners. Rather than serve as a comprehensive job description for teacher leaders, the

Standards instead describe seven domains of leadership. Each domain is further developed and supported by a list of functions that a teacher leader who is an expert in that domain might perform.

Effective team players must comprehend and demonstrate proficiency with the teacher leader standards in order for the teacher to increase student achievement (Heck & Hallinger, 2009; Ohlson, 2009); model leadership and teamwork (Mayo, 2002; Pounder, 1999); and advance professionally as team leaders and followers in ways that are positive and productive (Chi Keung, 2008; Tichenor & Tichenor, 2004–2005).

Teachers tend to approach their practices in two ways: individual work and group work (Pounder, 1999). When given opportunities to enhance individual work, teachers tend to show little or no change. When given opportunities to enhance group work, teachers may feel it is an intrusion on their time or an invasion of their expertise (Pounder, 1999). However, when given opportunities to enhance group work and teacher leadership featuring the components of trust, efficacy, agency, and mentorship, teachers tend to experience success and satisfaction that are both significant and sustained.

Teacher educators, like classroom teachers, may not have explored or experienced the four components of TEAM: trust, efficacy, agency, and mentorship. They may not have encountered the complexities associated with each component in concept or practice independently or as an integrated strength shared among the four components (Elliott, Isaacs, & Chugani, 2010). As teacher educators learn, practice, and teach the four components of TEAM, they become comfortable, competent, and confident. Administrators in higher education would be wise to provide professional development and teamwork opportunities for their faculty to build stronger comprehension and specific application of TEAM.

Thus, teacher educators provide the pivotal point for transforming TEAM-work. By adding TEAMwork to their teacher preparation courses and requiring TEAMwork during the clinical field placements both with P–12 students and among colleagues, teacher candidates will see, hear, and experience TEAMwork authentically and holistically. Teacher educators can model and reinforce TEAM leadership with candidates and colleagues. Additionally, teacher educators can articulate to candidates and colleagues the benefits of TEAMwork in the teacher educators' practices and research.

Conclusion

The power and presence of becoming a TEAM player paves the path of the classroom teacher's journey toward leadership. Although travels may begin on a single path, becoming TEAM players and teacher leaders quickly allows teachers to navigate (Sexton, 2008) many different paths previously unconsidered, either individually or with other team players. Teachers may serve as chairs of their departments or institution committees; they may participate on committees in their school districts and/or states. Teachers improve their abilities to guide and support teacher candidates and novice colleagues; they may earn graduate degrees and move into new positions as educational specialists or school administrators; some teachers may leave the classroom to move onto higher education, state departments of education, or other agencies. Teachers may join professional associations and become educational leaders.

When teacher educators and classroom teachers teach, practice, and pursue the four components of TEAM in order to increase student achievement, model leadership, and advance professionally, they discover that the members of their teams reap four rewarding outcomes (Kouzes & Posner, 2007). First, everyone asks more meaningful questions to establish context, identify challenges, and appreciate accomplishments. Next, the focus moves to the learners or the recipients of their teaching rather than concentrating on the teacher and the reasons that transformation is unlikely. Then, the team players share situations and strategies to enhance their transformations. Finally, the processes and products become shared experiences constructing a foundation to guide and support future team players and teacher leaders. Overcoming the generational perpetuation of practice theory and the propinquity effect, teachers discover greater success, satisfaction, significance, and sustainability in teaching, learning, and schooling when they learn what they live and live what they learn.

References

Bandura, A. (1997). *Self-efficacy: The exercise of control.* New York, NY: W.H. Freeman.

Bandura, A. (2006). Toward a psychology of human agency. *Perspectives on Psychological Science, 1*(2), 164–180.

Barth, R. S. (2001). Teacher leader. *Phi Delta Kappan, 82*(6), 442–449.

Bloor, M., Frankland, J., Thomas, M., & Robson, K. (2001). *Focus groups in social research.* Thousand Oaks, CA: Sage.

Borko, H. (2004). Professional development and teacher learning: Mapping the terrain. *Educational Researcher, 33*(8), 3–15.

Chi Keung, C. (2008). The effect of shared decision-making on the improvement in teachers' job development. *New Horizons in Education, 56*(3), 31–46. Retrieved from http://files.eric.ed.gov/fulltext/EJ832908.pdf

Danielson, C. (2007). The many faces of leadership. *Educational Leadership, 65*(1), 14–19.

Dirks, K. T. (1999). The effects of interpersonal trust on work group performance. *Journal of Applied Psychology, 84*(3), 445–455.

Donaldson, G. A., Jr. (2007). What do teachers bring to leadership? *Educational Leadership, 65*(1), 26–29.

Eby, L. T., Meade, A. W., Parisi, A. G., & Douthitt, S. S. (1999). The development of an individual-level teamwork expectations measure and the application of a within-group agreement statistic to assess shared expectations for teamwork. *Organizational Research Methods, 2*(4), 366–394.

Edmunds, H. (1999). *The focus group research handbook.* Lincolnwood, IL: NTC/Contemporary Publishing Group.

Elliott, E. M., Isaacs, M. L., & Chugani, C. D. (2010). Promoting self-efficacy in early career teachers: A principal's guide for differentiated mentoring and supervision. *Florida Journal of Educational Administration & Policy, 4*(1), 131–146.

Festinger, L., Schachter S., & Back, K. (1950). *Social pressures in informal groups: A study of human factors in housing.* New York, NY: Harper.

Gallavan, N. P. (2002). Gallavan cultural competence model. In J. Wink & L. Putney (Authors), *A vision of Vygotsky* (pp. 158–160). Boston, MA: Allyn & Bacon.

Gallavan, N. P. (2007). Seven perceptions influencing novice teachers' efficacy and cultural competence. *Journal of Praxis in Multicultural Education, 2*(1), 6–22.

Gallavan, N. P. (2013). *Advancing teacher education that matters in teaching, learning, and schooling: The roles and responsibilities of success, satisfaction, significance, and sustainability.* ATE presidential theme and discussion, 2013–2014. Manassas, VA, Association of Teacher Educators.

Gareis, E. (2010). Habermas to the rescue. *Business Communication Quarterly, 73*(2), 166–175.

Gordon, S. P. (2004). *Professional development for school improvement: Empowering learning communities.* Boston. MA: Pearson Education.

Heck, R. H., & Hallinger, P. (2009). Assessing the contribution of distributed leadership to school improvement and growth in math achievement. *American Educational Research Journal, 46*(3), 659–689.

Hellsten, L. M., & Prytula, M. P. (2011). Why teaching? Motivations influencing beginning teachers' choice of profession and teaching practice. *Research in Higher Education Journal, 13,* 1–19.

Hellsten, L. M., Prytula, M. P., Ebanks, A., & Lai, H. (2009). Teacher induction: Exploring beginning teacher mentorship. *Canadian Journal of Education, 32*(4), 703–733.

Kouzes, J. M., & Posner, B. Z. (2007). *The leadership challenge* (4th ed.). San Francisco, CA: Jossey-Bass.

Main, K. M. (2007). *A year-long study of the formation and development of middle years' teaching teams* (Unpublished PhD thesis). Griffith University, Brisbane. Retrieved from https://www120.secure.griffith.edu.au/rch/file/64a6473e-3a2b-f149-bd30-6e2033bbef0f/1/02Whole.pdf

Main, K. (2010). Teamwork—Teach me, teach me not: A case study of three Australian preservice teachers. *Australian Educational Researcher, 37*(3), 77–93.

Mangin, M., & Stoelinga, S. R. (2011). Peer? Expert? Teacher leaders struggle to gain trust while establishing their expertise. *Journal of Staff Development, 32*(3), 48–51.

Mawhinny, L. (2008). Coping with stress through validation: A tool of the teaching trade. *Journal of Ethnographic & Qualitative Research, 2*(4), 246–254.

Mayo, K. E. (2002). Teacher leadership: The master teacher model. *Management in Education, 16*(3), 29–33.

Mitra, D. L. (2008). *Student voice in school reform: Building youth-adult partnerships that strengthen schools and empower youth.* Albany: State University of New York Press.

Morgan, D. L. (1998). *The focus group guidebook.* Thousand Oaks, CA: Sage.

Mutch, A. (1998). Employability or learning? Groupwork in higher education. *Education + Training, 40*(2), 50–56.

Neumann, M. D., Jones, L. C. S., & Webb, P. T. (2012). Claiming the political: The forgotten terrain of teacher leadership knowledge. *Action in Teacher Education, 34*(1), 2–13.

Ohlson, M. (2009). Examining instructional leadership: A study of school culture and teacher quality characteristics influencing student outcomes. *Florida Journal of Educational Administration & Policy, 2*(2), 102–124.

Patton, M. Q. (1990). *Qualitative evaluation and research methods* (2nd ed.). Newbury Park, CA: Sage.

Pounder, D. G. (1999). Teacher teams: Exploring job characteristics and work-related outcomes of work group enhancement. *Educational Administration Quarterly, 35*(3), 317–348.

Rodriguez, C. M. (2009). The impact of academic self-concept, expectations and the choice of learning strategy on academic achievement: The case of business students. *Higher Education Research and Development, 28*(5), 523–539.

Rueda, R. (1998). *Standards for professional development: A sociocultural perspective.* Research Brief #2. Santa Cruz, CA: Center for Research on Education, Diversity & Excellence. Retrieved from http://www.cal.org/crede/pdfs/ResBrief2.pdf

Sexton, D. M. (2008). Student teachers negotiating identity, role, and agency. *Teacher Education Quarterly, 35*(3), 73–88.

Shulman, L. S. (1986). Those who understand: Knowledge growth in teaching. *Educational Researcher, 15*(2), 4–14.

Teacher Leadership Exploratory Consortium. (2011). Teacher leader model standards. Retrieved from http://www.teacherleaderstandards.org/index.php

Tichenor, M. S., & Tichenor, J. M. (2004–2005). Understanding teachers' perspectives on professionalism. *Professional Educator, 27*(1–2), 89–95.

Van den Bossche, P., Gijselaers, W., Segers, M., Woltjer, G., & Kirschner, P. (2011). Team learning: Building shared mental models. *Instructional Science, 39*(3), 283–301.

12

TEACHER LEADERS INTERNATIONALLY

Edward Owens

This chapter examines teacher leadership from an international perspective to better understand different countries' innovative approaches to teacher leadership. Particular attention is paid to teacher leaders' impact on students, schools, communities, and profession. Classroom teachers in other countries have served in various roles as teacher leaders and, by studying these authentic accounts and best practices, teachers and schools in the United States can replicate and benefit from these approaches (Swaffield & MacBeath, 2009). This chapter looks specifically at the unique perspectives of teacher leadership in Singapore, England, Australia, and New Zealand. Information about teacher leadership is taken from these international examples and is woven together with what is known from research about teacher leadership in the United States. All cited studies are American unless otherwise noted.

Understanding the Teacher Leadership Role

Who are teacher leaders? Barth (2001) defined teacher leaders as school-based reformers with a vested interest in their schools and communities. Following Barth's categorization is that of Fullan and Hargreaves (1996), who described teacher leadership as the "capacity and commitment to contribute beyond one's classroom" (p. 13). Analogous to this definition is that of Danielson (2007), who declared that "In every good school, there are teachers whose vision extends beyond their own classrooms" (p. 14). The research literature validates these definitions, asserting that teacher leaders are faculty members who are willing to work alongside others to create a better future, foster hope and goodwill, tackle obstacles and impediments, and build a better community while improving their schools, communities, and profession. On the other hand, not all is glamorous for those who serve in a teacher leadership role. Teacher leaders often face daunting challenges in their effort to drive change and improvement in their local schools and communities.

After gaining independence in 1965, Singapore policymakers faced issues of extreme poverty, limited natural resources, malaria, opium addiction, and ethnic strife among religious groups (Stewart, 2010). Despite these odds, the country rose from the shackles of poverty to become a global hub of trade, finance, and transportation. Singapore built an impressive education system that ranks high on the list of the world's best performing schools (Tan, 2012). Most observers agree that good teachers and effective school leaders form the cornerstone of the country's education system. Their high-quality teacher workforce did not happen by chance. Singapore created a comprehensive system for selecting, training, compensating, and developing teachers and principals. These valiant efforts have paid off tremendously, and now their teacher leaders are revered by educators around the world.

Bowman (2004), a scholar in the field of teacher leadership, surmised that teachers in the United States would face similar obstacles and demands as their traditional roles as educators are challenged. The implication is that teachers' active involvement and administrators' support of teacher leadership are paramount. Many educational scholars and reformers believe that teacher leaders must play an active role in any effort to increase student learning and school improvements. Katzenmeyer and Moller (2001) used the metaphor *awakening the sleeping giant* to raise awareness about the underutilization of teachers as resources. The awakening of the sleeping giant, they reason, will occur only when effective teacher leadership programs are firmly established.

In the United States, research has shown that in most successful schools, teacher leaders supported by school administrators have been able to help improve schoolwide policies and programs, teaching and learning, and communications (Danielson, 2007). This finding raises the question: If the concept of teacher leaders is so consequential, why are so few teachers contributing to school life outside the classroom (Barth, 2001)? Another scholar, Lambert (2003), stated that it is necessary to understand the context in which teacher leaders serve in order to answer this question. Coincidentally, a major premise of this chapter is that school administrators need to build more collaborative and cooperative arrangements within their schools if they want to meet their teacher leaders' diverse needs (Beachum & Dentith, 2004).

The Context of Teacher Leaders

In many countries, most notably England and Australia, teacher leadership responsibilities are assigned to a principal or headteacher, who is held accountable for improving the school. Swaffield and MacBeath (2009) conducted an international research project that examined the relationship between leadership and learning in schools. The participants for their study originated from seven countries

(Australia, Croatia, Greece, Portugal, Romania, Spain, and Turkey), six international cities (Athens, Brisbane, Copenhagen, Innsbruck, London, and Oslo), and two American cities (Seattle, Washington, and Trenton, New Jersey). The participants included university researchers, school principals, and teachers. What emerged from the study, also known as the Leadership for Learning Project (LfL), were five principles that school administrators, teachers, and students can use to promote leadership and learning. The five principles are

- maintain a focus on learning as an activity;
- create conditions favorable to learning as an activity;
- create a dialogue about leadership for learning;
- share leadership; and
- share a sense of accountability. (Swaffield & MacBeath, 2009, p. 14)

The five principles are interrelated, with dialogue forming the relationship between leadership and learning; the environmental context creating favorable conditions for shared leadership and learning; and accountability allowing self-evaluation at the classroom, school, and community level to ensure sustainability. When examining how decisions were made at these schools, Swaffield and Mac-Beath (2009) initially reported that the policymakers placed the decision making and leadership responsibilities in the hands of the principal or headteacher.

To better understand the relationship between leadership and learning, these researchers further analyzed the context in which leadership occurred by investigating eight of the most disadvantaged schools in England for more than 3 years. The findings from this follow-up study indicated that teacher leaders in the eight evaluated schools were unsuccessful even though the schools were heavily financed by the government for the first 3 years. The teacher leaders did not have the full support of administrators. Unfortunately, the teacher leaders' efforts were curtailed shortly thereafter because they were unable to provide evidence to support improvements. These schools, like others across England, faced overwhelming odds and adverse conditions, such as economic and social disenfranchisement; lack of social capital; racism, violence, and intimidation; lack of family mobility and know-how; transience and disillusionment; and media images, rumor, and disinformation.

Although the outcome was negative for teacher leaders in Swaffield and MacBeath's (2009) study, Frost (2004) discovered that headteachers and teachers working together in England can make a huge difference inside the classroom. He witnessed that in schools where headteachers shared their leadership responsibilities, the schools developed and improved. This shared leadership model sometimes involved teachers, support staff, students, parents, and others in the community. The findings in this study are consistent with the principle of shared leadership recommended by Swaffield and MacBeath (2009) described earlier. Frost (2004) also examined teacher leadership and the role of headteachers in supporting teacher-led development workshops. By drawing heavily on interview data collected from a previous research study called the Impact Project (Frost & Durrant, 2002), in which teachers who had worked as teacher leaders in their respective schools were asked about the conditions that allowed them to be most effective in their role. Frost (2004) summarized that teachers felt best about situations where the leadership

- recognized and understood the potential for leadership in teachers;
- developed a culture that was conducive to teacher-led development work;
- provided time and access for external support;
- ensured the existence of facilitated organizational structures; and
- provided critical friendship to teachers. (paraphrased, p. 1)

Both the Swaffield and MacBeath (2009) and the Frost (2004) research studies were in search of some common meaning and understanding of leadership and learning that could be applied in different contexts. Based on the findings, these studies support the argument that promoting and creating an environment conducive to the development of teacher leaders is crucial to improving schools, leadership, and learning.

Teacher Leadership Development

Danielson (2007) professed that not every school welcomes the idea of developing teacher leaders. This resistance is the reason that school administrators play such a vital role in creating the conditions that promote and encourage teacher leadership. In addition, Beachum and Dentith (2004) stated that school structures, organizational patterns, internal processes, use of external resources, and strong community relationships can also influence the development of teacher leaders.

In his work in England, Frost (2004) initiated an impact project study to determine the effectiveness of teacher-led development workshops. Through a series of interviews, the research team searched for a conceptual framework that headteachers could use to help facilitate and support teacher-led development workshops. The interviewees were teachers who had initiated teacher-led development workshops in their schools within the context of encouraging and supporting external school improvement programs, such as obtaining a master's degree. The schools entered into partnerships with universities in order to support teacher-led development workshops by providing

- frameworks of support and friendship for leadership change;
- guidance in methodology and school-based inquiry;
- links with wider research and discourses; and
- expertise related to pedagogy and the development process. (Frost, 2004, p. 2)

The interviews also provided key insights into the role of headteachers. The teachers interviewed emphasized the importance of headteachers' creating favorable conditions, whereby teachers could exercise leadership and maximize the impact of their work. The teachers recognized the importance of the head-teacher in this regard and sought internal support in the following areas: cultural and structural, planning and research, extending internal and external networks, and recognizing and celebrating the potential for leadership in teachers.

Furthermore, Lovett and Cameron (2011) performed a case study in New Zealand and the United States to determine whether teacher leaders wanted to serve as specialists or consultants early in their careers as teachers. The hope of retaining early career teachers and enticing promising teachers to become leaders was at the center of this study. The study evaluated what effect these two formal teacher leadership roles—the consulting teacher (CT) in the United States and the specialist classroom teacher (SCT) in New Zealand—had on the early careers of teachers. The researchers wanted to know whether or not moving from a classroom teacher to a teacher leadership position was appealing. The position of consultant teacher was a more formal teacher leadership role that was intended for highly skilled educators who had obtained at least 4 years of classroom experience and wanted more leadership responsibilities. Consultant teachers were required to be full-time peer coaches over a period of 3 years for beginning teachers and underperforming veteran teachers. Each consultant received stipends in addition to their annual salaries to cover 20 days of extra professional development assistance needed to perform their roles. As part of the contract agreement, the consultants promised to return to the classroom after 3 years as a consultant and teach for a minimum of 2 additional years. In contrast, the specialist classroom teacher role was established for secondary schools in 2004 after a teachers' collective bargaining agreement settlement. Educators in this role mentored beginning teachers across departments and subject areas, including experienced teachers who sought assistance. Two primary goals of the specialist role were to promote professional learning and improve classroom practice.

As part of their study, Lovett and Cameron (2011) conducted four interviews and two surveys over a 5-year period with a young female English teacher who had stumbled into the teaching profession and had secured a position with a school on the outskirts of London. The school was under special measures and at risk of being closed. The students were disengaged, and the teacher was not given due consideration of a beginning teacher. Although challenging, the teacher survived through her own efforts. Shortly thereafter, she returned to New Zealand and secured her first permanent job with an urban secondary school. Once again, she encountered disengaged learners and another challenging teaching assignment. Her first taste of leadership happened when she accepted the leadership role of assistant head of department (HOD). When commenting about the dual role of a classroom teacher and assistant HOD, she lauded the enjoyment of teaching but frowned upon the additional leadership responsibilities. Trying to juggle the dual role provoked feelings of frustrations and anxiety. As a result, she did not view her initial leadership experience as rewarding or satisfying because the position took away time from teaching, required too much paperwork, and included additional responsibilities that were unsatisfying. After performing the leadership responsibilities, she felt drained and did not possess the same level of energy and motivation inside the classroom. In addition, she cited long hours, the potential for burnout, and the inability to create work-life balance as problematic. In fact, she considered leaving the profession. Having noticed the pressures this teacher was experiencing, a senior staff member intervened and strongly advocated to the school management that the teacher needed better support. Once she began to receive better support, she found the work more rewarding and was later appointed to the role of specialist classroom teacher (SCT). In the SCT role, she combined classroom teaching with her SCT and assistant HOD work. The findings from this study suggested that the dual role of teaching and leading can be potentially rewarding and satisfying when given the support from the school's administration.

The study by Lovett and Cameron (2011) also examined how the SCT role in New Zealand and its companion role of the CT in the United Sates impacted teachers in terms of job engagement. To compare the two roles, the researchers used information collected by Fiarman (2007), who had interviewed eight CT teachers to determine whether they found the CT role rewarding in terms of professional development. The findings indicated that all eight respondents had found the CT role professionally rewarding because the role allowed them to improve their teaching, foster meaningful collaboration, increase their independence and flexibility, learn new skills, and see the big picture of the school district. The opportunity to observe, discuss pedagogical practices, and remain connected to the classroom was viewed positively by early career teachers in the CT role.

International Teacher Leadership

In an effort to educate and develop the citizens in its country, Singapore has created a high-quality teacher workforce by recruiting and selecting individuals from the top one third of its university and college graduating classes. Teachers then receive ongoing training—100 hours of professional development annually—at the Nanyang Technological University, a research intensive public university. After 3 years of classroom experience, teachers may choose one of three career options: a master teacher, a school leader, or a specialist in curriculum or research. Teachers with the potential and desire to become school leaders are moved to middle management teams and receive specific training for their new roles as administrators. As a result of this highly structured training and support system, Singapore does not have the problems of massive attrition and ineffective teachers, challenges that plague many school systems in other countries (Stewart, 2010).

New Zealand shares a similar vision for creating a world-class education system (McPherson & Borthwick, 2011). Most noteworthy is the Ministry of Education's delegation of decision making to schools and their leaders. New Zealand practices a distributed teacher leadership model, an approach whereby teachers, students, and administrators share leadership responsibilities. The principal takes the lead role in implementing this model. New Zealand supports its teacher leaders through professional development, consultation on curriculum through the agency CORE Education, national conferences, and EDtalks, which are a free repository of videos to help educators improve their instruction. CORE Education is responsible for providing cluster schools, or a group of like-minded schools, with advice on how to implement New Zealand's national curriculum. Teacher leaders receive training from the education and business sectors and focus on topics such as facilitation of groups, new curriculum design, online communication practices, and international study abroad.

Like New Zealand, Australia views school leaders as central to its efforts to improve that country (Mulford, 2008). Australian schools face some serious challenges arising from emerging trends such as technological advancements, diversity of the Australian population, the push to become a knowledge-based society, and globalization of the country's economy and culture. In response to these challenges, Australia created a focused education reform agenda that led to its position in the international education rankings (Asia Society, 2010). These efforts were propelled by four factors: the adoption of a national curriculum, the close monitoring of schools and school systems, the transparent presentation of school performance, and increased governmental support of schools.

Australia publicizes its national curriculum online for citizens to view and requires schools to participate in national surveys and international benchmarking. The results of these assessments are studied, evaluated, and also published online. The intent of this transparency is to encourage collaboration among schools and communities with similar profiles and the sharing of best practices. Finally, the government has launched an ambitious plan to double school funding, target disadvantaged areas, and create a leadership institute.

Furthermore, England is raising the quality of teaching and striving to increase the standards of its schools. To raise the status of the teaching profession, England hopes to attract more of its best graduates to become educators. Teacher training is undergoing reforms so that teacher candidates can develop the necessary practical skills from the outset. Schools have flexibility over the recruitment and pay of their staff, and schools are encouraged to collaborate in the preparation and professional development of teachers and headteachers. To improve the ways teachers receive their initial training, England has vowed to

- introduce School Direct, a program that allows schools to recruit and train their own staff;
- ensure all preservice teachers pass skills tests in literacy and numeracy before starting their professional training; and
- offer training bursaries to top graduates who are interested in teaching.

To improve teacher preparation and professional development, the school leaders will

- establish a national network of approximately 500 alliances of teaching schools, comprised of consistently outstanding schools working with other schools to develop leadership and raise the quality of teaching;
- develop a curriculum and new National Professional Qualification for Headship;
- help talented teachers become school leaders;
- introduce new ways for teachers to improve their teaching based on evidence of what works; and
- fund degree-level specialist training for talented teachers who work with special needs children.

Theoretical Perspectives on Teacher Leadership

A comprehensive conceptual framework developed by York-Barr and Duke (2004) proposed a theory of action for teacher leadership. This framework is based on seven major components. The first three components are foundations for teacher leadership and are derived from the research literature. These are (a) the characteristic of teacher leaders; (b) the type of leadership work teacher leaders engage in; and (c) the conditions that support the work of teacher leaders. The next three suggest a path by which teacher leaders can affect student learning. These are (a) the means by which teachers lead; (b) the targets of their leadership influence; and (c) the results of changes in teaching and learning practices. Student learning is the seventh and final component rounding out the proposed theory of action. The theoretical implication for teacher leadership is student-focused learning and school improvement goals.

By contrast, Lambert, Collay, Dietz, Kent, and Richert (1996) viewed teacher leaders from a constructivist perspective. Constructivist teacher leaders reframe their roles and responsibilities in order to facilitate change in schools and communities of learners. Constructivist teacher leaders see themselves as different from more traditional and hierarchical leadership. Expanding this view, Lambert (2003) contended that teacher leadership has been shackled by archaic definitions and outdated assumptions. She suggested that the goals of building leadership capacity are to develop all adults within a school community. She insisted, "Any framework with promise must address learning for school improvement on multiple levels—individuals and groups, adults and students, schools and districts, and the promise of sustainable results" (Lambert, 2003, p. 426). An inclusive learning community embracing all participants is at the heart of building high-capacity leadership.

Meanwhile, educators in New Zealand are shifting from a humanistic or nurturing view of teacher leadership to a more pedagogical framework during the induction phase for new teachers. Main (2007) developed a theoretical framework for the induction of new teachers in New Zealand using qualitative and quantitative methods to study teachers in low-socioeconomic primary schools. Main's work was based on a model by Achinstein (2001), who had previously created a pedagogical framework and induction program for the New Teachers Center in California. The Achinstein approach cited collaboration, inquiry, purpose, and building leadership as prerequisites for new teacher induction programs. Main later used this same model to study teacher induction programs in New Zealand, with the central premise being that professional development requires more than a nurturing environment.

Evaluating the Impact of Teacher Leadership Practices

To examine the impact of Main's (2007) work, a more in-depth analysis of the study was performed. Main employed Achinstein's (2001) same techniques to assess induction practices for teachers in low-socioeconomic primary schools in New Zealand. As part of the induction process, first-year and second-year teachers submitted written documentation regarding their site-based induction programs in order to complete their registration. All beginning teachers are also required to submit 2 years' worth of documented reflection and provide insight regarding the frequency and benefits of the induction practices. The 202 participating novice teachers completed a survey and identified the following beneficial activities: meeting with a tutor teacher, attending external professional development, observing a tutor teacher-demonstration lesson, and videotaping lessons. The new teachers noted that a written record of induction activities was less beneficial, citing demonstration lessons as occurring less frequently, and meeting with a group of beginning teachers and having a lesson videotaped as also occurring less frequently. The survey also revealed that 82% of beginning teachers were engaged in some form of leadership and extracurricular activity, with social leadership being the most prevalent. These activities were shown to benefit teachers and students in New Zealand. What this suggests is that models of professional development are crucial to teacher development programs.

International Teacher Leadership Models

Singapore's teacher leadership model is often cited in research as one of the best in the field. This Asian country employs a holistic approach to teacher development by offering three distinct pathways to professional growth. First, Singapore strives to make teaching an attractive career choice through teacher recognition and remuneration programs. It recruits and pays teachers as civil servants during the initial and training phase—a practice that improves retention and the quality of applicants. The Ministry of Education also offers undergraduate and postgraduate scholarships for future teachers. Second, Singapore works to improve teachers' expertise by emphasizing mastery of content courses where teachers can become experts in the areas they teach. Third and most important is the evaluation phase. Singapore's teacher evaluations are formative in nature, not critical or summative. Once selected, teachers follow one of three career choices, each with its own unique type of performance evaluation. The leadership track helps prepare teachers for leadership positions as principals and department heads, while the teaching track focuses on excellence in the classroom. The specialist track is available for those who wish to specialize in certain areas such as curriculum and instructional design (Tan, 2012).

Like Singapore, New Zealand also follows an innovative teacher leadership model. The Ministry of Education in New Zealand supports teacher leadership development through a Cluster Model (McPherson & Borthwick, 2011). Clusters bring together a group of like-minded schools to leverage their resources and create a collaborative learning environment. The Cluster Model provides teacher leaders with opportunities for professional development, consulting, digital technology, and educational conferences. The education conferences provide enriched learning opportunities with information that educators can apply in the classrooms. As part of the Cluster Model, partnerships were formed with CORE, a nonprofit agency. CORE sponsors a program called EDtalks, a repository of videos featuring best practices of leaders and innovative educators to assist teachers in the development of their professional practice. A similar program exists in England. In the United States, the pathway to school leadership positions is through the National College for School Leadership (NCSL), which offers a more centralized and structured approach to developing teacher leaders. Although the NCSL and Cluster Model provide good examples of developing teacher leaders, it is necessary to remember that the prevailing attitudes of some school administrators and leaders have kept the realization and hope of developing potential teacher leaders to a minimum.

Summary

This chapter examined teacher leadership from an international perspective to identify best practices that could be modeled in the United States. The four countries mentioned earlier viewed teacher leadership as critical to the development of their country even though it was determined that most teacher leadership roles and responsibilities are entrusted to either a headteacher or principal. More importantly, these countries have taken a proactive approach in the development of teacher leaders and include support and training, recruitment and selection, increased pay and incentives, professional development opportunities, and education and certifications. Moreover, teacher leaders have more autonomy and responsibility in these countries to improve their schools and communities. The question of how to reform education has been given lots of attention, and more consideration and the lessons learned internationally about teacher leadership can benefit educators and administrators in the United States.

References

Achinstein, B. (2001, April). *Building a community of learners and leaders for transformational induction programs.* Paper presented at the annual meeting of the American Educational Research Association, Seattle, WA.

Asia Society. (2010). *Australia strives for excellence and equity.* New York, NY: Author. Retrieved from http://asiasociety.org/education/learning-world/australia-strives-excellence-and-equity

Barth, R. S. (2001). Teacher leader. *Phi Delta Kappan, 82*(6), 443–449.

Beachum, F., & Dentith, A. M. (2004). Teacher leaders creating cultures of school renewal and transformation. *The Educational Forum, 68*(3), 276–286. doi: 10.1080/00131720408984639

Bowman, R. F. (2004). Teachers as leaders. *The Clearing House, 77*(5), 187–189. doi: 10.3200/TCHS.77.5.187-189

Danielson, C. (2007). The many faces of leadership. *Educational Leadership, 65*(1), 14–19.

Fiarman, S. E. (2007, March). *It's hard to go back: Career decisions of second-stage teacher learners.* Paper presented at the annual meeting of the American Educational Research Association, Chicago, IL.

Frost, D. (2004, August). What can headteachers do to support teachers' leadership? *Inform, 4,* 1–7.

Frost, D., & Durrant, J. (2002). Teachers as leaders: Exploring the impact of teacher-led development work. *School Leadership and Management, 22*(2), 143–161.

Fullan, M., & Hargreaves, A. (1996). *What's worth fighting for in your school?* New York, NY: Teachers College Press.

Katzenmeyer, M., & Moller, G. (2001). *Awakening the sleeping giant: Helping teachers develop as leaders* (2nd ed.). Thousand Oaks, CA: Corwin.

Lambert, L. (2003). Leadership redefined: An evocative context for teacher leadership. *School Leadership and Management, 23*(4), 421–430.

Lambert, L., Collay, M., Dietz, M. E., Kent, K., & Richert, A. E. (1996). *Who will save our schools? Teachers as constructivist leaders.* Thousand Oaks, CA: Corwin.

Lovett, S. & Cameron, M. (2011). Career pathways: Does remaining close to the classroom matter for early career teachers? A study of practice in New Zealand and the USA. *Professional Development in Education, 37*(2), 213–224.

Main, S. (2007). Toward a pedagogical framework: New Zealand induction. *International Professional Development Association, 33*(2), 237–240. doi: 10.1080/13674580701293093

McPherson, S., & Borthwick, A. (2011). Lessons from New Zealand: Leadership for learning. *Learning and Leading with Technology, 38*(5), 20–25.

Mulford, B. (2008). The leadership challenge: Improving learning in schools. *Education Review,* 53. Camberwell, Victoria: Australian Council for Educational Research.

Stewart, V. (2010). Dream, design, deliver: How Singapore developed a high-quality teacher force. *Phi Delta Kappan, 91*(7), 85–86.

Swaffield, S., & MacBeath, J. (2009, April). *Researching leadership for learning across international and methodological boundaries.* Paper presented at the annual meeting of the American Educational Research Association, San Diego, CA.

Tan, O. S. (2012). Singapore's holistic approach to teacher development. *Phi Delta Kappan, 94*(3), 76–77.

York-Barr, J., & Duke, K. (2004). What do we know about teacher leadership? Findings from two decades of scholarship. *Review of Educational Research, 74*(3), 255–316. doi: 10.3102/00346543074003255

13

NATIONAL BOARD CERTIFIED TEACHERS AS LEADERS

Mara Cawein
Patricia H. Phelps

Anna was passionate about her subject and her students. She fondly remembers bumping into a parent during the summer who commented, "I bet you cannot wait for school to start. My daughter had so much fun in your geometry class last year. Do you get bored by the end of the summer?" Anna actually enjoyed her school breaks but also loved learning more about teaching and learning. She belonged to several professional teaching organizations and attended conferences because she wanted to improve her classroom skills. Anna had been a classroom teacher for 8 years and was always looking for ways to improve her effectiveness. She created class activities based on ideas from the conferences, such as a stained glass project that involved using graphs to form artistic patterns. She also added relevance for her math students by adapting lesson plans from educational journals.

The story of Anna is similar to that of many classroom teachers, that is, until she decided to challenge her professional knowledge and skills against the national board standards. Anna felt that she was a good teacher, but she sometimes questioned herself when other teachers in the district did not agree with her methods. National certification was an opportunity to assess her teaching practices and hopefully to validate her personal beliefs about teaching.

Anna first learned about national board certification from a state Department of Education representative at a teaching conference. Having only a few nationally certified teachers, the state was actively promoting the process with incentives and assistance. Anna listened along with two of her friends; one would become certified after Anna and the other encouraged all colleagues in their professional growth. Anna investigated the certification process and became a candidate the next school year. She was the only teacher in her district going through the process, but she connected with a few candidates in a nearby district for support. The additional workload was similar to taking on a part-time job as she created the required teaching portfolio.

The national board process was an opportunity for Anna to challenge her effectiveness for the sake of her students. She wanted to be assessed at a national level to reaffirm her professional beliefs and teaching practices. Once she achieved national certification, she joined a state organization that assisted other national board candidates as they navigated through the certification process. Anna's increased confidence enabled her to expand her leadership. Before certification, her leadership activities were centered on her students. For example, she led a group of students in a national math modeling competition after hearing about it at a math conference. Additionally, Anna had taken risks in her classroom, had helped with departmental functions, and had continued to learn from professional reading and conferences. However, after becoming certified, she found herself for the first time leading other teachers and expanding her influence. She realized that impacting the classroom practices of another teacher resulted in having a broader influence on students beyond her own. Anna saw her influence increase because of her new professional credential and her greater confidence.

When Anna became certified, there were only 300 National Board Certified Teachers (NBCTs) in her state. She was very satisfied in the classroom, but when she received a job announcement from a local university, it was an opportunity she found hard to resist. The university wanted national board teachers in its college of education. Although Anna's school district had recognized her achievement, her daily life at school had not changed markedly with certification. Her principal did not know much about it, and there were still no other teachers considering the process. Anna's expanded activities since certification were mostly outside her district, working with the state Department of Education helping with new candidate orientation and support and also networking with other NBCTs in a newly formed state organization for national board certification. Anna saw the university recruitment letter as an opportunity to remain a teacher but also function as a teacher of teachers. After 2 years as a national board certified teacher in a public high school, Anna began teaching undergraduate education majors at a university. National certification opened doors for Anna and provided an avenue to expand her teacher leader role.

Anna's story is very similar to that of one of the authors of this chapter and probably many other NBCTs. Nationally certified teachers are passionate about their jobs, especially as their jobs relate to student learning. Many teachers perceive certification as a challenge in their career. Eager to see whether their teaching practices measure up to the national standards, they are pleasantly surprised with the process itself and how it provides an exhilarating professional learning opportunity. The accomplishment also increases confidence so that NBCTs who might not have felt confident before certification now more readily take on teacher leader opportunities. Teachers like Anna have reached the "expert" stage in the life cycle of the career teacher (Steffy, Wolfe, Pasch, & Enz, 2000). Driven by self-improvement, expert teachers adhere to the highest of standards. They are capable of becoming nationally certified or have successfully done so. In this developmental stage, expert teachers serve as exemplary models for other teachers. They are in a prime position to lead.

Being Nationally Certified

Nationally certified teachers are teacher leaders. NBCTs have stepped forward to test their practice and in the process, learned more about themselves and their profession. They are approximately 3% of the total teaching force (National Board for Professional Teaching Standards [NBPTS], 2013). They show themselves as leaders by taking the risk to become certified, and they have credentials to proudly display and to start conversations about accomplished teaching. NBCTs are leaders through having sufficient evidence in their portfolio to demonstrate active participation in their professional learning community. Evidence of teacher leader activities must be included for certification. One portfolio entry requires teachers to document activities outside the classroom that go above and beyond what is generally expected of teachers. Professional membership, leadership in the school and beyond the school, family and community involvement activities, and life-long learning provide valuable evidence to present to the national board evaluators. To illustrate, Anna included in her portfolio her participation in an educational conference that led her to develop an improved lesson plan. Her explanation of the lesson demonstrated that she used her acquired professional knowledge to improve student learning in a sustainable and responsible way.

Designing and Conducting a Study of NBCTs

The authors designed and conducted an original research study of NBCTs using protocols in accordance with the research review process at their southeastern university. The purpose of the study was to identify activities and perceptions of NBCTs relative to teacher leadership. In the fall of 2012, the authors mailed surveys to NBCTs to learn about leadership activities that they participated in and to determine their beliefs about leadership opportunities in their school buildings. Surveys were sent within one southern state to teachers certified at an Early Adolescence or Adolescent/Young Adult developmental level. In addition, only the following four content areas were considered: English language arts, social studies, mathematics, and science. To obtain at least 100 valid addresses from online school directories, the surveys were sent to the last 2 years of newly certified teachers in the state. These names were listed in the NBCT Directory on the NBPTS website and also available by year on the state's Department of Education website in a downloadable file. Each potential survey recipient was then looked up on the school district website to verify the assigned school building in order to have a valid mailing address. Some potential recipients could not be located, and therefore surveys were not sent to all NBCTs on the list.

Surveys were sent to 112 national board certified teachers and 47 teachers responded, a 42% return rate. The respondents' years of experience were fairly well spread across different periods of service, with 26% having 3–9 years, 42% having 10–19 years, and 32% having 20 or more years. Most of the respondents (47%) were in school districts with student populations of 751 to 2,500; while 8% were from smaller districts, 25% were from districts with student populations of 2,501 to 10,000, and 20% were from districts of more than 10,000 students.

The survey consisted of two sections, one with questions about leadership activities and the other with questions about teacher attitudes and perceptions. One section of the survey instrument listed 11 activities in which teacher leaders might engage. This list was based on the works of Barth (2001a), Danielson (2006), and Burgess (2009). Barth (2001a) indicated ten aspects of school life where teachers fulfill important leadership roles. Our survey covered nine of these including selecting new teachers, providing policy input, and shaping the curriculum. Additionally, Burgess (2009) presented four areas of responsibility for teacher leaders, such as academic facilitator and administrative liaison. The activity items listed in the survey were also categorized according to Burgess's (2009) areas. Further, Danielson's (2006) framework for teacher leadership consists of three areas of impact: teaching and learning, schoolwide policies and programs, and communications and community relations. The 11 activities on the survey were divided among these three areas with five items under teaching and learning and three items each falling within the other two areas. Thus, having made correlations with these three research sources, the survey items represented a broad range of possible teacher leader actions. In response to the list of activities, the NBCTs were asked to indicate how frequently they had been involved in each activity over the last 2 years.

The second part of the survey was a series of ten belief statements. A 6-point Likert scale was used for respondents to select their degree of agreement with each statement. These statements addressed teachers' perceptions of various aspects of school life that might influence their leadership. Four items dealt specifically with the impact of the certification process on the NBCTs' leadership and relationships. The remaining six items focused on the cultural context of the sample teachers' schools. Recognizing the powerful nature of school culture on teacher leadership (Danielson, 2006), these perceptual statements examined this critical factor. In particular, several items emphasized collegial relationships and administrative support, which Barth (2001a) identified as possible barriers to teacher leaders.

Survey data were divided into different groupings by district size, grade level, and years of experience. Statistical tests were conducted, specifically using chi-square for analysis of fit. None of the questions revealed any statistical difference when the subgroupings were compared to the whole-group results. NBCTs responded similarly to the items regardless of whether they had 5 or 25 years of experience. There was also no difference between teachers from schools in rural districts and those from larger school districts in or near urban areas. NBCTs as a group exhibited consistent perceptions and activities across the range of our survey questions.

Responding as NBCTs

As previously described, the first section of the survey instrument addressed various leadership activities. Respondents were asked to identify their level of involvement for each activity, utilizing four categories. Figure 13.1 displays the results for each of the 11 activities. Of the leadership activities included in the survey, the one in which the sample NBCTs were most frequently involved was providing input on curricular matters (72%). In view of the recent adoption of the Common Core State Standards, this is not surprising. In fact, this finding may be similar among all teachers currently, whether NBCT or not. Responding to the new curriculum standards, most teachers are diligently revising local and state-level curriculum documents and materials. In a related area, participating in initiatives to improve academic achievement had the next highest frequency of involvement, by 62% of the NBCTs. This may also be an area of high involvement for all teachers presently. The impact of No Child Left Behind and standardized testing requirements may have contributed to this result. However, there could also be nontesting-related reasons for such improvement initiatives. Although the survey did not ask for specific examples, follow-up information about the nature of these initiatives would be enlightening.

Other leadership activities with more than one third of the sample reporting a frequent level of participation were as follows: serving as mentors for newer

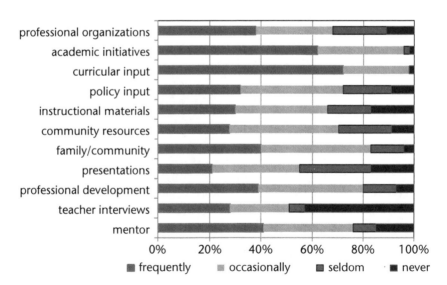

FIGURE 13.1 NBCT Leadership Activities

teachers, assisting with professional development for teachers, participating in school programs involving family/community, and participating in at least one professional organization. As was to be expected, NBCTs reported a frequent (41%) or occasional (35%) level of involvement in mentorship. Nationally certified teachers are the type of teachers that schools should want to have directly influencing new teachers.

As Danielson (2006) posited in her teacher leadership framework, spheres of influence for teachers who lead can reach outside the classroom to a teacher's team or department, across the school, or even beyond the school. Participation in professional organizations and connecting with families and the community are activities that reach beyond the school. Unsurprisingly, the sample NBCTs demonstrated leadership in these areas. Additionally, NBCTs reported occasional involvement (43%) in developing projects that linked community resources with the school.

In the realm of professional development, 80% of the NBCTs indicated either frequent or occasional involvement in assisting other teachers with this important activity. However, 45% reported seldom or never making presentations outside their school building. These findings may point to the NCBTs' involvement in less formal professional development activities that impact other teachers. The authors were disappointed that 43% reported "never" helping to interview or select new teachers. Their being asked for input would seem invaluable in recognizing potential excellence in novice teachers.

For the most part, our findings match the experiences of Anna. She was more than happy to take part in those activities that directly engaged students: curricular matters, initiatives to improve academic achievement, and family/community involvement. It required some additional time and increased confidence before Anna expanded her leadership activities not only to network with peers, but also to instruct them in the classroom and actually lead conference presentations. Some teachers need administrative leadership and support to enlarge their sphere of influence from students and their families to a larger sphere within and beyond the school. However, it was not until Anna moved into higher education that she participated as a member of a search committee to help in selecting a new colleague.

Perceiving Leadership

The second section of the survey instrument addressed the attitudes or perceptions of the NBCT sample. Each response in this section was based on a 6-point Likert scale. The mean scores are displayed in Figure 13.2. All mean averages fell within the positive half of agreement, with 4.15 being the lowest and 5.51 being the highest average levels of agreement. Within this set of ten statements, the highest mean response among the NBCTs was the belief that the certification process helped them to grow as teacher leaders. Other studies have found similar evidence in support of the national certification process's positive impact on

FIGURE 13.2 Leadership Perceptions

teachers' professional growth (Bohen, 2001; Hunzicker, 2011; TeacherSolutions, 2008). The sample NBCTs also tended to agree that they had been school leaders before completing the certification process. However, to a lesser degree (mean of 4.57), they saw opportunities for leadership increase after certification.

One research study of North Carolina teachers showed that NBCTs desired more leadership opportunities than non-NBCTs do (Petty, O'Conner, & Dagenhart, 2003). Their study showed that not only did NBCTs desire a voice in decision making, but they also wanted time to read professional literature to expand their knowledge base. This finding would likewise explain why Anna looked for opportunities to learn and grow as a professional as well as for ways to help her students achieve at an ever higher level. As a professional, Anna believed that academic success was within each student's reach and sought opportunities to make that happen. Being given time to devote to this quest would have expanded her impact.

"After I became nationally certified, professional relationships with my colleagues improved." Of all the statements in the second section of the survey, this one elicited the lowest level of agreement (4.15 mean with a variance of 0.94). Perhaps as Danielson (2007) pointed out, the "tall poppy syndrome" comes into play whereby teachers do not want another to stand out (or above others) for fear of negative consequences. As Barth (2001a) noted, sabotage by colleagues can frequently undermine teacher leadership efforts. This unfortunate situation may discourage NBCTs from becoming more involved in leading school initiatives. Anna was similar to many of the surveyed teachers; she did not receive any new respect, new responsibilities, or more voice in decision making after attaining national board certification. This finding also matches another NBCT's comment from our research, "For reasons I am unaware of, administration in my school does not seem to care if teachers are [nationally] certified or not. No special attention or duties are given." Anna would argue that administration is missing an opportunity to tap individuals who are willing and eager to go above and beyond for students' academic well-being.

Administrative support is a key factor in determining the expanse of influence that NBCTs are willing or able to provide. Four of the ten items in the perceptions section of the survey dealt with the NBCTs' view of administrative support. Of these statements related to the principal, the item that received the lowest mean level of agreement was the NBCTs' rating of their administration's willingness to give teachers control over instructionally related decisions (a mean score of 4.68 with a variance of 0.99). The variance was among the greatest; thus, some administrators are comfortable with utilizing these teachers' expertise. However, as Barth (2001a) identified, an obstacle to teacher leaders' becoming leaders is the principal's tendency to maintain control or power. Furthermore, Goetze (2006) suggested that principals should learn more about certification and the leadership potential of NBCTs. Her study on job satisfaction reported that two NBCTs changed jobs specifically because the principal was negative about national certification. With more knowledge and awareness on the part of administrators, this kind of situation is avoidable.

Focusing on Actions

The findings of this study have implications for helping teachers to develop at the preservice and inservice levels. This section describes approaches and actions that teacher educators and school administrators can take. Fostering leadership among teachers will ultimately have a positive impact on students (Danielson, 2006; Katzenmeyer & Moller, 2001). At the preparation level, future teachers need to be aware of the expectation that they will serve as leaders. A strong case exists for incorporating teacher leadership knowledge, skills, and dispositions at the preservice level of teacher preparation (Bond, 2011). Such a foundation might address leadership theories, roles and functions of teacher leaders, and critical dispositions (Bond, 2011; Phelps, 2008). Moreover, the new InTASC Model Core Teaching Standards specifically target Leadership and Collaboration in Standard #10 (Council of Chief State School Officers, 2011). Including assignments and field experiences that offer leadership opportunities in professional education coursework is a meaningful way to promote the development of teacher candidates' leadership abilities. Giving teacher candidates chances to engage in team projects engenders leadership skills. Whether teachers become nationally certified or not, their commitment to being open to leadership opportunities is vital for the future of the teaching profession. Further, as Helterbran (2010) noted, "Confidence is at the heart of any leadership role" (p. 365). Therefore, teacher educators should continually seek ways to build confidence among novice teachers.

The roles of teacher leaders, as identified by Lieberman and Miller (2004), provide useful concepts for preservice teachers' understanding. Specifically, these roles are *advocates, innovators,* and *stewards.* As advocates, teachers are willing to challenge the status quo. Being innovators requires a desire to function as change agents; and stewards strive to raise the perception of and respect for the teaching profession. NBCTs can and do fulfill all three roles. During the early years of becoming teachers, candidates who view their purpose through the lenses of these three roles are more likely to emerge as leaders. Becoming nationally certified is a fruitful way to obtain more recognition for the professionalism of teachers (Lieberman & Miller, 2004). Teacher educators can encourage future teachers to set their sights on the goal of becoming nationally certified.

School administrators play a highly significant role in promoting leadership among teachers. Recall from the case of Anna how searching for validation of her professional beliefs motivated her pursuit of national certification. How might building principals offer this type of validation as well? Drawing upon the work of Merideth (2007), the authors developed the following set of questions for administrators' reflection:

1. Do you recognize teachers for showing initiative?
2. Do you build community among teachers (or do you foster competition)?
3. Do you let teachers control their own professional development as much as possible?
4. Do you value teachers as professionals? Do you seek their perspectives?
5. Do you enlist teachers' help in solving school problems?
6. Do you actively seek ways to remove obstacles that impede teacher growth?
7. Do you encourage and reward risk taking among teachers?

Risk taking is a critical behavior among teachers who lead (Barth, 2001b). One of the authors of this chapter teaches a graduate course on teacher leadership. During each class session, the students (i.e., practicing teachers) are asked to share any risks they have taken recently in their schools. At first, class members are hesitant to engage in risk taking and there is limited discussion; but as the semester progresses, most become eager to share their risk taking experiences such as trying a new approach, speaking up during a meeting, asking for help, and offering assistance to other teachers or administrators. Engaging in behaviors such as these serve to reinforce and build teachers' leadership capacities. School administrators can similarly encourage and recognize risk taking among teachers. A starting point might be incorporating more shared talk about teaching in faculty meetings. The improvement of teaching and learning must neither become nor remain a nondiscussable topic in school settings (Barth, 2006).

Another important aspect of understanding how to utilize teachers as leaders is tapping the potential of networks. As Reeves (2006, 2008) found, communication in most organizations travels through networks in a nonlinear manner. Furthermore, a connection to a close colleague facilitates change more than hierarchical mandates do. Bureaucracy often serves as a barrier to change (Reeves,

2008). By promoting professional sharing among teachers, administrators can increase the impact of teacher leadership. One recommended structure for developing such networks is the creation of professional learning communities led by teachers. A recent study of National Writing Project participants confirmed the value of teacher networks in strengthening teachers as leaders (Lieberman & Friedrich, 2010).

One core proposition of the national board standards recognizes the effectiveness of teachers' working together to build a strong school program (NBPTS, 2002). Teachers can no longer be solo performers; they need to function as part of a larger community. Given the chance, NBCTs are willing and ready to accept leadership roles among peers. Some have already provided evidence of such leadership in their national portfolios. To maximize the resource potential of teacher leaders, their work should be aligned with school improvement goals (Mangin & Stoelinga, 2010). Administrators can guide this process. Additionally, teacher leaders should be included in the process of selecting future teaching colleagues. This will strengthen their voice, particularly of an advisory nature (Allen, 2004).

Beyond each school's boundaries exist other professionals. By encouraging teachers to join professional organizations, principals can help teachers connect to these extended networks. In the case of Anna, involvement in various organizations served to support her professional growth. Sometimes teachers need greater awareness of opportunities to interact with teachers outside their own schools and encouragement to do so. Additionally, conferences serve as valuable avenues to learn more about teaching and to contribute to others' development. Teachers become stronger leaders by sharing their knowledge and experiences with other teachers. Encouraging teachers to make presentations at conferences is one way to reinforce such leadership development.

Envisioning the Future

Roland Barth (1990), founder of the Principals' Center at Harvard University, made a strong argument in his book *Improving Schools from Within* that school improvement will best evolve from inside forces rather than outside ones. He advocated for teachers' seeing themselves as owners rather than tenants in schools (Barth, 1990). In most school environments, this mind-set is still in transition. As "the logical leaders of changed practice" (Mangin & Stoelinga, 2010, p. 50), teachers are critical in any school improvement initiatives. Addressing the unique role of teachers in educational reform, Dozier (2007) noted, "Because teachers know firsthand what is needed to improve student learning, promoting and supporting teacher leadership are crucial to the success of any education reform effort" (p. 58). Furthermore, in a reform report issued by the Institute for Educational Leadership (IEL, 2001), the IEL Task Force on Teacher Leadership recognized the leadership capacity of teachers to bring about educational change. Specifically, the Task Force (IEL, 2001) viewed the national board certification process as a means to "pave the way to teacher leadership" (p. 15). Therefore, the power to propel most school improvement efforts already exists within the teaching body, particularly NBCTs.

In considering teacher leadership through the lens of national board certification, the authors developed action checklists for education professionals to build upon the leadership experience of NBCTs. These suggested recommendations follow.

For Teacher Educators

- Design preparation programs using a leadership theme (Bond, 2011).
- Provide information about the national board process to preservice teachers.
- Incorporate course activities that develop leadership skills (e.g., structure team tasks that involve planning, facilitating, communicating, working with others).

For School Administrators

- Learn more about National Board licensure (see www.nbpts.org).
- Encourage teachers to undertake the national board certification process.
- Enhance collegial relationships among teachers to promote sharing.
- Encourage risk taking and innovation by all teachers.
- Enlist NBCTs to lead professional development sessions among peers.
- Invite teachers to serve on interview panels or search committees.
- Assign NBCTs as mentors to beginning teachers.
- Raise teachers' awareness of professional organizations and conferences for involvement.

For Teachers

- Look beyond the classroom for areas of impact to broaden your influence.
- Mentor another teacher (even if not officially assigned to someone).
- Learn from the experiences of NBCTs.
- Seek national board certification.
- Submit proposals to present at conferences (local, state, or national levels).

In general, these actions support the expansion of leadership among teachers. In her natural progression as a professional, Anna followed the recommended actions for teachers. Had she been more prepared for leadership in her teacher preparation program, she might have been more confident in her role as a teacher leader. Likewise, if Anna's school administrators had known more about national certification, then they might have provided more opportunities for her to lead before and after becoming certified. Our students deserve to have more educational professionals whose leadership potential has been realized.

Summary

The original research presented here reflects current writings on teacher leadership. For instance, Barth (2001b) identified risk taking as an important behavior for leaders. The national board process in and of itself is a risk-taking venture. It requires reflective analysis and has an evaluation system that may take 3 years to complete. According to the life cycle of a career teacher, NBCTs have reached the expert stage of their careers—a stage in which they are willing to lead (Steffy et al., 2000). NBCTs possess a teaching credential that does not ensure leadership but enhances the potential leadership of teachers like Anna. One can certainly be a teacher leader without national certification, but the process itself involves considerable risk taking, extensive reflection, and intensive self-improvement, which, in turn, further develops teachers' leadership potential. The education community would greatly benefit by looking more closely through the lens of national board certified teachers as a way to foster leadership, improve education, and strengthen students' academic achievement.

References

Allen, L. (2004). From votes to dialogues: Clarifying the role of teachers' voices in school renewal. *Phi Delta Kappan, 86*(4), 318–321.

Barth, R. S. (1990). *Improving schools from within.* San Francisco, CA: Jossey-Bass.

Barth, R. S. (2001a). Teacher leader. *Phi Delta Kappan, 82*(6), 443–449.

Barth, R. S. (2001b). *Learning by heart.* San Francisco, CA: Jossey-Bass.

Barth, R. S. (2006). Improving relationships within the schoolhouse. *Educational Leadership, 63*(6), 8–13.

Bohen, D. B. (2001). Strengthening teaching through national certification. *Educational Leadership, 58*(8), 50–53.

Bond, N. (2011). Preparing preservice teachers to become teacher leaders. *The Educational Forum, 75*(4), 280–297.

Burgess, J. (2009). *Other duties as assigned: Tips, tools, and techniques for expert teacher leadership.* Alexandria, VA: ASCD.

Council of Chief State School Officers. (2011). *InTASC Model Core Teaching Standards: A resource for state dialogue.* Washington, DC: Author.

Danielson, C. (2006). *Teacher leadership that strengthens professional practice.* Alexandria, VA: ASCD.

Danielson, C. (2007). The many faces of leadership. *Educational Leadership, 65*(1), 14–19.

Dozier, T. K. (2007). Turning good teachers into great leaders. *Educational Leadership, 65*(1), 54–59.

Goetze, I. (2006). *The perspectives of national board certified teachers on how leadership activities impacted job satisfaction* (Doctoral dissertation). University of Georgia, Atlanta. Retrieved from http://athenaeum.libs.uga.edu/handle/10724/23119

Helterbran, V. R. (2010). Teacher leadership: Overcoming "I am just a teacher" syndrome. *Education, 131*(2), 363–371.

Hunzicker, J. (2011). Teacher learning through national board candidacy: A conceptual model. *Teacher Education Quarterly, 38*(3), 191–209.

Institute for Educational Leadership. (2001). *Leadership for student learning: Redefining the teacher as leader,* A Report of the Task Force on Teacher Leadership. Washington, DC: Author.

Katzenmeyer, M., & Moller, G. (2001). *Awakening the sleeping giant: Helping teachers develop as leaders* (2nd ed.). Thousand Oaks, CA: Corwin.

Lieberman, A., & Friedrich, L. D. (Eds.). (2010). *How teachers become leaders: Learning from practice and research.* New York, NY: Teachers College Press.

Lieberman, A., & Miller, L. (2004). *Teacher leadership.* San Francisco, CA: Jossey-Bass.

Mangin, M. M., & Stoelinga, S. R. (2010). The future of instructional teacher leader roles. *The Educational Forum, 74*(1), 49–62.

Merideth, E. M. (2007). *Leadership strategies for teachers* (2nd ed.). Thousand Oaks, CA: Corwin.

National Board for Professional Teaching Standards. (2002). *What teachers should know and be able to do.* Arlington, VA: Author.

National Board for Professional Teaching Standards. (2013, January 8). *Number of board-certified teachers tops 100,000 as new studies show significant gains in student achievement.* Arlington, VA: Author. Retrieved from http://www.nbpts.org/nbpts-2013–01–08-nbct-student-achievement

Petty, T., O'Conner, K., & Dagenhart, D. (2003). *Identifying the wants and needs of North Carolina teachers.* Chapel Hill: University of North Carolina.

Phelps, P. H. (2008). Helping teachers become leaders. *The Clearing House, 81*(3), 119–122.

Reeves, D. B. (2006). Of hubs, bridges, and networks. *Educational Leadership, 63*(8), 32–37.

Reeves, D. B. (2008). *Reframing teacher leadership to improve your school.* Alexandria, VA: Association for Supervision and Curriculum Development.

Steffy, B. E., Wolfe, M. P., Pasch, S. H., & Enz, B. J. (Eds.). (2000). *Life cycle of the career teacher.* Thousand Oaks, CA: Corwin.

TeacherSolutions. (2008). *Measuring what matters: The effects of national board certification on advancing 21st century teaching and learning.* Carrboro, NC: Center for Teaching Quality.

14

COOPERATING TEACHERS AS LEADERS IN THE ACCREDITATION OF EDUCATOR PREPARATION PROGRAMS

Frank B. Murray
Christine Carrino Gorowara

The Council for the Accreditation of Educator Preparation (CAEP) is an independent, nongovernmental organization that assesses the quality of educator preparation programs in the United States. To receive accreditation, universities submit documentation demonstrating quality in one of three ways: (a) the program completers teach caringly and effectively; (b) the program's innovative features link to the quality of the program completers' teaching; or (c) the changes made in the program over time are true improvements. Each way, while different in emphasis, directness, and sensitivity to program variations, depends in the end on the accreditor's satisfaction that the graduates can teach competently. CAEP's goal is to accredit only the programs that show unequivocally that the graduates are competent teachers, that the program contributed to the competence, and that the program has a system for further improving the graduates' competence. As part of the accreditation process, CAEP relies on outside review teams comprised of university and K–12 educators to examine the program's documentation; conduct site visits to talk to professors, staff, and students; and solicit feedback from K–12 cooperating teachers who work directly with the program completers in the schools.

Two aspects of the CAEP process are noteworthy. First, information from multiple sources is gathered and analyzed before making the final determination about accreditation. These data attempt to provide convincing evidence of the quality of the educator preparation program. Second, practicing K–12 teachers, not just university professors, contribute to the accreditation process by serving as reviewers and providers of information for the submitting university. By involving practicing teachers in the accreditation process, CAEP acknowledges teachers' expertise, experience, and perspective about the quality of the educator preparation program and its graduates. Teachers who serve in these reviewer and information provider roles are, in essence, acting as leaders in the education profession. These teacher leaders fulfill one of the roles described by Danielson (2007), who said that the teacher leader's "involvement may take place within the teacher leader's own department or team, across the school, or beyond the school" (p. 17). This chapter describes two ways that teacher leaders serve "beyond the school" by participating in the accreditation process of educator preparation programs. The first section describes the role of the cooperating teacher, while the second section explains teachers' responsibilities on site visit teams and decision panels. The chapter concludes with some ways that teacher leaders can use their expertise to make assessments about the quality of teaching at the K–12 levels.

Cooperating Teachers' Evaluation of Student Teacher Competence

While conducting onsite visits of the educator preparation program, accreditors must be wary of how representative the opinions they are hearing are. As a way to cast a wider net for more accurate information, CAEP (formerly Teacher Education Accreditation Council [TEAC]) developed an online survey in 2008. The survey asks cooperating teachers to rate the adequacy of the program graduates' knowledge and skill and to assess aspects of the program such as the courses, facilities, resources, and support services. The respondents rate the aspects as *inadequate, barely adequate, adequate, more than adequate,* or *excellent.* Completed surveys are returned to a third-party vendor and are not seen by the institution. On average, approximately 30% are returned, a return rate that comfortably exceeds the return rate of 15% for satisfactory interpretable survey results (Fosnacht, Howe, Peck, & Sarraf, 2013).

Since the beginning of CAEP's existence, 684 cooperating teachers from 40 accredited programs have completed the survey. Overall, the ratings have been at the high end (4.0+) of a 5-point scale (see Table 14.1) and have shown that the cooperating teachers concluded that both their student teachers and the program were *more than adequate* and often close to *excellent* with regard to the student teachers' knowledge and skills. The cooperating teachers' ratings of their own understanding of the program, the training they received, and their relationship with the program faculty were significantly lower statistically but still in the *adequate* range of the *inadequate* to *excellent* scale. The cooperating teachers who reported that they were better trained and had a better understanding of the program were the most satisfied with the student teachers' knowledge and skills.

These cooperating teachers arguably know the level of teaching competence of the student teachers more thoroughly and accurately than do any other teacher educators who teach this group prior to the student teaching semester (Knowles & Cole, 1996). On average, cooperating teachers have spent close to 600 hours mentoring and observing the novices (U.S. Department of Education, 2011) and are, on the whole, the more experienced and higher degreed members

TABLE 14.1 Mean Cooperating Teacher Ratings (1–5) of Their Student Teacher's Competence and Some Program Features (N = 684) in Three Clusters (I–III)

	Number of Raters	Minimum Rating	Maximum Rating	Mean Rating	Standard Deviation
Student Competence					
I. Teaching Skill	672	1	5	4.57	0.71
II. Subject Matter	682	1	5	4.27	0.85
Pedagogy	681	1	5	4.13	0.88
Diversity Perspectives	616	1	5	4.23	0.83
Technology	653	1	5	4.26	0.87
Independent Learning	675	1	5	4.32	0.91
Overall Preparation	672	1	5	4.24	0.88
Program Features					
III. Faculty Relation	603	1	5	3.81	1.13
Training	631	1	5	3.53	1.05
Understanding	665	1	5	3.84	1.02

Scale: 1 (Inadequate), 2 (Barely adequate), 3 (Adequate), 4 (More than adequate), 5 (Excellent)

of the teaching profession (McIntyre, Byrd, & Fox, 1996; Murray & Stotko, 2004; Zimpher & Sherrill, 1996).

Table 14.1 presents the cooperating teachers' mean ratings (minimum, maximum, and standard deviations) of the student teachers in six areas of competence and of the three program features. As Table 14.1 shows, the cooperating teachers' ratings of the student teachers and the program features are clustered in three levels of magnitude (I–III), with the highest mean rating being the adequacy of the student teachers' teaching ability (4.57/5.00), a finding that is consistent with the university faculty survey ratings of the student teachers and with the student teachers' self-ratings (Murray, 2010). The second cluster of ratings includes the cooperating teacher ratings of the adequacy of the student teachers' knowledge of the subject matter and pedagogy (including related topics) and also their ratings of the student teachers' overall preparation for success (4.13–4.32/5.00). All of these ratings are in the *more than adequate* to *excellent* range. The cooperating teachers' ratings of their own understanding of the program, the training they received, and their relationships with the program faculty are significantly lower but still in the *adequate* to *more than adequate* range (3.53–3.84/5.00).

While the ratings may suffer from the so-called Widget effect (Weisberg, Sexton, Mulhern, & Keeling, 2009), namely, uniformly high ratings, they are not simply undifferentiated ceiling effects as the cooperating teachers do make statistically significant differentiations among survey items. The results reveal that cooperating teachers have a consistent, logical, nuanced, and coherent, if perhaps inflated, view of their student teachers. The teacher ratings were lawful and consistent as shown by a Cronbach's *alpha* for the ten-item survey of 0.88.

These survey results align with the evidence cited by the programs in their own accreditation self-studies (grades, license scores, ratings by employers and alumni, rates of accomplishments, portfolio, and work sample evaluations). Consequently, the findings are not exceptions to the main lines of other evidence and show again that the teachers were capable of coming to the same conclusions about the evidence on which accreditors typically rely. For example, the reported mean GPA for the student sample of online survey takers (N = 2658) was a high 3.67/4.00 (minimum 2.00, maximum 4.00, SD = 0.37), and the pass rates on the various license examinations were in the 90–100% ranges. The cooperating teacher survey results are also in line with the online surveys given to students (N = 2658) and faculty (N = 943), who rated the same program's students and also found that they were in the *more than adequate* to *excellent* range with regard to each area of teaching competence.

Furthermore, the survey form afforded the cooperating teachers an opportunity to make comments. Approximately 73% of the comments pertained to the program's quality or the student teachers' achievements, and the largest percentage of these (32%) comments focused on the high quality of the students and their accomplishments, particularly in the area of technology. About 10% found fault with the students' subject matter knowledge, and another 17% found the students poorly prepared in pedagogy, particularly in the area of classroom management. Problems were also cited with the programs themselves regarding poor organization, being too theoretical, and using assessment rubrics that were unclear or difficult to use. Approximately 20% of the comments portrayed weaknesses in the faculty's presence or interest in student teaching, but another 5% were impressed by the faculty's engagement. Ten percent reported that they were not trained, although some said they were experienced teachers who felt training was unnecessary.

A puzzling finding in the results from the faculty and student surveys (Murray, 2010) was that the students' teaching skill was rated significantly higher than their knowledge of the subject matter being taught and higher than the pedagogical knowledge that presumably undergirds teaching practice. While this finding seems to suggest that the whole of teaching is greater than the sum of its parts, it may also mean that the indicators of superior teaching skill are not closely linked to subject matter and pedagogical understanding. Still, it is unusual that the cooperating teachers think the student teachers' teaching ability is superior to their knowledge of the teaching subject or pedagogy, an instance in which performance exceeds prerequisite knowledge.

The cooperating teacher surveys, along with the surveys of the student teachers and the university faculty, are given in the context of the program's self-study accreditation report as a way of corroborating the program's own evidence of quality. While the surveys are reliable, as noted by Cronbach's *alpha,* the cooperating teachers' responses are also valid insofar as the results are in line with the equally high grades these program students receive, the high ratings they earn on the program's rubrics for clinical experiences and portfolios, the high pass rates on the state's licensure examinations, and the survey results from the students and faculty about the same students.

The findings cannot be solely explained by rating inflation and bias because there are genuine differences in the ratings of the various survey items. Table 14.1 shows that minimum ratings were given for each survey item and the standard deviations are approximately one rating unit. Obviously, given the variation in the individual ratings, the findings cannot be chalked up solely to ceiling effects, indiscriminate rating, or the so-called Widget effect. The real and meaningful information in these inflated results resides to the right of the decimal point in the ratings.

Unlike the faculty and students, who also gave uniformly high ratings, the cooperating teachers had less at stake in whether the program was accredited, but they still gave high ratings. It is notable that the better trained cooperating teachers and those who understood the program better were more satisfied with the teaching competence of their student teachers and with the program's potential for ensuring the student teachers' successful teaching careers. The results could have been the other way around because those who were more aware and better trained might have been expected to have downgraded their ratings of the preparation the students received for success had the programs and students been truly weak. The cooperating teachers did just the opposite. Overall, the overwhelming number of cooperating teachers from these accredited programs expressed high levels of satisfaction with the quality of their student teachers, the quality of the program, and their roles in the program.[1]

These results contrast with those of the prevailing national narratives, in which claims are routinely made that teacher education is *broken* and that today's new teachers are unprepared for their roles (Duncan, 2009, 2010; Greenberg, Pomerance, & Walsh, 2011; Levine, 2006). It is somewhat strange and worthy of further investigation that those most familiar with and knowledgeable about teacher education programs consistently come to conclusions about the graduates' competence that differ markedly from the conclusions of those who view these same programs from a distance (Aldeman, Carey, Dillon, Miller, & Silva, 2011; Conant, 1963; Crowe, 2010; Judge, Lemosse, Paine, & Sedlak, 1994; Kanstoroom & Finn, 1999; Koerner, 1963; Mitchell & Barth, 1999). Accreditation is perhaps a reasonable way to bridge this odd gap as it provides both an "up-close" visit and intimate review with a measure of detached national objectivity. Drawing upon the expertise of teacher leaders adds another important perspective to the accreditation process.

Teachers as Contributors to Site Visit Teams and Decision Panels

A challenge accreditors in teacher education faced as CAEP sought recognition by the U.S. Department of Education was adding classroom teachers to its audit teams and decision-making bodies. It was difficult to find on a recurring basis substitute teachers for the classroom teachers who served on the audit teams. The inclusion of teachers was a requirement for federal recognition. A substantial record maintained by the previous accrediting bodies before CAEP has shown the influence classroom teachers have had on the accreditation of programs, the insights they have provided, the nature of their deliberations, and the tasks they have performed during site visits.

At first, some stakeholders in the accreditation process were concerned that teachers would not be up to the task because the audit process, which requires verification and probing of claims made by programs that their graduates are competent, has proven difficult for university faculty and administrators to master. In spite of these worries, the K–12 teachers were, in all but a handful of cases, the equal of the university faculty members of audit teams and panels in their insight, arguments, and capacity to influence the accreditation findings and decision. The contributions of the teachers who have served as auditors have been documented in the surveys and in the record of audit reports and panel reports. A sample of these teachers (N = 24) were asked about their experiences as audit team members with regard to whether they *strongly disagreed, disagreed, were not sure, agreed,* or *strongly agreed* with the statements in Table 14.2. The other nonteacher members of the audit teams (N = 25) were similarly surveyed on the same topics with regard to the teachers who were members of their audit teams.

As shown in Table 14.2, the auditors and teachers on the whole had indistinguishable levels of agreement with the statements surveyed, and these levels were mainly in the *agree* to *strongly agree* range. For eight of the ten items, the teachers were more in agreement with the statement than other auditors were, and in four instances, the differences were statistically significant by a *t* test: items 2, 8, 9, and 10. The other auditors apparently had some reservations about the teachers' level of knowledge and whether they were truly essential in the audit. There were no differences in several key areas: the contributions the teachers made to the team, the benefits the team derived from the teacher, and the value of the teacher's local knowledge. Cronbach's *alphas* for the surveys were 0.83 for the teacher survey and 0.85 for the auditor survey for the ten items.

Both the teachers and the other auditors thought the teachers were helpful in assisting the team come to the "right decision" about the program (item 5), and the responses of both groups to this item correlated significantly (0.30–0.66) with the ratings of all but two other items (6 and 9). These results indicated that getting the right answer, in the view of the other auditors and teachers, was related to the teachers' overall experience of the audit, their background knowledge and experience, the benefits their knowledge and experience conferred on the team, their treatment as peers by the team, the influence they had on the team, the excellence of their own program, and the degree to which the accreditation system was seen to depend on teachers' participation. Overall, the survey respondents commented that the opportunity was "priceless," "outstanding," "symbolic," "highly professional," "demanding," and "mutually beneficial."

TABLE 14.2 Minimum, Maximum, Mean Ratings (1–5) and Standard Deviations From Lead Auditor (N = 25) and Teacher (N = 24) Members of TEAC Audit Teams

Ten Survey Items for Lead Auditor (A) and Teacher (T) Members of Audit Teams	Min	Max	Mean	SD
1. A: I found the overall experience of having a local practitioner (classroom teacher) on the team rewarding and enjoyable.	2.00	5.00	**4.56**	0.82
T: I found the overall experience of being a TEAC academic auditor rewarding and enjoyable.	3.00	5.00	**4.71**	0.55
2. A: I believe our local practitioner had the knowledge and experience to recognize a quality education program.	2.00	5.00	**4.24***	0.56
T: I believe I have the knowledge and experience to recognize a quality education program when I see one.	4.00	5.00	**4.79**	0.41
3. A: I felt it was important that our team had the benefit of our local practitioner's knowledge about the program and its context.	2.00	5.00	**4.44**	0.82
T: I felt it was important that the team had the benefit of my local knowledge about the program and its context.	4.00	5.00	**4.75**	0.44
4. A: I treated our local practitioner as a peer member of the audit team.	4.00	5.00	**4.80**	0.40
T: I was treated as a peer member of the audit team.	2.00	5.00	**4.58**	0.88
5. A: I felt our local practitioner helped the audit team come to the right decisions about the program.	2.00	5.00	**3.96**	0.97
T: I felt I helped the audit team come to the right decisions about the program.	2.00	5.00	**4.37**	0.76
6. A: I think our local practitioner benefited professionally by being a member of an audit team.	4.00	5.00	**4.44**	0.50
T: I benefited professionally from being a member of an audit team.	3.00	5.00	**4.62**	0.57
7. A: Our local practitioner was able to influence the other members of the audit team.	1.00	5.00	**3.76**	1.05
T: I was able to influence the other members of the audit team.	1.00	5.00	**3.79**	1.06
8. A: I felt our local practitioner's own professional undergraduate education program was excellent	3.00	5.00	**3.41***	0.71
T: My own professional undergraduate education program was excellent.	2.00	5.00	**4.29**	0.95
9. A: I felt that the experience of the audit caused our local practitioner to think about program quality differently.	3.00	5.00	**4.20***	0.57
T: Since the audit, I now look at my own professional program differently.	1.00	5.00	**3.41**	1.13
10. A: I felt the local practitioner's presence on an audit team was essential to the TEAC system uncovering whether or not a program is a quality program.	2.00	5.00	**3.56***	1.08
T: I felt the TEAC system could uncover whether or not a program is a quality program.	2.00	5.00	**4.50**	0.78

Scale: 1 (Strongly disagree), 2 (Disagree), 3 (Not sure), 4 (Agree), 5 (Strongly agree)

* Indicates a statistically significant difference between the means by *t* test

Teachers also participated on accreditation decision panels, in which five to seven educational experts evaluate the evidence that has been verified by the audit team to determine whether the preponderance of that evidence supports the claim that the graduates can teach effectively and caringly. At least one member of each panel is a teacher, and he or she, in consultation with an auditor, prepares an analysis of the evidence for a case that is coming before the panel. This audit team determines whether the evidence is consistent or inconsistent with what is needed to support the program's claims.

The other members of the panel are typically professors, administrators, state representatives, and members of the public. As with the audit teams, the teacher members of the panel are as insightful and informed as the other members. The teachers' postsession ratings of their confidence in their own decisions and in the entire panel's decisions are indistinguishable from those of the other members of the panel.

The results from a sample of 20 panelists' debriefing forms in 2008–2009 show mean ratings in the *certain* to *very certain* range (the top rating) about all aspects of program decision categories, with very little variance among the panelists. The mean standard deviation was a marginal 0.42 on a 5-point scale. The cases the panelists considered were not problem-free, with some displaying problems that were severe enough that they had to be corrected within 2 years for the program to maintain its accreditation. On a scale of 0–3 with regard to the severity of the problems the panel found, the mean problem rating was 1.10 with considerable variation among the cases (SD = 1.12). Panelists had significantly more confidence in the panel's group decisions than in their own individual decisions (4.37 vs. 4.18), a fact that is consistent with the view that the nonteacher panelists valued the teachers' contributions. Otherwise, they would have had more confidence in their view of their own decision than in that of the panel, as the panels always included the contributions of the teacher participants. In short, classroom teacher leaders played an important role in the site visit teams and decision panels.

Teacher Leaders as Future Accreditors of K–12 Education

Policymakers and regulators are seemingly preoccupied at the moment with finding metrics by which to hold K–12 teachers accountable for their teaching. These same people have been stymied by the enormous variation among the nation's schools and within schools that make "one-size-fits-all" assessments and metrics patently unjust and unfair. Policymakers think that they may have now found a fair solution to this problem in the use of value-added assessments, which allegedly correct for the uneven starting points of each pupil's schooling. Of course, the obstacles to an acceptable implementation of these value-added methods are many: contested calculation method variations (McCaffrey, Koretz, Lockwood, & Hamilton, 2004), confidentiality of student test scores, nonrandom assignments of students to teachers, selective and sporadic grade and subject area assessments, standardized curriculum assessments of unproven validity, and the blatant and ever-present consequences of Campbell's law[2] (Nichols & Berliner, 2007).

An alternative solution to these problems is applying to the K–12 setting the same accreditation principles and procedures that are used to hold universities accountable. By following this approach, teachers themselves would make their own claims about their "excellence." They would have to muster supporting evidence for their claims, make the additional case for why their evidence should be trusted as valid, and have in place a classroom system that yields evidence about pupil accomplishment and that enables the teacher to monitor and improve classroom learning. The teacher who makes such a case would have it checked and verified by a third party, like an accreditor. This process would put schools in a compelling position to withstand the current critics who claim that teaching is "broken."

In this new model, the teacher would write a report documenting the fact that her class learned what it was supposed to learn during the allotted time. The report would not focus on whether the teacher believed that all children can learn, but whether those students did learn. The report would include all features of the program *Inquiry Brief.* Teachers would make a case for the validity of their assessments, describe the system they put in place for class monitoring and for improving the quality of student learning, show how they rely on the evidence of student learning to improve their teaching, and demonstrate that they have the capacity to teach in an accomplished manner. More importantly, the case for teacher quality would shift to evidence the teacher has that her students learned something and to evidence that the class in question achieved what it was supposed to achieve.

The trustworthiness of the evidence presented is the one aspect of most quality assurance schemes that is in the most doubt. This uncertainty arises because either the evaluators are not onsite to see quality for themselves, or, when they are onsite, they do not check the primary sources in the manner of the audit. Instead, they rely primarily on hearsay and interviews.

This concern would be addressed, as it is in program accreditation, through an onsite audit of the evidence. For example, if a teacher cited the state's standardized curriculum test mean score as evidence of her students' subject matter understanding, an auditor might (a) recalculate the mean from the teacher's data; (b) check to see whether the sample of scores was entered correctly from the test-maker's score report; (c) examine the test's specifications; (d) check other sources of evidence to determine whether the pupils in the class truly understood the items on which they answered correctly and truly did not understand those on which they answered incorrectly; (e) interview pupils about the test; and (f) then follow a similar plan for each line of evidence (grades, portfolios of pupil work, parental satisfaction, growth in pupil understanding, and motivation) that the teacher cited as evidence of her teaching accomplishments in an effort to show that the teacher's evidence was just as she said it was.

The reports that the teachers write would be analogous to reports prepared by university programs for accreditation. In time, the reports would have a role in accreditation that would trump almost all other categories of evidence because they would provide the best available evidence the field has that teaching was taking place at a high standard. Were the graduates of the program to have such reports, demonstrating that the graduates were adding high levels of true academic value in their work, the program's case for accreditation would be more convincing than are the proxies the field has for the evidence of what kind of learning transpired in the teacher's classroom.

Conclusion

This proposed project, along with accreditation itself, is critically dependent upon teachers' exhibiting the kind of leadership that accreditors in teacher education have seen in their accrediting work so far that has engaged the active professional judgment of classroom teachers. To date, teachers have brought their independent perspectives and made significant professional contributions from the site visit to the final accreditation decision of the national accreditors in teacher education. These educators are serving as true teacher leaders who are bringing about positive change in the profession.

Notes

1. TEAC (the accreditation body before CAEP) has anecdotal evidence from its interviews of some cooperating teachers, who gave very high marks on the program's student teaching forms, that the teachers keep a set of public evaluations and a separate set of private evaluations. The former, reported to the college, are designed to aid the student teachers' career chances, while the latter are lower and are designed to truly mentor and guide the student to higher performance levels.
2. Campbell's law holds that high-stakes assessments have two predictable consequences: They tend to corrupt the assessment instrument, and they tend to corrupt the matter assessed.

References

Aldeman, C., Carey, K., Dillon, E., Miller, B., & Silva, E. (2011). *A measured approach to improving teacher preparation.* Washington, DC: Education Sector.

Conant, J. B. (1963). *The education of American teachers.* New York, NY: McGraw-Hill.

Crowe, E. (2010). *Measuring what matters: A stronger accountability model for teacher education.* Washington, DC: Center for American Progress.

Danielson, C. (2007). The many faces of leadership. *Educational Leadership, 65*(1), 14–19.

Duncan, A. (2009, October 9). *A call to teaching.* Speech delivered at the University of Virginia. Retrieved from http://www.ed.gov/news/speeches/call-teaching

Duncan, A. (2010). Teacher preparation: Reforming the uncertain profession. *Education Digest, 75*(5), 13–22.

Fosnacht, K., Howe, E., Peck, L., & Sarraf, S. (2013, April). *How much effort is needed? The importance of response rates for estimating undergraduate behaviors.* Paper presented at the meeting of the American Educational Research Association, San Francisco, CA.

Greenberg, J., Pomerance, L., & Walsh, K. (2011). *Student teaching in the United States.* Washington, DC: National Council on Teacher Quality.

Judge, H., Lemosse, M., Paine, L., & Sedlak, M. (1994). *The university and the teachers: France, the United States, and England. Oxford Studies in Comparative Education* (Vol. 4, 1&2). Oxford, UK: Symposium Books.

Kanstoroom, M., & Finn, C. E. (1999). *Better teachers, better schools.* Washington, DC: Thomas B. Fordham Foundation.

Knowles, J. G., & Cole, A. L. (1996). Developing practice through field experiences. In F. B. Murray (Ed.), *The teacher educator's handbook: Building a knowledge base for the preparation of teachers* (pp. 648–688). San Francisco, CA: Jossey-Bass.

Koerner, J. D. (1963). *The miseducation of American teachers.* Boston, MA: Houghton Mifflin.

Levine, A. (2006). *Educating school teachers.* Washington, DC: Education Schools Project.

McCaffrey, D. F., Koretz, D. M., Lockwood, J. R., & Hamilton, L. S. (2004). *Evaluating value-added models for teacher accountability.* Santa Monica, CA: RAND Education.

McIntyre, J., Byrd, D., & Fox, S. (1996). Field and laboratory experiences. In J. Sikula, T. J. Buttery, & E. Guyton (Eds.), *Handbook of research on teacher education: A project of the Association of Teacher Educators* (2nd ed., pp. 171–193). New York, NY: Macmillan Library Reference.

Mitchell, R., & Barth, P. (1999). Not good enough: A content analysis of teacher licensing examinations. How teacher licensing tests fall short. *Thinking K–16, 3*(1), 1–26.

Murray, F. B. (2010). Lessons from ten years of TEAC's accrediting activity. *Issues in Teacher Education, 19*(1), 7–19.

Murray, F. B., & Stotko, E. M. (2004). The student teacher as an agent of instructional reform: Effects of student teachers on supervising teachers. *Action in Teacher Education, 26*(3), 73–81.

Nichols, S. L., & Berliner, D. C. (2007). *Collateral damage: How high-stakes testing corrupts America's schools.* Cambridge, MA: Harvard Education Press.

U.S. Department of Education. (2011). *Preparing and credentialing the nation's teachers: The secretary's eighth report on teacher quality based on data provided for 2008, 2009, 2010.* Washington, DC: Office of Postsecondary Education.

Weisberg, D., Sexton, S., Mulhern, J., & Keeling, D. (2009). *The widget effect: Our national failure to acknowledge and act on differences in teacher effectiveness* (2nd ed.). New York, NY: New Teachers Project.

Zimpher, N. L., & Sherrill, J. A. (1996). Professors, teachers, and leaders in SCDES. In J. Sikula, T. J. Buttery, & E. Guyton (Eds.), *Handbook of research on teacher education: A project of the Association of Teacher Educators* (2nd ed., pp. 279–305). New York, NY: Macmillan Library Reference.

PART III

Influence and Impact of Teachers Who Lead

15

LEADING AS A MORAL IMPERATIVE*

Learning From Culturally Responsive and Socially Just Teachers

Sonia Nieto

Teachers who work in what are euphemistically called "urban," "high-need," "under-achieving," and "problem" schools typically teach Latino/a, African American, and Native American students along with Asian American students who struggle in school—especially Cambodian, Hmong, and Laotian students—as well as immigrants, English language learners, those labeled as "disabled," and White students living in poverty. Yet for a variety of reasons, numerous teachers, both veteran and novice, do not feel prepared to teach such students (Ready & Wright, 2011). This may be so for a number of reasons, including the harsh realities of working in under-resourced schools, a lack of personal and professional experience with students of diverse backgrounds, poor preparation in their teacher education programs, personal biases about the children of diverse backgrounds, or inservice programs with an inadequate focus on diversity.

Evidence about teachers' discomfort or inability to teach students of diverse backgrounds comes from a variety of sources. For example, although one survey found that 61% of teachers said they were able to differentiate instruction according to students' needs, this means that nearly 40% were not (MetLife, 2011). In another survey, more than 600 first-year teachers indicated that their coursework on diversity was comprehensive and useful, yet nearly half still felt underprepared for the challenges of dealing with diversity in their classrooms (Rochkind, Ott, Immerwahr, Doble, & Johnson, 2008). Another study found that all teachers, whether traditionally prepared or not, needed positive support systems, some classroom experience prior to beginning teaching, and instruction on diversity and assessment (Zientek, 2007).

In spite of the challenges of teaching in high-poverty schools, some teachers *are* successful at teaching students of diverse backgrounds. What makes the difference, and what can we learn from teachers who are leaders in their schools (and beyond) about what it takes? The research on which this chapter is based focuses on 23 teachers who are enthusiastic about, and effective in, teaching students of diverse backgrounds (Nieto, 2013). They range from a first-year teacher to one who had been in the classroom for nearly 40 years, and they reflect a variety of ethnic backgrounds, native languages, subject areas, pedagogical styles, and geographical locations. In this chapter, I focus on three of these teachers.

Throughout the interviews with the teachers, it became clear that one of the responsibilities they took most seriously was instilling in their students enduring values to help them become moral human beings with consequential lives. These include empathy and responsibility for others, values consistent with an ethic of care (Noddings, 1992). Although they certainly want their students to shine intellectually, these teachers also recognize that trying to understand others who are different from themselves and demonstrating responsibility for others are important human values that need to be nurtured.

All the teachers I interviewed, whether neophytes or veterans, are teacher leaders because they exemplify the qualities of good leaders everywhere. Exemplary leadership, according to James Kouzes and Barry Posner (2007), is similar across all disciplines and all professions, including teaching. According to them, exemplary leaders model the way, inspire a shared vision, challenge the process, enable others to act, and encourage the heart. Amber Bechard, Adam Heenan, and Carmen Tisdale (the real names of these teachers), as you will see in this chapter, do all of these things.

In what follows, the three teachers are introduced, along with a description of where and what they teach. Using the teachers' words and examples of their values and teaching practices, two themes are explored: *teaching with a moral perspective as instilling values of empathy and responsibility;* and *demonstrating a moral perspective through a culturally responsive pedagogy.*

Teachers' Perspectives on the Moral Dimensions of Teaching

What does it mean to view teaching as a moral endeavor? In their interviews, the teachers gave many examples. These include modeling strong ethical values, creating a classroom environment that promotes trust and confidence, presenting a multicultural curriculum through various lenses, and becoming culturally competent educators, among other values and classroom practices. The remainder of this chapter focuses on how the focal teachers embody two specific aspects of the moral dimension of teaching, both of which are also linked closely with teachers as leaders: *teaching as instilling values of empathy and responsibility in their students,* and *teaching as culturally responsive pedagogy.* Teachers who are leaders, in addition, not only work at instilling values in their students and honoring their students' identities and experiences, but they also recognize that they are learners who need to look critically at both their talents and their limitations, a characteristic that these three teachers possess.

Teaching as Instilling Values of Empathy and Responsibility

Although they want their students to be academically successful, Amber Bechard, Adam Heenan, and Carmen Tisdale also recognize that learning to understand and appreciate others who are different from them, as well as demonstrating responsibility for others, are also important human values that need to be nurtured.

Carmen Tisdale. A teacher at Carver Lyon Elementary School in Columbia, South Carolina, Carmen Tisdale has been teaching for 14 years, mostly in her home state. Carmen defines teaching in terms of a moral commitment, saying, "I'd like to think that I'm giving them goodness for their hearts along with the education I'm providing." In fact, she said that helping her students become moral human beings was primary among the reasons she teaches, "I just want them to be good people, and if I haven't taught them how to be good people, that's failure to me." For Carmen, there has to be a balance between teaching students the skills they need and helping them become ethical people. For example, when asked what *thriving* meant to her, Carmen was quick to respond that it meant helping students develop both intellectually and socially, adding, "The first day of school I tell my children how important it is to be a person of good character and to be a good person in the world. I say if you have a good heart, it speaks volumes about you, so much more than if you are the smartest kid in my class."

All teachers recognize that their profession is often undervalued and that it is unlikely that they will become rich or famous. They also recognize that teaching, even in the best of circumstances, is a difficult job. But even in challenging circumstances, teachers want to make their mark. Carmen describes teaching as "hard and heavy because there's so much more to it than a book and a pencil." As a result, even when she feels she hasn't done her best, she is aware of the onerous moral responsibility she has as a teacher, saying, "Teaching is so much more than putting information in their heads. You're helping to form people that are going to lead this world, and if you look at it that way, you take it more seriously." Carmen was sorely tested, for example, by Geneva, one of her most difficult students. Nonetheless, knowing that she wants to make a difference in their lives, Carmen shared that it "makes me go in tomorrow and try to love Geneva more [than yesterday]." A couple of years after Geneva went on to another school, a substitute teacher approached Carmen with a note from Geneva telling her how much she loved her. Though Carmen expressed her surprise, the woman told her that of all the people at this school, Geneva had asked only about Carmen, saying, "She asks about you every time I see her." That was confirmation for Carmen that she had done her best.

Adam Heenan. The sense of teaching as a moral endeavor to educate good people can also be seen in comments made by Adam Heenan, a social studies high school teacher in a large urban high school in Chicago. Because he attended schools with large numbers of African American students and because he made it a point to learn Spanish, Adam, who is White, is comfortable teaching his students, most of whom are African American and Latino/a. Also, he teaches with a decidedly multicultural and social justice perspective.

As a senior in high school, Adam was nominated by the superintendent of his school district for the Golden Apple Award, a scholarship that pays a large part of the cost of college for 100 high school students in Illinois who want to pursue teaching and agree to teach for at least 5 years in a "school of need." Adam was thrilled about this award because he had already been contemplating teaching as a career. He reflected, "This is a way for me to serve my community and do what I love and kind of make it my career, make it what I am as a person."

Adam spoke about the values that are important to him as a teacher, the same kinds of values he wants to instill in his students, "Honesty and resilience, dignity, resourcefulness and consistency: those are the things that have been able to construct my teacher identity so far." On the other hand, he made sure to clarify that he was not just speaking about standards as currently defined in many school districts. He explained, "I have high expectations, I just have them with my kids, they know I have them; I don't need standards to tell them."

Although Adam realizes that his students may not think of his social studies classes as the most important thing in their lives, the intrinsic values he tries to model for his students are even more essential. He explained,

> So, do I think they come away from my classroom being better human beings? Yeah, I think so. I think they're better off because I am here. That [sounds] so egotistical! But I like to think that my students come away learning from my class even if they didn't learn exactly what I had in mind. They come away with a broader worldview.

Adam gave the example of a project on homelessness in his economics class in which his students were engaged. Besides developing empathy for others, he also expected them to learn research skills, take responsibility for their work, and learn to take initiative, all the while also being innovative. The students had to demonstrate what they had learned and also develop an action plan. He explained that he wanted the project to benefit their community; it was not just for a grade. He said, "For me, they have to create something of value for other people, not just themselves."

Amber Bechard. The third teacher highlighted in this chapter, Amber Bechard, had been teaching kindergarten in a very privileged, almost exclusively White, private school in Massachusetts when her husband was told he would be transferred to Chicago. Knowing that she would be teaching a much more diverse student body, she took it upon herself to learn more about student diversity and pedagogy. She took a class in multicultural curriculum and for the first time, as a White woman, she felt she had permission to teach with a multicultural perspective, something that she then tried out in her nearly all-White kindergarten class before moving to Chicago. She said, "I just needed someone to say, 'You don't have to be Black to do this.' I needed you to say it's okay if you don't know it." For Amber, being given the freedom to bring up conversations about race and privilege in the classroom was relevant even in her all-White kindergarten class.

After moving to the Chicago area, Amber was hired to teach language arts to middle school students in Plainfield, an urbanized suburb that was rapidly becoming extremely diverse. She explained that she loves teaching her middle school students as much as she had loved teaching her kindergarten children. Although it was starkly different from her previous school, rather than be intimidated, Amber was eager to begin her new job because more than anything, it is the process of learning that fascinates her.

Working with her colleagues in other subject areas, Amber instills values of responsibility and empathy through the curriculum. For example, after reading the memoir of Aaron Elster (Elster & Miller, 2007), a Holocaust survivor, she engaged the students in doing memoirs of their own lives, gathering recipes, anecdotes, photographs, and stories, as well as interviewing parents and grandparents, and writing their families' immigration stories. As she explained, "In my classroom I teach what I'm supposed to teach, what the state tells me to teach that's good for kids, but I also teach kids to embrace themselves and each other."

In this project, the art teacher had the students make beautiful covers for their memoirs and then taught them how to bind them. As Amber said, "They left the last day of the school year with their yearbook in one hand and their memoir in the other, and they valued who they were, and they valued their stories." This was true even of the boys, she said, who one might think would not care about such things, or as Amber said, "14-year-old boys going off to high school, with their ego in one hand and memoir in the other."

Beyond just a focus on their own lives, however, Amber and the other eighth-grade teachers wanted the students to understand what it means to have a moral obligation to others. Extending the study of memoir, they invited Aaron Elster to do a read-aloud of his book. The students took charge of the entire activity, planning the visit, placing posters all over the school, and pulling quotes from his memoir as well as other relevant quotes from the Dalai Lama and Thomas Jefferson. Amber said,

> When this man walked into our school, he was amazed. Three hundred and thirty eighth graders sat in complete silence while this man walked in and [they] went into a standing ovation without being coached! Then he spoke to the class and on three occasions, he broke down in tears. At the end of the talk, a hundred kids purchased his book even though they had already heard

the entire story. They valued his story, they valued his message. For eighth graders to value the story of an 87-year-old man who was a 10-year-old escapee from the Polish ghetto: That was amazing.

The postscript to this story is that when the Illinois Holocaust Museum opened a few years ago with Bill Clinton as the star attraction, Aaron Elster invited the team of teachers who had used his memoir in the curriculum to the museum opening, giving them tickets to sit with Holocaust survivors. When he approached the teachers with his son, Aaron Elster said to him, "I want to introduce you to these teachers from JFK," and his son said, "Oh, this is the one you haven't stopped talking about." Aaron responded, "This is the school that has touched me in a way that no other school ever has. I speak all the time and I've never been so impacted. The kids really understood and respected my message."

Teaching as Culturally Responsive Pedagogy

The field of culturally responsive pedagogy has grown enormously in the past two decades. Spurred by such books as Gloria Ladson-Billings's *The Dreamkeepers* (1994/2009) about effective teachers of African American students, the field has since expanded to include Latino/a, American Indian, and students of other racial and ethnic backgrounds (Gay, 2000/2010; Irizarry, 2011; Irvine, 2003). Culturally responsive pedagogy is not an explicit set of strategies to use with students of particular backgrounds, but rather a mind-set that respects and honors students' cultures, experiences, and histories, and that looks for ways to include them in the curriculum and pedagogy. Culturally responsive teaching entails affirming students' identities while at the same time expanding their worldview; it means having admiration for them and their communities and also holding high expectations for them. It means learning about and infusing students' cultural and family practices and values in the curriculum. It means teaching students that their voices are just as important as everybody else's. It means teaching students that they have the power and the responsibility to care for themselves and others, as well as the power to change the world. In the end, culturally responsive teaching is a belief that students are capable of achieving high standards and worthy of a quality education. In what follows, Carmen, Amber, and Adam discuss what cultural responsiveness means to them.

Carmen Tisdale. Feeling the responsibility to "give back" to her community is a major reason that Carmen is a teacher. Teaching in a predominantly African American school, she believes that children need to see their culture and race reflected in the professionals around them, something that many children of color do not get to see. Carmen experienced a sense of joy and pride as a child, she said, when she saw other African Americans in positions of responsibility and status, and she wants the same for her students. She explained,

As a Black woman, I have to convey to them, especially at the school that I'm at now—it's not just African American, it's [also] low socioeconomic—that they are valuable and that they are smart and that they can be so much more.

Offered four jobs when she returned to South Carolina, Carmen chose Carver Lyon Elementary. Not only was the student body mostly African American, but so were the majority of staff members and the principal. Having these role models in the school, she wants her students to look beyond the limited choices they see in the community, and she makes sure to remind them frequently of such possibilities. She gave the example of her student Jamal, who told her that he wanted to be a bus driver. She responded, "I want you to think about owning a fleet of buses." Although she said that there's nothing wrong with being a bus driver, she felt that Jamal chose this job because that was one of the few jobs he saw in his neighborhood. She concluded, "I think it's my place—not that it's not anybody *else's* place—but it's *my* place to show him that he can be more and that he needs to be more."

Carmen also spoke about being a "Black Momma," something that connects culturally with her African American students and that also demonstrates her caring. As she explained, all cultures have a certain way of talking. "There's a rhythm to it," she said, and she could tell that the White students she had taught previously were not accustomed to her style when they would first come to her classroom. She explained, "They were not used to what I term 'Black Momma.' It is just who I am. We all bring our culture to the classroom whether we realize it or not." She is the kind of teacher defined by Judith Kleinfeld (1975) as a *warm demander*. While communicating personal warmth, these teachers also practice what Kleinfeld calls "active demandingness," that is, they are unrelenting in their demands at the same time that they are nurturing and loving. Researchers Jacqueline Irvine and James Fraser (1998), picking up on this term, provided an example of how a warm demander teacher might speak to a student who is inattentive or lazy: "That's enough of your nonsense, Darius. Your story does not make sense. I told you time and time again that you must stick to the theme I gave you. Now sit down" (Irvine & Fraser, 1998, p. 56). This kind of talk is not often viewed as a positive thing, presumably because it might seem abrasive. Nevertheless, when it is done with care and knowledge of the individual, it gives students the undeniable message that the teacher both cares about them and expects a lot from them. In her all-Black classroom, Carmen Tisdale too enacts this kind of "demandingness" with her students who are not intimidated by her "Black Momma" stance and instead recognize it as expecting the best from them because she loves them.

In terms of how she used this approach in her current class, she explained, "I might say, 'Get your behind over there and sit down.' That's what your Black Momma would say and it's not to say every Black Momma would say it." As she explained, just using Black dialect created a mutual understanding with her students. Referring more specifically to the controversy about Ebonics (see, for example, Delpit & Dowdy, 2002; Miner, 1998), Carmen spoke about maintaining a balance between language that is socially accepted in the general society and helping children understand that their language is also a legitimate form of communication. She said, "I know I have to teach them language that is accepted in school, but I also give them confirmation that their home language is a real language. There is nothing wrong with it. In some ways, I feel like I offer them validation of who they are, and I understand them just because of who I am."

Beyond being their teacher, Carmen sees her job as being a family member to her students. She is, she said, their mom and more at school, explaining, "You're the social worker and advocate; you are the momma. 'I'm putting Shea butter on your little ashy face. That's what your momma does.'" In turn, students feel perfectly comfortable in saying, as if they were at home, "Ms. Tisdale, I need some Shea butter." She concluded, "I really am a part of that village it takes to raise a child."

Carmen incorporates African American culture in her classroom in other ways as well. During Black History Month, her brother, who is a rapper, composed a rap for her students about famous African Americans. She said, "It showed how much children learn through music!" Specifically, Carmen spoke about one of her students, April, who had a serious learning disability. Carmen was teaching them about Rosa Parks and asking who was the lady who refused to give up her seat to a White man. April was trying to remember it and looking for help from the other children who offered, "Michelle? Michelle Obama?" (Carmen explained that ever since Barack Obama was elected President, Michelle Obama was the answer to everything.) She said to April, "No, come on April, you can get it. You can get it." Carmen then began to rap the song and April immediately remembered Rosa Parks, the name that was coming next in the song. Carmen said, "It was just a beautiful thing and throughout the whole unit, whenever I would mention any of them, they would break out in song, like 'MLK, Dr. Martin Luther King' and I have to wait until they get to the end of the verse because they all would just join in."

What made the experience especially meaningful for Carmen was that the students did not just learn a watered down version of Black History, which is the norm in most history books. Instead, Carmen stretched their learning, explaining, "We did research projects and wrote letters to some of the people in the rap song. I was able to show them that these are real people who live real lives today. They could be one of these people." This idea was reinforced when one of the people to whom they had written responded with a letter to the class. He was no longer just a name; he became real.

Carmen Tisdale is African American as are most of her students, and this certainly helps to explain both her rapport and her success with them. But what about teachers who do not share the same culture as their students? Many teachers have had neither personal nor professional experiences with students whose identities are different from theirs and, consequently, they may feel uncomfortable trying to be culturally responsive. Amber Bechard used to be one of these teachers.

Amber Bechard. Amber, who began to learn about multicultural education shortly before moving to Chicago, brought her excitement for this field to Illinois, as well as her confidence in broaching difficult conversations about diversity and privilege. Because she had begun to broach these conversations with her kindergarten students, she said, "It gave me the courage to have those conversations with my colleagues and with 14- and 15-year-old kids in middle school later." Consequently, when she arrived at her new school, she found that while the racial and ethnic diversity was growing significantly (for example, there were now 32 languages represented in the school, not to mention many different ethnicities), it was a fairly new issue for that community. Amber felt that being willing to talk about these differences and comfortable enough to do so was necessary. Nonetheless, many teachers were silent and unsure about what to do about the changing demographics. Given her growing knowledge about and enthusiasm for diversity, Amber jumped in and started all sorts of projects, in addition to beginning (and successfully completing a few years later) a doctoral program in multicultural education.

Amber also took the initiative in promoting a multicultural perspective throughout her school. She started a Multicultural Club, the first one in the district. In the spring, her school hosts a Culture Fair where students and families display projects they have developed and videos they have made. The Culture Fair features student creations, including art, poetry, and other projects. For example, using music, one student made a video about prejudice, while another interviewed fellow students about why they sit at lunch with only students of the same race. Amber was animated when she talked about the Culture Fair and how it has generated so much excitement in the school and the larger community. She said that the previous year, she had "parents jumping on board." One group of African American parents did a large display on Barack Obama and another group prepared a display of the Little Rock Nine. In the current year, African American parents had mounted a display on hair: They brought in mannequin heads and showed students and other families how to do braids. A family from India did henna, and a mother from Indonesia brought Thai and Indonesian dancers to the fair. Parents also brought in Praise Dancers from a local church.

Amber was clearly proud of these efforts, saying, "This was our third annual and it's now at two different schools." As a result, her district now wants to extend the fair to be districtwide. For her, a really rewarding experience "is when it starts real little, for me as a passion, and it explodes beyond. So now it's not just the Amber Bechard Diversity Show [laughter], it's the district's." As a result of the fairs and the combined efforts of many other individuals, the district now has a diversity committee.

Because of her passion for teaching and for multicultural education, Amber has been a catalyst for much of what has started "real little" and has grown in her school and the larger community. She spoke about the ramifications of what began as simply a Culture Club in one school:

> The reward, I think, comes from the tiniest little thing like the kid who said this year, "I never knew I was related to Billie Holiday. That's really cool. I'm going to do my project on that." Then the mom who says, "Next year let's do this between three schools so that we can have the high school, the middle school, and the elementary school all together and we can make this even bigger."

As a result, more parents are visiting the school. What was especially satisfying for Amber was "to see that when YOU start a little fire, it can really get big. And it's getting bigger. It's awesome!"

Adam Heenan. For Adam Heenan, being able to talk naturally about race and other differences with his students is about creating a culturally responsive space. According to him, "We have to build a community about trust before we even get there." Being Jewish, Adam could relate to what it means to be a minority in certain contexts, mostly due to experiences he had as a child. He feels confident, he said, that his own identity "has enabled me to talk with students about our collective definitions of 'minority' and 'diversity' in new ways. We can take collective ownership of the many ways in which we are diverse as a class: ethnicity, religion, gender and sexual identity, disability, and in other ways." His comfort also derived as a result of the relationships he had built over time with students of color. As he said, "They tell me I am real; they tell me I am not trying to fake it."

It is clear, then, that for Adam, becoming a culturally responsive teacher means establishing close and caring relationships from the start with students. He told the story of how this came to be with one of his students, a girl named Jhesyka, who, he had been warned, was a "difficult" student. Not knowing how to pronounce her name, he wrote it on the chalkboard in the teachers' room and asked his colleagues whether anyone knew her. Mr. Roosevelt, one of the teachers, said that he knew her, saying, "I have had that student. Her name is 'Jhesyka' [pronounced just like Jessica]. Be careful around her, yeah, [she's] one of those students, kind of rambunctious; be ready for her!" Prepared with the correct pronunciation of her name, Adam described what happened on the first day of school as he read her name correctly,

> She kind of does this double take. Like I imagine no one has ever probably got her name right on the first day, right? And I had such a great relationship with her from day one. And maybe it is kind of over the hidden curriculum that other students see, like there is a teacher who cared enough to research how you say this girl's name.

Being culturally responsive also means including in the curriculum topics that are of consequence to students. For students of color, issues that impact their daily lives include discrimination, exclusion, and marginalization, topics not generally discussed in many classrooms. But when asked whether he thought all teachers should discuss these issues with their students, he was cautious, saying, "Well, I think it depends on *who* is talking about it and *how* they are talking about it." He said this because he feels that some teachers do not really understand poverty and discrimination, and they do not see their students as their equals. As a result, such teachers can do more harm than good in having these conversations. He explained,

> I think they are from the very much "pull yourself up by your bootstraps" mentality and they would never, you know, admit to the idea that some people don't have bootstraps, or don't have boots. Which, that is my camp, right?

Nevertheless, Adam believes that if teachers are willing to genuinely listen and have honest discussions about these matters, then they should have these conversations. He added, however, "When the topics are broached haphazardly and without a comfortable space, most often the outcome of the lessons will not be beneficial to anyone; it could result in further misunderstandings and deeper prejudices."

Conclusion: Teaching Is an Ethical Endeavor

There are many lessons to be learned from the examples of Adam Heenan, Amber Bechard, and Carmen Tisdale, but one is especially obvious: Teaching is always an ethical endeavor. Teachers need to understand that their actions, attitudes, and practices may have untold and long-standing repercussions, although these may be unintended, on their students' lives. Teacher leaders know this well. They know that their teaching has an impact, either positive or negative, on their students. Culturally responsive teachers can be a powerful influence on students whose identities and experiences have been invisible in the curriculum and pedagogy. By making them visible and affirming, teachers are sending an important message to students. They are saying, "You belong here. You are honored here. I believe in you." Whether it is about teaching students responsibility for themselves and their peers or learning about students' identities in order to become culturally responsive educators, the ethical nature of teaching is irrefutable. Although Carmen, Amber, and Adam are extraordinary teachers, they are in many ways no different from many other caring and compassionate teachers. Like many teachers, they demonstrate their commitment and leadership in innumerable ways through their teaching, their relationships with their students and their students' families, and their collaboration with colleagues.

Unfortunately, given the teacher bashing that is so prevalent today, these kinds of leadership qualities and ethical commitments are too often invisible. In spite of this reality, teachers know that their job is not simply a 9–3 affair, but that, as Adam said, for their students, "it's their *lives!*" He went on to explain that one of his goals is to make students lifelong learners. According to him, teachers need to be resourceful, to find out everything they can about what the community has to offer. He had a particularly powerful way of expressing this idea, saying, "It is the number one thing that you can be as a teacher for your kids: a pipeline to other opportunities, a pipeline outside the classroom." Adam understands that this pipeline can, and often does, provide the only option for students for a better life. It gives them the cultural and social capital to which youngsters from under-resourced communities usually do not have access.

As these teachers see it, teaching and being leaders in their classrooms and beyond is a moral endeavor in which they strive to help students be all they can be while also teaching them to care about others. Teaching as a moral endeavor also means respecting and affirming students' identities. Teachers know that in the end a quality education is the only way that children from marginalized communities can hope to have a chance of living a consequential life. In an era when there is so little talk about ethics in education, these teachers and others like them dare to believe in their students, honor who they are, and teach them to be responsible and moral human beings.

Note: All student names are pseudonyms.

References

Delpit, L., & Dowdy, J. K. (Eds.). (2002). *The skin that we speak: Thoughts on language and culture in the classroom.* New York, NY: The New Press.

Elster, A., & Miller, J. E. (2007). *I still see her haunting eyes: The Holocaust and a hidden child named Aaron.* Peoria, IL: BF Press.

Gay, G. (2010). *Culturally responsive teaching: Theory, research, and practice* (2nd ed.). New York, NY: Teachers College Press. (Original work published 2000)

Irizarry, J. G. (2011). Culturally responsive pedagogy. In J. M. Cooper (Ed.), *Classroom teaching skills* (9th ed., pp. 188–214). Belmont, CA: Cengage Learning.

Irvine, J. J. (2003). *Educating teachers for diversity: Seeing with a cultural eye.* New York, NY: Teachers College Press.

Irvine, J. J., & Fraser, J. W. (1998, May 13). Warm demanders. *Education Week, 17*(35), 56.

Kleinfeld, J. (1975). Effective teachers of Eskimo and Indian students. *School Review, 83*(2), 301–344.

Kouzes, J. M., & Posner, B. Z. (2007). *The leadership challenge* (4th ed.). San Francisco, CA: Jossey-Bass.

Ladson-Billings, G. (2009). *The dreamkeepers: Successful teachers of African American children* (2nd ed.). San Francisco, CA: Jossey-Bass. (Original work published 1994)

MetLife. (2011). *The MetLife survey of the American teacher: Preparing students for college and careers.* New York, NY: Author.

Miner, B. (1998). Embracing Ebonics and teaching Standard English: An interview with Oakland teacher Carrie Secret. In T. Perry & L. Delpit (Eds.), *The real Ebonics debate: Power, language, and the education of African-American children* (pp. 79–88). Boston, MA: Beacon Press.

Nieto, S. (2013). *Finding joy in teaching students of diverse backgrounds: Culturally responsive and socially just practices in U.S. classrooms.* Portsmouth, NH: Heinemann Publishers.

Noddings, N. (1992). *The challenge to care in schools: An alternative approach to education.* New York, NY: Teachers College Press.

Ready, D. D., & Wright, D. L. (2011). Accuracy and inaccuracy in teachers' perceptions of young children's cognitive abilities: The role of child background and classroom context. *American Educational Research Journal, 48*(2), 335–360.

Rochkind, J., Ott, A., Immerwahr, J., Doble, J., & Johnson, J. (2008). *Lessons learned: New teachers talk about their jobs, challenges, and long-range plans,* Issue # 3: Teaching in changing times. Washington, DC: National Comprehensive Center for Teacher Quality, and New York, NY: Public Agenda.

Zientek, L. R. (2007). Preparing high-quality teachers: Views from the classroom. *American Educational Research Journal, 44*(4), 959–1001.

16

THE ROLE OF INQUIRY IN TEACHER LEADERSHIP

Marilyn Cochran-Smith
Rebecca Stern

In discussions about educational improvement, practice has emerged as a key issue (e.g., Ball & Forzani, 2009; Bryk, 2008), and teachers have been identified as the lynchpins in educational reform (Cochran-Smith, 2005). Acknowledging that reform cannot be sustained without the participation of teachers and other practitioners is critical. Increasingly, however, teachers' participation has been constructed primarily as their correct implementation of "research-based" practices as embodied in mandated curricula and assessments, followed up with close monitoring and surveillance. In addition, teachers have increasingly been pinpointed as the cause of educational failure (e.g., Education Equality Project, 2008; Kumashiro, 2012), and teachers and other practitioners have been harshly disparaged in the media and elsewhere (e.g., Brill, 2009; Thomas, 2010).

In contrast, when teachers and other practitioners are researchers, they conduct their own systematic and intentional inquiries into practice informed by, but also critiquing, the knowledge and theories of others (Cochran-Smith & Lytle, 2009). Practitioner researchers investigate highly significant questions about the kinds of practices and approaches that provide all learners access to quality educational opportunities and have direct experience with the ways research-based policies play out in the day-to-day life of classrooms. In this era of accountability and standards, the role of teachers as leaders and researchers is more important than ever.

This chapter focuses on the role of inquiry in teacher leadership. It explores the multiple and complex relationships of inquiry and leadership by presenting five mini-cases of practice that illustrate the various facets and perspectives of these relationships. While the teachers we describe here are differently positioned from one another generationally and culturally, they all hold creative visions about the purposes of education, and they all engage in inquiry with the explicit intention of creating greater access to rich learning opportunities and equity in learning outcomes for all students.

Inquiry as Stance: A Framework for Understanding Teacher Leadership

As a framework for understanding the multiple roles of inquiry in teacher leadership, we use the idea of "inquiry as stance," developed over many years by Marilyn Cochran-Smith, the senior author of this chapter, in collaboration with her co-author and colleague, Susan Lytle (Cochran-Smith & Lytle, 1993, 1999a, 1999b, 2009). As Cochran-Smith and Lytle (1999a, 2009) have suggested, to call inquiry a "stance" is to regard inquiry as a worldview, a critical habit of mind, and a dynamic and fluid way of knowing and being in the world of educational practice that carries across professional careers and educational settings. This contrasts sharply with inquiry constructed as a time- and place-bounded classroom research project, as a method, or as a set of steps for solving problems. When inquiry is a project or set of steps, the message is that inquiry is something turned off and on at given points in time, which positions practitioners as receivers of information with little space for questioning the ways problems are posed in the first place or for problematizing the terms and logic of larger frames. Fundamental to inquiry as stance is the idea that educational practice is not simply instrumental in the sense of figuring out how to get things done, but also (and more importantly) it is social and political in the sense of deliberating about what gets done, why to get it done, who decides, and whose interests are served.

There are four key dimensions to Cochran-Smith and Lytle's (2009) concept of inquiry as stance, which encompass particular perspectives on knowledge, practice, communities, and democratic purposes. First, the view of knowledge central to inquiry as stance rejects the prevailing assumption that two kinds of knowledge— formal and practical—account for the universe of knowledge types for understanding teaching, learning, and schooling. When inquiry is a stance, local knowledge generated by practitioner researchers is also considered one of the keys to educational transformation. The second dimension is an expanded and transformative view of practice. Rather than accepting the dominant view that juxtaposes theory and research with practice, Cochran-Smith and Lytle suggest that practice is deeply contextual, theoretical, and interpretive, informed by teachers' nuanced sensemaking about learners, content, and pedagogy. The third dimension is communities, which are the primary mechanisms for enacting inquiry as stance. In the communities central to the concept of inquiry as stance, practitioners work together to uncover, articulate, and question their own assumptions about teaching, learning, and schooling, thus functioning as catalysts for change (Wood, 2007). Cochran-Smith and Lytle's final dimension of inquiry as stance is democratic purposes and social justice ends. They emphasize that learning communities are not simply tools for more effectively producing the nation's labor force. Instead, when practitioner researchers take an inquiry stance, they are engaged in work both within and against the system—an ongoing process of problematizing fundamental assumptions about the purposes of the existing education system and raising difficult questions about educational resources, processes, and outcomes.

Understanding Inquiry and Teacher Leadership: Five Cases of Practice

In the remainder of this chapter, we offer five mini-cases of teachers who lead through inquiry in a variety of ways, which we characterize as learning to lead, leading each other, leading inside to outside, leading with, and leading over a lifetime. Consistent with the basic premises of inquiry as stance and with the idea that practitioner researchers are not simply consumers of other people's knowledge, but generators of local knowledge, for each case, we stay as close as possible to the words and perspectives of the teachers by drawing on their writing or on excerpts from interviews with them. Except where indicated, all teachers' and school names are real and used with permission.

Learning to Lead: Gary McPhail

We describe the work of Gary McPhail as an illustration of what we call "learning to lead." By this we mean that for Gary, and for some other teachers who begin with a critical, questioning stance and who engage in inquiry early on, learning to lead can be a natural outgrowth of learning to teach.

When Gary began teaching, he was the only male on the faculty of his elementary school, a situation which brought gender issues into sharp relief almost immediately. Being referred to as the "token male" prompted him to focus on equity issues almost from the beginning. As he put it:

> This [term] infuriated me . . . but got me thinking about . . . what inequities I [saw] in a school setting that didn't have male representation on its faculty. . . . I had never been passionate about issues of gender inequity before. My own role as a male educator in female dominated territory propelled me to take a stance to begin to question things.
>
> (McPhail, 2013)

Over a number of years teaching first grade at Shady Hill School in Cambridge, Massachusetts, Gary noticed that the personal narrative focus of the first-grade writing curriculum (e.g., stories about day-to-day life experiences) was particularly appealing to many girls and not so appealing to many boys in his classes (McPhail, 2009a; 2009b). He wrote:

> As a male teacher in the primary grades, I have often been struck by the fact that my female students tend to both perform at a higher level with regard

to writing proficiency and are far more interested in writing than my male students. . . . Many boys come to realize that their interests are not worthy of being taught in the classroom and as a result come to view writing as more a female activity than male.

(McPhail, 2009b)

Through his analysis of research by others (e.g., Newkirk, 2002; Smith & Wilhelm, 2002), Gary learned that the "gendered" achievement gap in writing was an educational phenomenon nationally and internationally. Based in part on the interests of his students, he created a new year-long writing workshop curriculum that intentionally included some genres of writing he believed might appeal more to boys (e.g., action adventure stories), some that might appeal more to girls (e.g., personal narratives), and some new to everybody (e.g., letter writing). As he implemented the new curriculum, Gary systematically collected all the students' written work, whole class and individual student interviews, ongoing classroom observation notes concentrating on several boys who had differing levels of writing skill, and biweekly entries in a teacher research journal.

He found that, for the most part and with some overlap across genders, the boys and girls in his class did indeed have differing literacy interests (McPhail, 2011). But, even more important, he discovered that both boys and girls performed at higher levels when they were writing in genres that were of interest to them. With the new writing curriculum, some boys who had never performed well began to blossom. Some girls who had always excelled at personal stories struggled, but also learned additional skills when writing in new genres. Eventually, Gary presented his research at conferences, in print, and in university classes. Just as importantly, he shared what he had found with his entire school faculty and invited others to join him in a teacher inquiry group focused on students' writing. The inquiry group worked together for several years to interrogate their writing practices, unpack their assumptions about boys and girls, and create a new schoolwide writing curriculum that responded to the interests of all writers.

Currently, Gary is the head of the Meadowbrook Lower School in Weston, Massachusetts. He was hired in part because of his experience engaging in teacher research as a form of leadership. He is now facilitating four faculty inquiry groups related to gender and how boys and girls experience school differently, concentrating on gender and literacy, gender and STEM (science, technology, engineering, math), gender and behavior/expectations, and gender and the outdoor classroom. Each group has formed its own research questions and planned for design and implementation. Gary is now involved in linking the inquiry work at Meadowbrook to the efforts of a national center on gender and schooling. As he suggested, "My charge is now about putting teacher inquiry front and center because teachers are the best at asking the most relevant emic questions because they are there with the students in the moment, seeing the learning, struggles, and successes in action" (McPhail, 2013).

Leading Each Other: Gill Maimon

From almost the beginning of her career as a teacher, Gill Maimon was aware of the importance of engaging in systematic inquiry with other teachers about the complicated issues of teaching, learning, and schooling. Here we present Gill's case as an example of what we call teachers "leading each other," or the process of like-minded practitioners meeting regularly in the context of inquiry communities to construct local knowledge together. In these communities, teachers lead each other by rotating formal leadership roles, conjoining their experience and understandings, and generating new collective insights. Margaret Himley (1991) suggested that the purpose of this kind of shared leadership is to "open up intellectual space [and] to understand more fully and richly a shared focus of interest . . . through language and the power of collective thought" (p. 59).

Gill began teaching in a large, urban school district more than 15 years ago, after completing a university-based teacher preparation program that supported the development of inquiry in its teacher candidates. Like most first-year teachers, Gill struggled upon entering the classroom. While she felt supported by some of her colleagues who shared materials and offered a listening ear, she received no meaningful support from her officially designated "mentor," nor was her critical stance welcomed by her principal. In what she told us was an act of "desperation" about how to improve her practice as a teacher, Gill began to attend the Philadelphia Teachers Learning Cooperative (TLC), a practitioner inquiry group she had learned about during her teacher preparation program (Cochran-Smith, 2012).

TLC is a teacher-led, cross-school group of educators committed to improving the learning and life chances of students in urban schools. The group has met weekly in each other's homes for more than 35 years. Influenced strongly by Patricia Carini and her colleagues at the Prospect Archive and Center for Education and Research, TLC employs a variety of reflective protocols that use observation and description of students, classrooms, and practices to improve teaching and learning in its members' classrooms. According to El-Haj (2003), who spent 5 years observing and working with the TLC, the inquiry engaged in by the group "has supported TLC practitioners to speak back to policies and practices that perpetuate, rather than redress, educational inequalities" (p. 818).

Along with her supportive school colleagues, Gill credited the TLC group as "her saving grace" during her first year of teaching (Cochran-Smith, 2012, p. 114). When her first teaching placement failed to support her in ways she found meaningful, Gill turned to the TLC group, which viewed asking questions and admitting uncertainties as signs of learning, not signs of failure (Cochran-Smith, 2012). Part of what TLC did was to expose the normally shadowed, private happenings of teachers' individual classrooms and open them up to the collective eyes and ears of other committed practitioners. As Gill pointed out, when teachers lead each other in planned ways, their collaborative inquiries not only deepen each individual teacher's capacity to "see" their own students, but also lead teachers to capture, examine, and act upon their unique knowledge as practitioners, which Gill views as "essential to efforts to improve educational opportunities for all children" (Maimon, 2013). Gill's subsequent years as a teacher in urban elementary schools were profoundly shaped by her experiences in TLC and other contexts where she and her colleagues lead each other through detailed descriptions of students, sometimes emotionally charged journal reflections, and honest, often raw, exposure to the joys and heartbreaks of teaching. Gill reflected:

> Observing and describing my work in writing, and in work with communities of teachers, is what has sustained me. Teacher networks [are of profound] importance. Looking together with like-minded practitioners increases what I am able to see. I both literally and figuratively open my classroom door to other observers.
>
> (Maimon, 2013)

From Gill's perspective, it is this ability to see her students through the eyes of other colleagues that has sustained and nourished her over her career as a teacher. Describing collaborative inquiry through the TLC and other teacher learning communities, Gill emphasized the importance of local knowledge to school change and to challenging inequities. She wrote:

> [The fact that] educational inequities abound is itself a reflection of a systemic crisis of perception. It is for this reason that knowledge like mine, which is the product of intentional work to attend to the particular, is essential to efforts to improve educational opportunities for all children. Practitioner inquiry should be a cornerstone to providing equitable educational access for all.
>
> (Maimon, 2013)

Leading, Inside to Outside: Kirstin McEachern

Our next mini-case examines the work of Kirstin McEachern, focusing on an inquiry she engaged in over several years about gender issues at her all-boys, single-sex school. We use this work to illustrate what we call "leading, inside to outside." By this phrase, we mean that from the outset of her inquiry about gender, Kirstin, like some other practitioner researchers, was not interested only in the potential "inside" influence the local knowledge her inquiry generated might have on the participants and culture of her own school site. Rather she was also centrally motivated by the contribution her insider research might make "outside"—in the sense of connecting with and informing important issues related to gender and schooling more broadly. Kirstin's inquiry illustrates how teachers lead by engaging in inquiry intended to generate local knowledge that also provides new perspectives on larger, more public issues.

Kirstin has been an English and journalism teacher for more than a dozen years in several settings. She currently teaches at a single-sex boys school:

> For the past 10 years, I have taught English at "St. Albert's Preparatory School," an all-boys suburban secondary school serving over 1,200 students in the Northeast. As a teacher at this school, I am conflicted about the value of single-sex education for boys. The school regularly speaks of fostering a brotherhood among the students, and I see evidence of this on a daily basis. However, St. Al's has not been an easy place to work. My own experience is consistent with research studies that have found all-boys schools to be more sexist environments than all-girls schools (Lee, Marks, & Byrd, 1994), where students generally afford their female teachers less respect than their male teachers. (Keddie, 2007; Keddie & Mills, 2007; Robinson, 2000)
>
> (McEachern, 2013c)

From the beginning of her inquiry, Kirstin was interested in leading, inside to outside, as indicated by her comments. These comments were prompted by discussion among the members of her inquiry group in the university course where she began the gender inquiry 5 years earlier. The group had read several critiques of practitioner research by academics who treated it as second class and had discussed these critiques both online and in class:

> [One member of our group] asserted that teacher researchers' priority is to their sites of practice, so acceptance in the academy should not be an issue. I could not disagree more, as I see teacher research benefiting a site of practice *and* contributing to the field. My project might have larger, direct benefits to my school, but that does not mean that I don't care if the work is well regarded in the university world. . . . What does it mean that I'm not satisfied with influencing my site of practice alone? Why can't I seek to benefit both worlds?
>
> (McEachern, 2008)

In keeping with this initial intention, Kirstin has presented her ongoing inquiry in multiple regional and national research conferences, and is currently finishing a doctoral dissertation based on her inquiry, which she intends to publish. Kirstin stated:

> [My study] addresses some of the silences in the literature on how gender construction occurs in single-sex classrooms, specifically in a Catholic, all-boys secondary school. [I ask]: As the classroom teacher, what role do I play in the construction of gender in my classroom via my pedagogy, and interactions and relationships with my students? How do students construct

gender? How do these constructions of gender shape the ways my students and I as a teacher navigate the school outside of our classroom?

(McEachern, 2013b)

As this book goes to press, Kirstin's study is nearing completion. She has found that:

> Despite stated goals of inclusivity and acceptance of all, and a mission of caring for the whole person, the larger culture of the school fosters exclusivity and reinforces stereotypical gender norms that limit community members. . . . In this way, they create a "brotherhood" that is ostensibly inclusive of the school community and bonds them together, but actually alienates a significant portion of the community.
>
> (McEachern, 2013a)

Kirstin's analysis reveals that all the members of the school community—to greater or lesser degrees—are complicit in creating the "brotherhood" through three key processes: silencing of dissenting voices, "othering" of girls and women, and exclusion of them from the fraternity. Kirstin's analysis has the potential to help change the culture of her school. In addition, because she is a teacher committed not only to her own school, but also to gender equity writ large, Kirstin's case demonstrates the power of leadership when inside inquiry moves outside to influence other contexts as well.

Leading With: Victoria Ekk

Although school administrators are sometimes pitted against the teachers they lead, we present the case of Victoria Ekk as an example of a principal who "leads with" the teachers in her school. She described herself "as an insider working with other insiders, namely teachers, parents, and students" (Ekk, 2013, p. 54). Victoria has been the principal of Southeastern, a large middle school in Massachusetts for 10 years, all of which have been influenced by the implementation of the far-reaching requirements of the No Child Left Behind Act of 2001 (NCLB, 2002). In her work as principal, Victoria has chosen to work alongside her teachers and community to navigate the stressful, confusing, and often maddening pressures of NCLB while simultaneously fostering a positive, joyful middle school for each of the 1,300 students who attend.

Southeastern Middle School is a suburban, traditionally high-performing middle school. As principal, Victoria wrote:

> I often experienced frustration and anxiety over the No Child Left Behind Act's (NCLB) increasingly negative influence on the school's reputation and morale. While the Commonwealth [of Massachusetts] consistently rated Southeastern

as very high in English language arts and high in mathematics, NCLB's rating, based on one group of students failing to meet proficiency targets, labeled the school in need of improvement in 2004, moved to call for corrective action in 2006, and recommended school restructuring in 2008. It seemed to me, a veteran of over 30 years in the education field, that the discrepancy between labels was confusing at best, distracting our staff from their strong commitment to build a professional, democratic, and positive school culture.

(Ekk, 2013)

Victoria had always envisioned herself as a teaching principal, one who is "a promoter of the professionalism I believed should be recognized by all" (Ekk, 2011). Struggling with the imposed mandates of NCLB, Victoria chose to enroll in a doctoral program in curriculum and instruction in order to model constant learning and reflection for her teaching staff. Through her doctoral work, Victoria was exposed to research, theory, and practice that helped guide her as a collaborative leader. During her tenure, Southeastern Middle School teachers participated in a series of schoolwide reform efforts to address the needs of all of the students. As a principal, Victoria worked alongside her staff in small learning communities engaged in collaborative inquiry cycles around issues of access, curriculum, assessment, and school culture. These learning communities demonstrate Victoria's commitment to leading *with* teachers. She wrote:

Lit by the fire of Paulo Freire's *Pedagogy of the Oppressed* (1970/2000), my desire to fight for socially just educational change has fueled my drive to uphold teacher empowerment as an ethical and moral duty, which has resulted in the provision of increased opportunities for shared decision-making and professional collaboration. As a teacher/learner, I am grounded in the tradition of practitioner research, rooted in constructivism, and informed by the concept of "inquiry as stance" (Cochran-Smith & Lytle, 2009). Thus I take on the task to use inquiry as stance to ask, answer, analyze, and re-ask questions that investigate what has been happening at Southeastern, inviting the voices of fellow Southeastern educators who are contributing to the work.

(Ekk, 2013)

While the pressures of NCLB have not disappeared, and the mandates of Race to the Top are looming ever closer, Victoria's inquiry with teachers has proven to be somewhat of an antidote to the common response of simplifying and standardizing the work of teaching in order to increase student scores on a single test. Instead, teachers are working with Victoria to create a dynamic learning environment that models inquiry and reflection as integral parts of school culture. Recently, a math teacher named Janie approached Victoria to tell her about a new teaching method she was experimenting with in her classroom. Janie said she "want[ed] to make sure they [were] all focused on thinking math, not just getting problems done" (Ekk, 2011). Janie's focus on developing inquiry in her students, not just increasing their test scores, reflects the cultural shifts that were the result of intensive collaborative inquiry at Southeastern—the direct result of Victoria "leading with" her teachers.

Leading Over a Lifetime: Diane Waff

We use the case of Diane Waff as an illustration of leading from an inquiry stance over a lifetime. Over a professional lifetime, there may be changes in positions and contexts as well as shifts—sometimes dramatic—in educational policy and the political climate. For example, when Diane began teaching in the Philadelphia public schools in 1985, it was just after the publication of *A Nation at Risk* (National Commission on Excellence in Education, 1983), and there was an intense focus on increasing teacher professionalism. This was nearly two decades before No Child Left Behind legislation and only the beginning of the now "common sense" assumption that teacher quality is the key to the health of a nation's economy. This was also well prior to the now firmly entrenched neoliberal, market-based approach to educational reform (Cochran-Smith & Fries, 2011). One constant in Diane's professional work, across almost three decades and in the face of enormous changes in education policy and practice, was an inquiry stance.

Initially, Diane was a special education teacher who supported the learning of students with moderate special needs. Early in her career, she was part of an inquiry community that profoundly influenced her. As Diane recounts, in one inquiry group session, each group member had written a journal entry about issues of practice. Diane wrote about her experience using a short story about a young woman who was raped by a man who offered her a ride home. Diane noted that in response to this story, her students seemed engaged in new ways. She wrote:

> As my colleagues and I discussed my lesson, I began to understand just how much I had been using the "special education" label as an excuse for not nurturing intellectual curiosity and a desire for further learning. This began a transformation in attitude for me as well as my students, when I began to intellectually engage and challenge them.
>
> (Waff, 1994)

As the inquiry group discussion continued, another teacher's journal entry called attention to the way ability grouping and tracking in mathematics were reproducing societal social stratification patterns and inequalities. Diane commented on the group's response:

> Why didn't we know Black and Latino students were being routinely routed to general math? Why hadn't we noticed the composition of the

advanced math classes? What other kinds of tracking were taking place at the school? These kinds of questions politicized our work and caused all of us to think critically about the need for continuous dialogue about teaching and learning.

(Waff, 1994)

The group's response to this entry was intense and signified a turning point in their work collectively and for Diane individually.

After 10 years in the classroom, Diane took on an administrative position, serving as the coordinator of teaching and learning, designing professional development and coordinating school/classroom-based support for 700 teachers in nine schools. Later she became vice principal of a large high school in Trenton, New Jersey, and she is currently a teacher educator at the University of Pennsylvania, working with experienced teachers in the public schools as they tackle the new Common Core State Standards (CCSS, 2010). Not surprisingly, they are working from an inquiry perspective.

One of the frustrations of the group was the scripted curriculum that had been put into place in Philadelphia in order to meet NCLB adequate yearly progress requirements, which "took away much of the classroom teachers' autonomy and did little to promote the development of teachers' knowledge of content, pedagogy, and assessment" (Waff, 2012, p. 2). The hope was that the CCSS' higher expectations for students would move things beyond the tightly scripted curriculum. Working with the group, Diane established what she referred to as "inquiry routines," which "helped teachers examine and reframe their teaching of literacy and mathematics" (Waff, 2012, p. 3). Diane commented, "The resulting re-conceptions of literacy teaching and learning generated a changed teacher repertoire of classroom practices and resulted in . . . higher student engagement and self-direction, higher expectations for student performance, and more frequent collaboration between and among teachers and students" (Waff, 2012, p. 5).

In commenting on the role of inquiry in her professional life and her own engagement with inquiry communities over the professional lifespan, Diane wrote:

My inquiry into the constraints and possibilities of school reform from my vantage point as an African American female teacher/leader/administrator working in the midst of school change initiatives [has centered] on . . . the influence teacher research and participation in teacher inquiry communities have had on my practice and my understanding of the social and cultural contexts that have shaped who I am, what I believe, and how I interact in the world both as a teacher and as a colleague.

(Waff, 2008)

Inquiry and Teacher Leadership: Concluding Comments

In the current era of educational standardization, it is common for schools to attempt to implement "best" practices in ways that exclude teachers' reflections and insights from educational conversations and replace teachers' local knowledge with scripted curricula, multiple choice tests, and national standards. As our five mini-cases show, there are exceptions to this situation. In local pockets of resistance all over the country, teachers and other educators are pushing back against highly prescriptive curricula that they believe are not in the best interests of the students they teach. Some of these teachers, such as those in our cases, are leading through inquiry. And they are clearly having an impact—in each of their contexts, teaching, learning, and schooling are improving as a result of inquiry-centered leadership; and the local knowledge they are disseminating through presentations and writing beyond their own schools is also having a positive impact.

Understood in the ways we have presented it here, an inquiry perspective values local knowledge, teacher and student exploration of ideas and content, and community building as a foundation of shared learning, values that cannot be supported in a tightly controlled educational system. Standardization often leads teachers, students, and schools away from the personal and local. If leadership is understood as a process of joining educational stakeholders together to move toward a shared vision, inquiry is a necessary partner on that journey. Moving from scripted and standardized education to student- and community-centered education requires leaders to question many aspects of schooling and to join with others to reimagine it in a new way.

These five mini-cases suggest five different, yet overlapping, examples of how the dynamic relationship between inquiry and teacher leadership actually plays out in schools and other contexts where teachers work together for change. In varying ways, all five examples highlight the importance of local knowledge, meaningful and purposeful practice, learning communities, and the democratic purposes and social justice ends of education (Cochran-Smith & Lytle, 2009). By leading with and through inquiry, these educators are creating an alternate, and profoundly hopeful, vision of educational leadership and its potential effects on all students.

References

Ball, D. L., & Forzani, F. M. (2009). The work of teaching and the challenge for teacher education. *Journal of Teacher Education, 60*(5), 497–511.

Brill, S. (2009, August 31). The rubber room: The battle over New York City's worst teachers. *The New Yorker.* Retrieved from http://www.newyorker.com/reporting/2009/08/31/090831fa_fact_brill

Bryk, A. (2008, November 19). *The future of education research: An address by Anthony S. Bryk.* Washington, DC: American Enterprise Institute.

Cochran-Smith, M. (2005). The new teacher education: For better or for worse? *Educational Researcher, 34*(7), 3–17.

Cochran-Smith, M. (2012). A tale of two teachers: Learning to teach over time. *Kappa Delta Pi Record, 48*(3), 108–122.

Cochran-Smith, M., & Fries, K. (2011). Teacher education for diversity: Policy and politics. In A. F. Ball & C. A. Tyson (Eds.), *Studying diversity in teacher education* (pp. 339–362). Lanham, MD: Rowman & Littlefield.

Cochran-Smith, M., & Lytle, S. L. (1993). *Inside/outside: Teacher research and knowledge.* New York, NY: Teachers College Press.

Cochran-Smith, M., & Lytle, S. (1999a). Relationships of knowledge and practice: Teacher learning in communities. *Review of research in education, 24,* 249–305.

Cochran-Smith, M., & Lytle, S. L. (1999b). The teacher research movement: A decade later. *Educational Researcher, 28*(7), 15–25.

Cochran-Smith, M., & Lytle, S. L. (2009). *Inquiry as stance: Practitioner research for the next generation.* New York, NY: Teachers College Press.

Common Core State Standards Initiative. (2010). *Common Core State Standards for English language arts & literacy in history/social studies, science, and technical subjects.* Washington, DC: National Governors Association Center for Best Practices and Chief State School Officers.

Education Equality Project. (2008). Stand for children [Website]. Retrieved from http://stand.org/national/two-education-champions-join-forces

Ekk, V. B. (2011, April). *Unintended consequences: A practitioner researcher's study of the impact of No Child Left Behind on middle school special education students.* Paper presented at the annual meeting of the American Educational Research Association, New Orleans, LA.

Ekk, V. B. (2013). *The long roller coaster ride: Ten years with NCLB, AYP, and RTTT—An insider's perspective.* Unpublished doctoral dissertation, Boston College, Boston, MA.

El-Haj, T. R. A. (2003). Practicing for equity from the standpoint of the particular: Exploring the work of one urban teacher network. *Teachers College Record, 105*(5), 817–845.

Freire, P. (2000). *Pedagogy of the oppressed* (30th anniv. ed., M. B. Ramos, Trans.). New York, NY: Bloomsbury Academic. (Original work published 1970)

Himley, M. (1991). *Shared territory: Understanding children's writing as works.* New York, NY: Oxford University Press.

Keddie, A. (2007). Issues of power, masculinity, and gender justice: Sally's story of teaching boys. *Discourse: Studies in the Cultural Politics of Education, 28*(1), 21–35.

Keddie, A., & Mills, M. (2007). *Teaching boys: Developing classroom practices that work.* Crows Nest NSW, Australia: Allen & Unwin.

Kumashiro, K. K. (2012). *Bad teacher! How blaming teachers distorts the bigger picture.* New York, NY: Teachers College Press.

Lee, V. E., Marks, H. M., & Byrd, T. (1994). Sexism in single-sex and coeducational independent secondary school classrooms. *Sociology of Education, 67*(2), 92–120.

Maimon, G. (2013, April). *Images of inquiry: Why we need practitioner research to challenge educational inequities.* Paper presented at the annual meeting of the American Educational Research Association, San Francisco, CA.

McEachern, K. (2008). *Advanced classroom research portfolio.* Unpublished manuscript, Boston College, Boston, MA.

McEachern, K. P. (2013a). *Dissertation assertions.* Unpublished manuscript, Boston College, Boston, MA.

McEachern, K. P. (2013b). *Welcome to his-land: Make your own map.* Unpublished manuscript, Boston College, Boston, MA.

McEachern, K. P. (2013c, April). *"You're the (wo)man!" A female teacher researcher's study of an all-boys, Catholic high school.* Paper presented at the annual meeting of the American Educational Research Association, San Francisco, CA.

McPhail, G. (2009a). Teaching the "bad boy" to write. *Learning Landscapes, 3*(1), 89–104.

McPhail, G. (2009b). The "bad boy" and the writing curriculum. In M. Cochran-Smith & S. Lytle (Eds.), *Inquiry as stance: Practitioner research for the next generation* (pp. 193–212). New York, NY: Teachers College Press.

McPhail, G. (2011). *Finding freedom as a writer: Genre, gender and identity in a first grade writer's workshop.* Dissertation, Boston College, Boston, MA.

McPhail, G. (2013, April). *Images of inquiry: Why we need practitioner research to challenge educational inequities.* Paper presented at the annual meeting of the American Educational Research Association, San Francisco, CA.

National Commission on Excellence in Education. (1983). *A nation at risk: The imperative for educational reform.* Washington, DC: U.S. Department of Education.

Newkirk, T. (2002). *Misreading masculinity: Boys, literacy and popular culture.* Portsmouth, NH: Heinemann.

No Child Left Behind (NCLB) Act of 2001, Pub. L. No. 107-110, §115, Stat. 1425 (2002).

Robinson, K. (2000). "Great tits, Miss!" The silencing of male students' sexual harassment of female teachers in secondary schools: A focus on gender authority. *Discourse: Studies in the Cultural Politics of Education, 21*(1), 75–90.

Smith, M. W., & Wilhelm, J. D. (2002). *"Reading don't fix no Chevys": Literacy in the lives of young men.* Portsmouth, NH: Heinemann.

Thomas, E. (2010, March 5). Why we must fire bad teachers. *Newsweek.* Retrieved from http://mag.newsweek.com/2010/03/05/why-we-must-fire-bad-teachers.html

Waff, D. (1994). Girl talk: Creating community through social exchange. In M. Fine (Ed.), *Chartering urban school reform: Reflections on public high schools in the midst of change* (pp. 192–203). New York, NY: Teachers College Press.

Waff, D. (2008, March). *An insider voice: Leading as a teacher.* Paper presented at the annual meeting of the American Educational Research Association, New York, NY.

Waff, D. (2012, April). *Hybrid learning in a school-university partnership: Teacher research integrating common core standards, scripted curricula, and innovative practice.* Paper presented at the annual meeting of the American Educational Research Association, Vancouver, British Columbia, Canada.

Wood, D. (2007). Teachers' learning communities: Catalyst for change or a new infrastructure for the status quo? *Teachers College Record, 109*(3), 699–739.

17

MEASURING THE IMPACT OF TEACHER LEADERS

Pamela Scott Williams
Joni M. Lakin
Lisa A. W. Kensler

With the clamor for quality education, the general public has placed increasing pressure on schools to improve performance. Stagnating state-level standardized test results are drawing serious attention among practitioners, educational stakeholders, and policymakers in the educational sector. Students in the United States do not fare well in international comparisons (Darling-Hammond, 2009; Dillon, 2010). When explaining the underperformance of students, scholars have identified the critical role that principals and school leadership play in facilitating student academic success (Hallinger & Heck, 1996; Ross & Gray, 2006; Witziers, Bosker, & Kruger, 2003). However, individual principals play many different roles in schools and typically cannot lead and manage alone (Olson, 2008). In response to these concerns, teacher leadership has been widely acknowledged by anecdotal evidence and qualitative studies as a potentially powerful tool for raising student achievement (Katzenmeyer & Moller, 2001; York-Barr & Duke, 2004). Brown and Medway (2007) explained that teacher leaders may directly support their colleagues in improving instruction, or they may exert some indirect pressure in that direction. The continuous improvement of instruction resulting from pressure or support from teacher leaders is linked to improvement of students' performance and learning (Nasser-Abu Alhija & Fresko, 2010).

The array of research on this subject strongly suggests that teacher leadership is a possible solution to low achievement (Leithwood, 2003; Ryan, 1999; Snell & Swanson, 2000). In fact, the educational field is already responding to this possible link by developing more teacher leadership degrees (Rebora, 2012), and the National Board for Professional Teaching Standards (nbts.org) is in the process of developing National Board Teacher Leadership Certification. Despite this effort to increase teacher leadership, there is limited research directly connecting teacher leadership to student achievement, as well as a dearth of quantitative studies on the subject. Additional studies are required for a conclusive argument for the effect of teacher leadership on student achievement (Harris & Muijs, 2004). As York-Barr and Duke (2004) concluded in their extensive review of teacher leadership literature, "There are many well-reasoned assertions and even some data-based inferences about the effects of teacher leadership on student achievement, but little evidence to support these claims" (p. 285). Thus, the field needs further quantitative studies on the subject to more broadly establish the relationship between teacher leadership and student achievement.

This chapter will present a new tool for measuring teacher leadership. We begin the chapter with a brief summary of the foundational literature and then describe the development of the tool, Teachers' Perception of Teacher Leadership (TPTL) Survey. We end the chapter with a discussion of the impact of teacher leadership and future research opportunities.

Summary of the Foundational Literature

The purpose of this chapter is to illuminate the need for research on teacher leadership and then present a theory-driven, quantitative survey instrument to be used in future research. A review of the literature revealed that only a handful of instruments have been used to measure teacher leadership and that they present mixed findings. See Table 17.1 for a summary and Scott Williams (2013) for a full review of this literature. The literature indicates that although qualitative studies have highlighted the integral role of teacher leadership in students' achievement (Ryan, 1999), quantitative studies relating teacher leadership to students' performance are quite limited and fail to consistently show strong or statistically significant relationships between teacher leadership and student achievement. The limitations associated with the quantitative studies cast doubts on their findings. In the existing research, many surveys used too few items to measure teacher leadership and/or used measures of teacher leadership that were indirect. As a result, it remains unclear whether the mixed results have been due to methodological issues or indicate a true nonsignificant relationship between teacher leadership and student achievement (York-Barr & Duke, 2004).

Even though the six studies outlined in Table 17.1 all measure teacher leadership, they are strikingly different in many ways. First, each study used various constructs to measure teacher leadership. For example, Louis, Dretzke, and Wahlstrom (2010) and Angelle and Dehart (2010) included shared leadership as a construct of teacher leadership while the other four did not. Similarly, the number of facets chosen to define teacher leadership varied from two to seven. By the same token, the number of items that measured teacher leadership were as few as three (Leithwood, Jantzi, & Steinbach, 1999) to as many as 37 (Scott Williams, 2013). Moreover, the constructs chosen as dimensions of teacher leadership ran the gamut from collegiality to trust in principal to sharing leadership. Another difference is in the selection of theories or frameworks. While Taylor and Bogotch (1994) and

TABLE 17.1 Summary of Teacher Leadership Studies Using Survey Instruments

Study	Theory/Framework	Number of Items	Factors/Constructs/Dimensions	Results
Leithwood, Jantzi, and Steinbach (1999)	Distributed leadership	3	Perceived influence of teacher and principal leadership in the school	Nonsignificant relationship between teacher leadership and student engagement.
Taylor and Bogotch (1994)	None specified	19	Associated technology Managerial Instructional materials Core technology	Nonsignificant relationship between teacher leadership and student achievement.
Louis, Dretzke, and Wahlstrom (2010)	Theory assumes that the teacher leaders' effects on students are almost entirely indirect	6	Focused instruction Teachers' professional community Shared leadership Instructional leadership Trust in principal	Shared leadership indirectly related to student achievement through the effects of professional community and focused instruction. Student math achievement scores were significantly associated with focused instruction, professional community, and teachers' trust in the principal.
Angelle and Dehart (2010)	None specified	17	Sharing expertise Sharing leadership Supra-practitioner Principal selection	Findings indicate significant differences between elementary school teachers and middle/high school teachers, teachers with a bachelor's degree and teachers with graduate degrees, and formal teacher leaders and teachers in no leadership position.
Ngang, Abdulla, and Mey (2010)	Katzenmeyer and Moller (2001) model of teacher leadership	25	Developmental focus Recognition Autonomy* Collegiality Participation Open communication* Positive environment*	Significant relationship ($R^2 = 0.565$) between three dimensions of teacher leadership and self-reported measure of school effectiveness.
Scott Williams (2013) (Current study)	Teacher Leadership Consortium	37	Collaborative culture Research Professional learning Instruction and student learning Student learning Outreach and collaboration Assessments and data	Nonsignificant relationship between teacher leadership and student achievement.

* Ngang et al. (2010) found that only these three factors appeared in their item-level analyses

Angelle and Dehart (2010) did not have an underpinning theory or framework, the other studies chose varying theories or frameworks. Moreover, the studies also differ in their results: The results of Leithwood et al. (1999), Taylor and Bogotch (1994), and Scott Williams (2013) show nonsignificant and the other three show significant relationships to measures of student achievement.

It is evident just from the literature that research on teacher leadership is inconsistent and inconclusive; therefore, more research is needed. A fair amount of the inconclusiveness of quantitative studies on teacher leadership and student achievement possibly stems from survey development. Therefore, a theory-driven, quantitative survey instrument was developed using the framework of the Teacher Leadership Exploratory Consortium (2011). The framework is comprised of seven major domains that interact with one another to define teacher leadership. The seven domains build a pathway to the final outcome of high student achievement. The main goal of these model standards is "to stimulate dialogue among stakeholders of the teaching profession about what constitutes the knowledge, skills, and competencies that teachers need to assume leadership roles in their schools, districts, and the profession" (Teacher Leadership Exploratory Consortium, 2011, p. 3). The final standards, which followed a format similar to that of the Interstate School Leaders Licensure Consortium State Standards for School Leaders, came up with a set of "domains" that specifically define the critical context and dimensions of teacher leadership. The Teacher Leader Model Standards (Teacher Leadership Exploratory Consortium, 2011) domains are as follows:

- Domain I: Fostering a Collaborative Culture to Support Educator Development and Student Learning
- Domain II: Accessing and Using Research to Improve Practice and Student Learning
- Domain III: Promoting Professional Learning for Continuous Improvement
- Domain IV: Facilitating Improvements in Instruction and Student Learning
- Domain V: Promoting the Use of Assessments and Data for School and District Improvement
- Domain VI: Improving Outreach and Collaboration with Families and Community
- Domain VII: Advocating for Student Learning and the Profession

Developing the Survey

To fill the gap in research investigating the relationship between teacher leadership and students' performance, we developed a new measure of teacher leadership, the Teachers' Perception of Teacher Leadership Survey. A copy of the survey is included in Appendix 17.A at the end of this chapter. The TPTL Survey is a 37-item instrument that measures teachers' perceptions of teacher leadership in their schools. We developed four to six items to sample each of the seven domains discussed in the previous section. The Teacher Leadership Model Standards and two existing surveys informed the development of our survey items: the Leadership Capacity Staff Survey (Lambert, 2003) and the Leadership Development for Teachers Survey (Katzenmeyer & Moller, 2001).

All 37 items are simple descriptive statements. The appropriateness of item content was established through two rounds of expert reviews, cognitive interviews, and a field test, while the level of reliability of the survey results was determined by examining internal consistency (Desimone & Le Floch, 2004). The response scale asks teachers to indicate the extent to which each statement characterizes all of the teachers in their school (not simply their individual practice) on a 5-point Likert-type scale. The scale includes the following choices: None = 1; Few = 2; Some = 3; Most = 4; All = 5. The overall score for the TPTL Survey is simply the mean score of all the items; thus, the mean score represents the teacher's average perception of the extent to which teachers in the school exhibit teacher leadership.

Collecting the Data

We collected data from 630 teachers drawn from 49 different schools in Alabama. We also gathered the publicly available results of the Alabama Reading and Math Plus (ARMT+) for the 2011–2012 school year (the annual accountability assessment in Alabama) for participating schools so that we could investigate the relationship between perceived presence of teacher leadership and the achievement of the students. The study sought to address three research questions:

1. Does the TPTL appear to measure seven distinct factors of teacher leadership?
2. What is the relationship between teachers' perception of their schools' leadership and average student achievement in schools?
3. What is the relationship between teacher leadership and student achievement when controlling for school socioeconomic status and school size?

Establishing Content Validity for the TPTL Survey

The appropriateness of the TPTL Survey's item content was established in three ways, providing evidence that survey results can be interpreted with an acceptable level of validity, meaning that the survey actually measures teacher leadership. First, a group of four expert educational researchers in the field of teacher leadership provided feedback on the quality of survey items during item development. Expert judgment and feedback related to the design of the instrument is an essential part of establishing content validity (Lissitz & Samuelsen, 2007).

The second method of assessing item appropriateness was cognitive interviews. Three teachers were asked to participate in cognitive interviews to detect unanticipated misinterpretations of the survey statements. Cognitive interviews involve interviewing potential respondents to learn how specific statements are interpreted so that higher-quality data can be gathered and the validity and reliability of surveys can be improved (Desimone & Le Floch, 2004). Finally, the revised survey was pilot-tested with a group of five teachers. Pilot testing is an effective way of detecting errors of content, form, and clarity by giving the survey to respondents similar to ones who would be included in the actual study under realistic administration conditions (Sireci, 2007). We revised the survey items as suggested by the expert, interviewees, and pilot study participants.

Establishing the Factor Structure of the TPTL Survey

Our first research question asked about the seven domains of teacher leadership. Although the framework suggested seven distinct domains, we needed to explore whether or not the statistical analyses indicated that the domains were measuring different aspects of teacher leadership or actually measuring a more unified conception of teacher leadership. To explore this question, we examined the descriptive statistics and interrelationships of survey items. The results indicated perhaps too much agreement among the seven domains. All of the domain scores were highly correlated with the total score (r ranged between 0.97 and 0.99). Thus, the seven domains of teacher leadership did not seem to actually measure different aspects of teacher leadership; rather, they measured a single construct. Exploratory factor analysis confirmed this conclusion by showing a strong single factor underlying the 37 item responses. These results indicate that, although the items were derived from a theory with seven domains, a much shorter survey of leadership skills could be used to get similar reliability and a single dimension of teacher leadership.

Exploring Correlations Between Teacher Leadership and Student Achievement

In response to our second research question, "What is the relationship between teachers' perception of their schools' leadership and average student achievement in schools?" we calculated school-level averages of teacher responses to the survey. We also gathered publicly available information on the percent of students in each school who were proficient in reading and math. The results indicated a nonsignificant relationship between perceived level of teacher leadership and student achievement in mathematics and reading ($r = -0.076$; $p = 0.303$; and $r = -0.035$; $p = 0.406$, respectively).

To assess the hypothesis that teacher leadership predicts reading and mathematics percent proficient after controlling for the effects of socioeconomic status

(SES) and school size (the third research question), a hierarchical multiple regression analysis was employed to test the relative influence of teacher leadership when schools were statistically equated in terms of SES and school size. Results indicated that neither SES nor school size significantly predicted student achievement as measured in this study. Thus, our hypothesis about the relationship between these variables was not supported. A number of factors could have potentially masked the relationship between teacher leadership and math and reading percent proficient. We explore these explanations next.

Interpreting the Results

If the United States is to compete in the global market, then there is a need to increase student achievement by improving the quality of instruction. Cultivating teacher leadership has become a popular school improvement strategy to meet this goal. Theory indicates that teacher leadership should be related to student achievement, but quantitative findings have been mixed. Of the studies on teacher leadership and student achievement, several found that teacher leadership is not related to student achievement on standardized tests or to teachers' reports of student academic performance (Leithwood et al., 1999; Scott Williams, 2013; Taylor & Bogotch, 1994), while others have found positive relationships (Angelle & Dehart, 2010; Louis et al., 2010; Ngang, Abdulla, & Mey, 2010).

Consistent with other studies (e.g., Taylor & Bogotch, 1994), we did not find a statistically significant relationship between our new measure of teacher leadership and student performance on state math and reading tests. One possible explanation for the lack of correlation between teacher leadership and student achievement may relate to our dependent variable, the ARMT+ percent proficient score. Although individual student tests are scored on a continuous (and likely normally distributed) scale, the publicly available ARMT+ results are simply the percent of students in a school who tested proficient or better. The public data also showed that many Alabama schools had high percent proficient, leading to a distribution of achievement scores that is severely nonnormal (which makes statistical analyses less interpretable). Averaging percent proficient scores across grade levels within schools may also have eliminated grade-level effects of teacher leadership programs. Collectively, these measurement concerns highlight the importance of dependent variable selection in research. In our case, this was the only publicly available measure. Future studies should explore using other measures of student achievement, including proxies for achievement, such as student engagement, and scale score averages, which are not always publicly available.

Although survey research is efficient and often effective, self-reported data contain several potential sources of bias that should be noted as potential limitations of this study: over- or underreporting of behaviors, social desirability bias, and misunderstandings of the questions or statements (Brutus, Aguinis, & Wassmer, 2013). The survey in this study could be laden in particular by social desirability bias, meaning the participants responded to questions with answers that reflected their desire to be "right" more than to be honest (van de Mortel, 2008). These biases may be what led to an unexpected finding in our data, that low-performing schools showed higher averages on the teacher leadership measure. In other words, teachers from lower-performing schools tended to report higher levels of school-wide teacher leadership practice. It is quite possible that teachers from under-performing schools felt social pressure to report that their practices were in line with research-based practices; they may have been inclined to report that they were doing more of what they knew they should be doing rather than what they actually were doing. We believe that teachers in the lower-achieving schools may be (intentionally or unintentionally) protective of themselves and their colleagues in their responses, not wanting to place blame on their faculty. Such a potential response bias would inhibit the efforts to find a relationship between teacher leadership and school achievement. An alternative explanation could be that these lower performing schools have active teacher leadership initiatives in place (that is, teachers were reporting accurately) and that there is a substantial lag time between teacher leadership initiatives and achievement test score improvement. Further research is clearly needed to better understand the relationship between teacher leadership and student achievement.

Implications of Teacher Leadership for Promoting Student Achievement

Even with a new theory-driven measure of teacher leadership and high-quality student achievement data, there may not be a direct relationship between teacher leadership and student achievement. This would not mean that teacher leadership is unimportant or unrelated to student performance. It may simply mean that the impact of teacher leadership on student achievement is indirect, rather than direct. An indirect relationship means that teacher leadership may be linked through others factors with student achievement. For example, the seven domains of the Teacher Leader Model Standards do not measure teachers' direct work with students. The standards also do not capture teachers' pedagogical strategies or relationship quality with students. Rather, the standards seek to measure the degree to which teachers provide influence on the conditions and behaviors in the classroom that then have a more direct impact on student learning, performance, and achievement.

Teacher leadership has been operationalized using a wide number of dimensions and construct definitions in the literature. This has led to mixed results that do not conclusively inform current efforts to promote teacher leadership and its impact on student achievement. The inconsistency of results in studies measuring teacher leadership and student achievement should propel us to take a look at extended efforts to develop quantitative measures of teacher leadership. Although we did not have access to precise achievement data to fully and effectively test the relationship between teacher leadership and student achievement in our study, we do believe we have presented an instrument worthy of further development and testing. There are strengths to the TLTP Survey, including a strong theoretical grounding and rigorous survey development procedures, as well as opportunities for refinement. Our recommendation for future researchers is to explore other methods of measuring teacher leadership to reduce issues arising from self-reporting.

References

Angelle, P., & Dehart, C. (2010, May). *Measuring the extent of teacher leadership: Construction, testing, and factors in the teacher leadership inventory.* Paper presented at the annual meeting of the American Educational Research Association, Denver, CO.

Brown, K. E., & Medway, F. J. (2007). School climate and teacher beliefs in a school effectively serving poor South Carolina (USA) African-American students: A case study. *Teaching and Teacher Education, 23*(4), 529–540.

Brutus, S., Aguinis, H., & Wassmer, U. (2013). Self-reported limitations and future directions in scholarly reports: Analysis and recommendations. *Journal of Management, 39*(1), 48–75.

Darling-Hammond, L. (2009). President Obama and education: The possibility for dramatic improvements in teaching and learning. *Harvard Educational Review, 79*(2), 210–223.

Desimone, L. M., & Le Floch, K. C. (2004). Are we asking the right questions? Using cognitive interviews to improve surveys in education research. *Educational Evaluation and Policy Analysis, 26*(1), 1–22.

Dillon, S. (2010, December 7). Top test scores from Shanghai stun educators. *The New York Times*, p. A1.

Hallinger, P., & Heck, R. H. (1996). Reassessing the principal's role in school effectiveness: A review of empirical research, 1980–1995. *Educational Administration Quarterly, 32*(1), 5–44.

Harris, A., & Muijs, D. (2004). *Improving schools through teacher leadership.* London, UK: Open University Press.

Katzenmeyer, M., & Moller, G. (2001). *Awakening the sleeping giant: Helping teachers develop as leaders* (2nd ed.). Thousand Oaks, CA: Corwin.

Lambert, L. (2003). *Leadership capacity for lasting school improvement.* Alexandria, VA: Association for Supervision and Curriculum Development.

Leithwood, K. (2003). Teacher leadership: Its nature, development, and impact on schools and students. In M. Brundrett, N. Burton, & R. Smith (Eds.), *Leadership in education* (pp. 103–117). Thousand Oaks, CA: Sage.

Leithwood, K., Jantzi, D., & Steinbach, R. (1999). *Changing leadership for changing times.* Buckingham, UK: Open University Press.

Lissitz, R. W., & Samuelsen, K. (2007). A suggested change in terminology and emphasis regarding validity and education. *Educational Researcher, 36*(8), 437–448.

Louis, K. S., Dretzke, B., & Wahlstrom, K. (2010). How does leadership affect student achievement? Results from a national US survey. *School Effectiveness and School Improvement, 21*(3), 315–336.

Nasser-Abu Alhija, F., & Fresko, B. (2010). Socialization of new teachers: Does induction matter? *Teaching and Teacher Education, 26*(8), 1592–1597.

Ngang, T. K., Abdulla, Z., & Mey, S. C. (2010). Teacher leadership and school effectiveness in the primary schools of Maldives. *Hacettepe University Journal of Education, 39,* 255–270.

Olson, L. (2008, April 16). Lack of school leadership seen as a global problem: OECD study finds too few candidates at a time when the roles have expanded. *Education Week, 27*(33), 8.

Rebora, A. (2012, October 17). Teacher-leader degree designed as a vehicle for career fulfillment. *Education Week, 32*(10), 1.

Ross, J. A., & Gray, P. (2006). School leadership and student achievement: The mediating effect of teacher beliefs. *Canadian Journal of Education, 29*(3), 798–822.

Ryan, S. A. (1999, April). *Principals and teachers leading together.* Paper presented at the annual meeting of the American Educational Research Association, Montreal, Canada.

Scott Williams, P. (2013). *Teachers' perception of the presence of teacher leadership and ARMT+ percent proficient in Alabama's public elementary schools: A correlation study* (Unpublished doctoral dissertation). Auburn University, Auburn, AL.

Sireci, S. G. (2007). On validity and test validation. *Educational Researcher, 36*(8), 477–481.

Snell, J., & Swanson, J. (2000, April). *The essential knowledge and skills of teacher leaders: A search for a conceptual framework.* Paper presented at the annual meeting of the American Educational Research Association, New Orleans, LA.

Taylor, D. L., & Bogotch, I. E. (1994). School-level effects of teachers' participation in decision making. *Educational Evaluation and Policy Analysis, 16*(3), 302–319.

Teacher Leadership Exploratory Consortium. (2011). *Teacher leader model standards.* Retrieved from http://teacherleaderstandards.org/downloads/TLS_Brochure.pdf

van de Mortel, T. F. (2008). Faking it: Social desirability response bias in self-report research. *Australian Journal of Advanced Nursing, 25*(4), 40–48.

Witziers, B., Bosker, R. J., & Kruger, M. L. (2003). Educational leadership and student achievement: The elusive search for an association. *Educational Administration Quarterly, 39*(3), 398–425.

York-Barr, J., & Duke, K. (2004). What do we know about teacher leadership? Findings from two decades of scholarship. *Review of Educational Research, 74*(3), 255–316.

APPENDIX 17.A

Questionnaire

Directions: We would like to ask about your perceptions of your school and the role of teachers in your school. Please use the scale provided to indicate the option that best reflects your agreement with the statement.

	None	Few	Some	Most	All
Domain I: Fostering a Collaborative Culture to Support Educator Development and Student Learning					
Teachers at my school respond to their own and others' needs as they advance shared goals.					
Teachers at my school talk with other teachers about the curriculum.					
Teachers at my school create an inclusive culture where diverse perspectives are welcomed.					
Teachers at my school share successful instructional strategies.					
Teachers at my school consult with other teachers when addressing student learning challenges.					
Domain II: Accessing and Using Research to Improve Practice and Student Learning					
Teachers at my school use research-based practices.					
Teachers at my school gain new knowledge through reading professional articles.					
Teachers at my school participate in action research to improve student learning.					
Teachers at my school learn about educational research from reading journal articles or books.					
Teachers at my school facilitate analysis of research to improve student learning.					

	None	Few	Some	Most	All
Domain III: Promoting Professional Learning for Continuous Improvement					
Teachers at my school actively support the professional learning of other teachers by coaching and/or mentoring.					
Teachers at my school work together with school administrators to plan professional learning that is linked to school/district improvement goals.					
Teachers at my school engage in professional learning experiences aligned with their needs.					
Teachers at my school direct professional learning activities that correlate with the school's improvement goals.					
Teachers at my school seek support from professionals who have specialized expertise (e.g., special educators, media specialist, reading coach, ESL specialist) to design learning experiences.					
Teachers at my school model effective instructional practices for colleagues.					
Domain IV: Facilitate Improvements in Instruction and Student Learning					
Teachers at my school engage in reflective dialogue to improve teaching.					
Teachers at my school use school based student test results to identify opportunities to improve instruction and student learning.					
Teachers at my school use instructional strategies that promote diversity and equity in the classroom.					
Teachers at my school observe other teachers' classroom instruction to improve student learning.					
Teachers at my school connect with other educators around the globe to improve teaching and learning.					
Domain V: Promoting the Use of Assessments and Data for School and District Improvement					
Teachers at my school engage colleagues in conversations about student learning data.					
Teachers at my school facilitate collaborative interpretation of data results (e.g., data meetings, data rooms).					
Teachers at my school use assessment data results to promote changes in instructional practices.					
Teachers at my school use a variety of data (e.g., systematic observation, information about learners, research) to evaluate the outcomes of teaching and learning.					
Teachers at my school use data to differentiate instruction.					

(Continued)

	None	Few	Some	Most	All
Domain VI: Improving Outreach and Collaboration With Families and Community					
Teachers at my school model and/or teach effective communication and collaboration skills with families.					
Teachers at my school develop a shared understanding among colleagues of the diverse educational needs of families.					
Teachers at my school collaborate with families to develop comprehensive strategies to address the diverse educational needs of students.					
Teachers at my school collaborate with community members to develop comprehensive strategies to address the diverse educational needs of students.					
Teachers at my school work with colleagues to promote ongoing systematic collaboration with families.					
Domain VII: Advocating for Student Learning and the Profession					
Teachers at my school advocate for the profession in contexts outside of the classroom (local, state, or national level).					
Teachers at my school advocate for access to professional resources (e.g., financial support, human, and other material resources).					
Teachers at my school advocate for the rights and needs of students.					
Teachers at my school advocate for teaching and learning processes that meet the needs of all students.					
Teachers at my school share information with colleagues within and/or beyond the district regarding how state policies can impact classroom practices.					
Teachers at my school work in partnership with organizations engaged in researching critical educational issues (e.g., universities, Alabama Education Association [AEA]).					

18

THE IMPACT OF MENTORS AS TEACHER LEADERS IN INDUCTION PROGRAMS

Elizabeth A. Wilkins

Between 40% and 50% of teachers leave the profession by the fifth year. There is considerable evidence that among new teachers who stay, mentoring and induction efforts have an influence on whether beginning teachers stay or leave (Ingersoll, 1997; Ingersoll & Smith, 2003; Johnson & The Project on the Next Generation of Teachers, 2004; MetLife, 2012). Over the past three decades, mentoring has been the most frequently offered support to beginning teachers (Moir, 2009; U.S. Department of Education, 2004–2005). In an induction program, mentoring is a complex developmental process where one mentor or a team of mentors supports and guides the beginning teacher in becoming an effective educator and career-long learner. Mentoring also entails accelerating the beginning teacher's development to best address the complexities and demands of teaching.

In 2008, states began to create induction standards to guide the development and delivery of programs, which included mentor selection, assignment, and professional development. These standards brought attention to the important role mentors play in supporting beginning teachers and implicitly how mentors can serve as teacher leaders. Being a mentor to a beginning teacher does not automatically make one a teacher leader. Rather, a mentor becomes a teacher leader when he or she positively influences the beginning teacher's practice as well as purposely enlists support from colleagues and other members of the school community to improve the mentee's teaching and learning practices with the aim of increased student learning and achievement (York-Barr & Duke, 2004).

In the same year the induction standards were created, a national consortium developed teacher leader standards to delineate the knowledge, skills, and competencies that teachers need in order to assume leadership roles in schools. The mentoring process and the influence mentors can have on beginning teachers align with the view that "teacher leadership is a powerful strategy to promote effective, collaborative teaching practices in schools that lead to increased student achievement . . . and a dynamic teaching profession for the 21st century" (Teacher Leadership Exploratory Consortium, 2011, p. 3). Given the growing attention in the education profession about mentoring and teacher leadership, this chapter focuses on the role and influence of mentors as teacher leaders in inducting beginning teachers to the profession.

Background Information on Mentoring and Teacher Leadership

Mentoring programs for beginning teachers first emerged during the educational reform era of the 1980s. Before 1984, only eight states implemented policies requiring induction and mentoring programs. Over time, interest in delivering these programs steadily grew. By the early 1990s, 26 additional states offered support to beginning teachers, and half of those states created policies requiring mandated programming. By the turn of the 21st century, a strong upward trend of 83% of new teachers in public schools participated in these support programs (Ingersoll, 2006; Strong, 2009).

Different types of mentoring have also evolved over time with a paradigm shift away from the buddy system toward mentors who are purposely selected, prepared, and matched to a particular beginning teacher. When mentoring programs first began, it was not uncommon to be assigned a mentor who served more as a "buddy" (i.e., an informal and unstructured peer relationship requiring no specific roles/responsibilities) than one who helped strengthen the beginning teacher's instructional practice. Since that time various types of mentoring have emerged. One such type is the traditional, one-on-one support for a beginning teacher typically provided by a veteran teacher from the same content area or grade level and who has received formal preparation to be a mentor (Odell & Huling, 2000). A second type is called "intensive mentoring," mentoring focused on improving beginning teacher professional practice and student learning through collaboration, reflection, and inquiry into practice. This kind of mentoring occurs during regular visits over extended periods of time (Moir, Barlin, Gless, & Miles, 2009; Stanulis & Floden, 2009). A third type of mentoring involves "mentoring teams"; this approach entails groups of individuals in various roles providing support and professional development to a beginning teacher. In this approach, mentoring tasks are divided among several educators who share the mentoring responsibilities based on their individual strengths (Sweeny, 2008). All types of mentoring, except for the "buddy" approach, provide the opportunity for mentors to serve as teacher leaders, when the emphasis is on improving teaching and learning practices with the aim of increased student learning and achievement.

In 2008, various states created standards for high-quality induction programs to assist schools and districts in supporting new teachers. California and Illinois led this initiative (e.g., California Commission on Teacher Credentialing, 2008; Illinois State Board of Education, 2008). Explicit in the standards were specifics about the mentoring component in induction programs. The standards codify the components into mentor selection, assignment, and professional development. Likewise, the Teacher Leader Standards "stimulate dialogue among stakeholders . . . [as to] what constitutes the knowledge, skills, and competencies that teachers need to assume leadership roles in their schools, districts, and the profession (Teacher Leadership Exploratory Consortium, 2011, p. 3). Properly defined, a teacher leader is someone who influences his or her colleagues and other members of the school community to improve teaching and learning practices with the aim of increased student learning and achievement (York-Barr & Duke, 2004). To show the relationship between being a teacher leader and being a mentor, all three sets of standards are listed in Table 18.1.

TABLE 18.1 Side-by-Side Comparison: Teacher Leader Standards and State Induction Standards Focused on Mentoring

Teacher Leader Standards	California Induction Standards	Illinois Induction Standards
Domain I: Fostering a Collaborative Culture to Support Educator Development and Student Learning **Domain II:** Accessing and Using Research to Improve Practice and Student Learning **Domain III:** Promoting Professional Learning for Continuous Improvement **Domain IV:** Facilitating Improvements in Instruction and Student Learning **Domain V:** Promoting the Use of Assessments and Data for School and District Improvement **Domain VI:** Improving Outreach and Collaboration with Families and Community **Domain VII:** Advocating for Student Learning and the Profession (Teacher Leadership Exploratory Consortium, 2011)	**Standard 4: Mentor Selection** A rigorous mentor selection process is required. **Standard 5: Mentor Training** Foundational training and ongoing professional development for mentors is required. **Standard 6: Mentor Assignment and Caseload** Criteria include how mentors are assigned to beginning teachers, keeping caseloads manageable, and providing release time for mentors. (California Commission on Teacher Credentialing, 2008)	**Standard 5: Mentor Selection and Assignment** Mentors are recruited, selected, and assigned using a comprehensive strategy that includes a clearly articulated, open process and specific criteria that are developed by and communicated to all stakeholder groups. **Standard 6: Mentor Professional Development** Mentor professional development provides a formal orientation and foundational mentor training before they begin their work with beginning teachers and should continue over the course of the mentor's work with beginning teachers. Mentors have time, supported by the program, to engage in this mentor learning community and are consistently supported in their efforts to assist beginning teachers in their development, with a focus on student learning. (Illinois State Board of Education, 2008)

A Statewide Study: Mentors as Teacher Leaders in Induction Programs

To better understand how mentors can serve as teacher leaders, a statewide study was conducted. A mixed-method approach was used to answer six research questions.

1. How are mentors prepared for their role (i.e., selection, training, and accountability)?
2. What kind of mentoring activities are provided and not provided to beginning teachers?
3. What other supports are provided to beginning teachers to enhance mentoring?
4. Is mentoring a predictor of beginning teacher self-efficacy?
5. What do mentors cite as the successes they achieved through mentoring?
6. What are the barriers or obstacles to becoming a successful mentor?

The population for the study included state-funded induction programs chosen from a competitive proposal process provided by the Illinois State Board of Education. Programs that received funding were from varied settings (i.e., urban, suburban, and rural) as well as configurations (e.g., community unit districts, single school districts, consortiums, and partnerships with Regional Offices of Education and universities). Both beginning teachers (n = 1,973) and mentors (n = 1,323) involved in 39 state-supported induction programs participated in the study.

Data were collected using a simple descriptive approach. A one-shot survey gathered mentor and beginning teacher knowledge about induction and mentoring. The two survey instruments (created, validated, and used by SRI International) contained both closed- and open-ended items (Weschler, Caspary, Humphrey, & Matsko, 2010). The Mentor Survey solicited information about (a) Mentor Background, (b) Mentor Training, (c) Support Provided to Teachers, and (d) Perceived Growth of Mentees in Various Dimensions of Teaching; whereas the Beginning Teacher Survey gathered information about (a) Demographic Background, (b) School Context, (c) Induction Supports Received, and (d) Teacher Efficacy. Because of the mentors and beginning teachers' comfort with, ease of, and accessibility to technology, the survey was distributed online. In April, at the close of the school year, all mentors and beginning teachers in the 39 funded induction programs received the survey with electronic reminders to encourage participation. The response rate for the mentors and beginning teachers was 77% and 61%, respectively. Analysis of the quantitative data from the surveys used descriptive and inferential statistics. The qualitative data analysis used open, axial, and selective coding (Corbin & Strauss, 2008). The categories that emerged were distinct and were evaluated by multiple researchers with expertise in qualitative methodology.

Lessons Learned About Mentoring and Teacher Leadership

The following sections describe the role and influence of mentors as teacher leaders on beginning teachers.

Mentor Requirements

The most frequent requirement for mentor selection was that an individual had to complete a mentor training program prior to selection (49%). All other selection criteria occurred less often: minimum number of years (38%), formal application (34%), recommendation (21%), interview (14%), and classroom observation (13%). These findings reveal there is limited application of selection criteria, which also contradicts best practice, according to California Induction Standard 4 and Illinois Induction Standard 5.

Next, nearly all of the mentors (96%) attended a professional development session to prepare for their role and responsibilities. Of those, only 67% received that training before they met their beginning teachers. Even fewer (58%) received ongoing professional development throughout the school year to help them support their mentees. These data indicate that those who prepare mentors to support beginning teachers need to monitor when mentors receive their initial training and how often mentor professional development occurs during the school year. Both the California and Illinois standards encourage programs to provide consistent high levels of training.

There were very few requirements for holding mentors accountable for their work. Logging of mentoring hours (49%) and summaries of mentoring meetings (36%) were the two most reported requirements. Three other accountability measures existed but with a 12% or lower response: summary of mentoring goals, formative evaluation, and summary evaluation of target teacher. Neither the California nor the Illinois mentor standards address the issue of accountability; however, within the teacher–leader standards, Domains I and III implicitly address accountability through ongoing collaboration and continuous improvement.

Mentoring Activities With Beginning Teachers

Mentor and mentee pairs spent time together in a wide range of activities. The most common mentoring activity was discussing instructional issues and problems, which were experienced by 50% of the beginning teachers. The next most common activity for mentors and beginning teachers was talking about the strengths and/or needs of specific students (41%). Discussing assessment data and sharing materials were the mentoring activities experienced less frequently, 28% and 26%, respectively.

There were certain mentoring activities that a considerable number of beginning teachers never experienced (Figure 18.1).

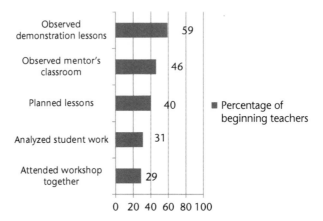

FIGURE 18.1 Mentoring Activities Never Experienced

These results, particularly the large percentage of beginning teachers who never had the opportunity to see their mentors demonstrate lessons, observe their mentor's teaching, jointly plan lessons, analyze student work, or attend a workshop together, suggest a lack of mentor/mentee activities with high potential for improving instructional practice. Unfortunately, school schedules do not traditionally allow for adequate release time during the school day for mentors and beginning teachers to work together to observe instruction and discuss strategies for assessment and pedagogical improvements.

Other Supports Provided to Beginning Teachers to Enhance Mentoring

Although mentoring is the support provided most often to beginning teachers, there were other supports offered as part of induction programming. The major support that beginning teachers sought to enhance mentoring was a professional network. Such a network provided camaraderie as well as a forum for the beginning teachers to share instructional ideas, voice successes, and share fears. Specifically, time to interact with other teachers occurred the most on a monthly/weekly basis and was considered moderately to extremely valuable by more than three quarters of the beginning teachers. In contrast, two other supports identified as enhancing beginning teacher development and support occurred only infrequently: (1) beginning teachers meetings, workshops, and seminars; and (2) release time.

Mentoring and Beginning Teacher Self-Efficacy

The composite variables used for the regression analyses in Weschler et al. (2010) predicted teacher self-efficacy. The combined composite variable predictors accounted for 23.9% variance in teacher self-efficacy, and all were individually significant predictors of teacher self-efficacy: $b = 0.17$, $p < .001$, school context; $b = 0.04$, $p = .014$, intensity of mentoring; $b = 0.11$, $p < .001$, focus on instruction; and $b = -0.1328$, $p < .001$, need for support. All composite variables were positively related to teacher self-efficacy except need for support. Analysis of residuals of the full regression model indicated homoscedasticity and normality. These data indicate that intensity of mentoring, in combination with other variables, is a predictor of beginning teacher self-efficacy.

When asked about their professional growth, the beginning teachers identified three areas where they felt they grew the most: instructional techniques (70%), reflection on teaching practice (67%), and creation of a positive learning environment including classroom management (65%). Although self-reported data are limiting, they do provide insight into what the beginning teachers believed they gained from working with their mentors and from participating in their respective induction programs.

Successes Achieved Through Mentoring

One open-ended question asked mentors to describe noteworthy successes they achieved through mentoring. Of the 499 responses (Table 18.2), the majority (74%) reflected Growth and Workplace Relationships.

Subthemes (e.g., classroom management, instructional strategies, professional skills, confidence, and mutual growth) from coded responses helped the researchers to better understand what the mentors meant by Growth. Following are examples of how two mentors shared these feelings:

> Protégé continued to evolve as a first-year teacher and classroom management skills improved from first semester to second semester. I believe that he has matured to the point as a teacher where I don't have the daily talks I had in the beginning of the school year.

> My mentee finally realized he did not need to keep talking louder to present his information. When I would observe his class formally or just outside his room from the hall, he would have students talking and he would just get louder talking over them. I convinced him to begin the second semester differently—lower voice, higher expectations of respect from students—and it worked! He is no longer so loud that you can hear him all the way down the hall and through the wall.

TABLE 18.2 Noteworthy Successes Achieved Through Mentoring

Themes	Number of Responses	Percentage of Responses
Growth	242	48%
Building Workplace Relationships	130	26%

In addition to growth, the theme of Workplace Relationships emerged from the data. Collegial friendship, increased collaboration, and support/trust were sub-themes of workplace relationships. Below are some representative comments shared by the mentors:

> It brought me closer to a beginning teacher and made me realize what challenges new teachers are faced with.

> I feel like I have developed good rapport with my mentee, and I know she feels comfortable discussing anything with me—personal or professional, formal or informal.

Collectively, mentors saw development in their own practice by changing the lens through which they viewed their own work. Professional communication was usually at the heart of all improvement. These findings also revealed that being a mentor requires a genuine interest in helping beginning teachers, a practice that often resulted in an overwhelming feeling of pride and joy.

Barriers or Obstacles to Successful Mentoring

A total of 750 responses were provided about barriers and obstacles. The majority of the responses (66%) reflected time and mentor/mentee match (Table 18.3).

Because Time was such a large barrier, the responses were broken down into four subthemes: balancing professional responsibilities, limited opportunity for collaboration, limited time for observations, and scheduling conflict. Two mentors described the theme of time this way:

> There is very little time to interact during the school day with my target teacher. We are all overburdened with responsibilities.

> When you teach in a full-time position and then have to plan for your own classroom and meet with the others, it does become overwhelming.

The second largest barrier was mentor/mentee match. The subthemes included location, content area/grade level, and number of assigned mentees. One mentor shared her barrier thus:

> Finding time to meet with the new teacher being in a separate building. I believe that it is very difficult to have a positive experience for a new teacher when I am in a different building.

TABLE 18.3 Barriers and Obstacles Faced in Becoming a Successful Mentor

Themes	Number of Responses	Percentage of Responses
Time	277	37%
Mentor/Mentee Match	217	29%

Another mentor described a different type of obstacle in this way:

> I found it difficult at times to target my teacher's weaknesses. I would make a suggestion and he would not try it and that was frustrating to follow up with questioning as to why he did that.

These findings reveal that mentors want to support their new teachers by having ample time to plan, collaborate, and observe. Proximity and content area/grade level matches create opportunities for more successful mentor/beginning teacher relationships. However, increased workloads and professional responsibilities leave mentors little time to spend and work with new teachers.

Discussion

This study demonstrated that beginning teachers received support from and valued collaboration with their mentors. These professional relationships often took the form of collegial exchanges focused on improving instruction and student learning by investigating problems. This finding was evident through activities like discussing instructional issues and problems, and talking about the strengths and/or needs of specific students. Additionally, more than 80% of the beginning teachers worked in schools where they could seek and share advice about instructional issues (i.e., a school environment akin to a professional learning community). However, most of the beginning teachers never had the opportunity to see their mentors demonstrate lessons, observe their mentor's teaching, jointly plan lessons, analyze student work, or attend a workshop, all of which are activities strongly associated with improving instructional practice. Undoubtedly, without school schedules that reflect a belief in the importance of these activities, implementation of highly valued instructional supports cannot occur.

Quality, ongoing professional learning entails creating, valuing, and sustaining a community of collaboration. In this study, mentors readily used their knowledge and experience to promote an environment of collegiality, trust, and respect that focused on continuous improvement for beginning teachers as well as for themselves. The mentors could readily see growth and workplace relationships that resulted from their interactions with beginning teachers. According to York-Barr and Duke (2004), these interactions and relationships entail modeling, encouraging professional growth, and facilitating teacher learning through organization-wide processes. Additionally, mentoring, as a form of teacher leadership, is intended to draw upon the expertise of inservice teachers to not only support and accelerate the development of beginning teachers, but also to influence the school context in which all teachers work. As teacher leaders, these mentors advanced a community of both collaboration and continuous improvement for all teachers.

In reflection on the Teacher Leader Standards, there are clear connections among the roles, responsibilities, and actions of these mentors and how their efforts contributed to the profession through their leadership. Five questions frame the remainder of this discussion to enhance the conversation about mentors as teacher leaders. These questions also support the purpose of the Teacher Leader Standards (2008): "to stimulate dialogue among stakeholders in the teaching profession about what constitutes the knowledge, skills, and competencies that teachers need to assume leadership roles in their schools, district, and the profession" (p. 3).

Question 1: How could mentor selection and professional development be modified to enhance teacher leadership?

The most frequent requirement for being selected was to complete a mentor training program prior to selection; however, fewer than 50% of the mentors reported doing so. Equally concerning was the fact that a mere 58% received ongoing professional development to support their mentee in light of explicit induction standards about providing such training. Likewise, these limited experiences for mentors run counter to two of the Teacher Leader Standards. Domain I explicitly addresses how teacher leadership entails fostering a culture to support educator development as well as understanding the principles of adult learning (which is essential in working with beginning teachers). Additionally, in Domain IV, a teacher leader is cognizant of the need to be a continuous learner. Clearly, modifications to mentor selection and professional development are needed in order to be better aligned with the tenets of the Teacher Leader Standards. That is, for mentors to be as well prepared as possible, initial preparation and ongoing professional development need to occur much more frequently.

Question 2: What teacher leader qualities shared by mentors with beginning teachers are most valued?

The opportunities for ongoing communication, collaboration, and problem solving were teacher leader offerings that beginning teachers most valued in their mentors. New teacher self-efficacy was also impacted by the intensity of mentoring the beginning teachers received. In this study, the teacher leader qualities that were demonstrated by the mentors aligned with five of the seven domains. The mentors were able to support beginning teachers through (a) continuous improvement in instruction (Domain I); (b) systematic inquiry (Domain II); (c) knowledge that helps advance professional skills (Domain IV); (d) the use of assessment and other data to make informed decisions (Domain V); and knowledge of practices that support effective teaching and increase student learning (Domain VII).

Question 3: How could induction program delivery be modified to mitigate barriers and obstacles identified by the mentor in his or her role as teacher leader?

The mentors in this study unequivocally stated that they wanted to support their beginning teachers by having ample time to plan, collaborate, and observe. However, increased workload responsibilities, which limited their time to mentor, along with proximity and content area/grade level match with the mentee, were identified as barriers and obstacles. The Teacher Leader Standards are filled with action verbs such as uses *knowledge, models, facilitates*, and *collaborates*. For mentors to carry out these teacher leaders' actions, they need dedicated time to do so. Research also supports this point: To make a difference in teacher effectiveness, retention, or student achievement, mentors and beginning teachers need allocated time for discussions about instructional practice (Ingersoll & Strong, 2011; Strong, 2009). The most practical way for induction programs to meet this requirement for time is to approach mentor/mentee collaboration in the same way schools/districts are now making time available to establish professional learning communities that enhance professional development and focus on student learning.

Question 4: How does the role of the mentor as teacher leader impact beginning teachers' immersion into the professional community/school context?
In this study, the mentors provided the required one-on-one support, but they also modeled and encouraged the start of a professional network by nurturing cross-collaborative work with other colleagues. Beginning teachers valued this immersion into the school community. Time to interact with other teachers was found to occur on a regular basis, and more than three quarters of the beginning teachers reported that this collaborative support was moderately to extremely valuable. Domains I and III of the Teacher Leader Standards support this approach: fostering a collaborative culture to support educator development and promoting professional learning for continuous improvement. Unknowingly, these mentors were exhibiting qualities of teacher leaders by helping the beginning teachers become immersed in the professional community, which subsequently promotes a school culture where ongoing learning and development is embraced and expected.

Question 5: How could state induction standards be revised to better characterize mentors as teacher leaders?
Both the California and the Illinois Induction Standards could be revised to better characterize mentors as teacher leaders. One area of revision might be to simply utilize and integrate the phrase *teacher leader* into the language. The short descriptors found in Table 18.1 are explained in more detail in each state's respective induction documents. In those extended narratives, the qualities of teacher leadership and how those qualities align with mentoring could be expounded upon. For example, a mentor becomes a teacher leader when he or she positively influences the beginning teacher's practice as well as purposely enlists support from colleagues and other members of the school community to improve the mentee's teaching and learning practices with the aim of increased student learning and achievement.

Conclusion

In the words of the Teacher Leadership Exploratory Consortium (2011), "We must seek to use the expertise that already exists in the teaching force by ensuring opportunities for recognition and specific leadership roles for those who wish the added responsibilities that come with leadership" (p. 3). Mentors possess expertise, and they seek out added responsibility by agreeing to develop a relationship with beginning teachers to help them become both effective teachers in the classroom and active members of the school community. The Teacher Leader Standards describe the knowledge, skills, and competencies that teachers need in order to assume such a leadership role in schools. This study is but one step in justifying how serving as a mentor aligns with the domains that comprise the Standards. More research needs to be conducted to explore those connections and to continue dialogue among educational stakeholders as to how mentors do serve as teacher leaders. With almost half of all teachers leaving the profession in the first 5 years, the role and responsibilities of the mentor as teacher leader could not be more important. The process of mentoring creates timely opportunities for teacher leaders to support beginning teachers who are new to the profession through collaborative expertise.

References

California Commission on Teacher Credentialing. (2008). *Ensuring educator excellence: Induction program standards.* Retrieved from http://www.ctc.ca.gov/educator-prep/standards/Induction-Program-Standards.pdf

Corbin, J. M., & Strauss, A. (2008). *Basics of qualitative research* (3rd ed.). Los Angeles, CA: Sage.

Illinois State Board of Education. (2008). Illinois standards of quality and effectiveness for beginning teacher induction programs. Springfield, IL: Author. Retrieved from http://www.isbe.net/licensure/pdf/induction_mentoring_stds.pdf

Ingersoll, R. M. (1997). Teacher turnover and teacher quality: The recurring myth of teacher shortages. *Teachers College Record, 99*(1), 41–44.

Ingersoll, R. M. (2006, February). *Does teacher induction matter?* Presentation given at the Illinois New Teacher Collaborative Conference, Springfield, IL. Retrieved from http://intc.education.illinois.edu/resource/rod/does-teacher-induction-matter

Ingersoll, R. M., & Smith, T. M. (2003). The wrong solution to the teacher shortage. *Educational Leadership, 60*(8), 30–33.

Ingersoll, R. M., & Strong, M. (2011). The impact on induction and mentoring programs for beginning teachers: A critical review of the research. *Review of Educational Research, 81*(2), 201–233.

Johnson, S. M., & The Project on the Next Generation of Teachers. (2004). *Finders and keepers: Helping teachers survive and thrive in our schools.* San Francisco, CA: Jossey-Bass.

MetLife. (2012). *The MetLife survey of the American teacher: Teachers, parents and the economy.* Retrieved from http://www.metlife.com/assets/cao/contributions/foundation/american-teacher/MetLife-Teacher-Survey-2011.pdf

Moir, E. (2009). Accelerating teacher effectiveness: Lessons learned from two decades of new teacher induction. *Phi Delta Kappan, 91*(2), 14–21.

Moir, E., Barlin, D., Gless, J., & Miles, J. (2009). *New teacher mentoring: Hopes and promise for improving teacher effectiveness.* Cambridge, MA: Harvard Education Press.

Odell, S. J., & Huling, L. (Eds.). (2000). *Quality mentoring for novice teachers.* Washington, DC: Association of Teacher Educators. Indianapolis, IN: Kappa Delta Pi, International Honor Society.

Stanulis, R. N., & Floden, R. E. (2009). Intensive mentoring as a way to help beginning teachers develop balanced instruction. *Journal of Teacher Education, 60*(2), 112–122.

Strong, M. (2009). *Effective teacher induction and mentoring: Assessing the evidence.* New York, NY: Teachers College Press.

Sweeny, B. W. (2008). *Leading the teacher induction and mentoring program* (2nd ed.). Thousand Oaks, CA: Corwin; Reston, VA: National Association of Secondary School Principals.

Teacher Leadership Exploratory Consortium. (2011). *Teacher leader model standards.* Retrieved from http://teacherleaderstandards.org/downloads/TLS_Brochure.pdf

U.S. Department of Education. (2004–2005). *Become a teacher: Survival guide for new teachers* [Web content]. Washington, DC: Author. Retrieved from http://www2.ed.gov/teachers/become/about/survivalguide/message.html

Weschler, M. E., Caspary, K., Humphrey, D. C., & Matsko, K. K. (2010). *Examining the effects of new teacher induction.* Menlo Park, CA: SRI International.

York-Barr, J., & Duke, K. (2004). What do we know about teacher leadership? Findings from two decades of scholarship. *Review of Educational Research, 74*(3), 255–316.

Funding: This study was conducted through the financial support of the Illinois New Teacher Collaborative, Champaign, IL 61820.

19

THE IMPACT OF TEACHER LEADERS ON STUDENTS, COLLEAGUES, AND COMMUNITIES

Insights From Administrators

Sue Lutz Weisse
Suzanne M. Zentner

Every school has teachers who stand out: the teachers whom colleagues, students, and other staff members gravitate toward; the teachers who display their commitment to their students, school, and district in both action and word. These are the teachers who principals think epitomize the best the school has to offer. Here's an example we heard from a principal:

> We get many requests for tours. Parents move into the area and request a school tour when deciding which school would most benefit their child. We have the open enrollment option in our state. We get many requests from parents living in neighboring districts wanting to tour our school. When setting up these tours, I recommend that the children come and tour the school, too. Last year, I conducted over 25 such tours. I always try to take them into the grade-level classrooms of the child. Without fail, there is one teacher who will stop what her class is doing. She will ask the child his or her name, and the class will automatically welcome that child to the classroom by name in unison. The teacher then encourages the child to look around the room and say hi to the children. She makes the child feel comfortable. Without fail, when parents tour that teacher's classroom, they decide to come to our school. These small gestures have a huge impact. The teacher is not putting on a show for the parent; that is how the teacher is with everyone. Needless to say, her students achieve and also have a positive model of what a school community feels like. She is the leader in that classroom.

Teachers like these get the children whom other teachers "don't know what to do with." These teachers sit on school and district committees, stay current on research, and continuously revise their practices based on research. These teachers attend and support community events, work collegially with others, motivate students, and positively impact the school in a manner that extends beyond the walls of a classroom. They gain the respect of their students and colleagues through their words and actions (Leithwood & Riehl, 2005). These are the most effective teachers; these are the *teacher leaders* of the school.

The purpose of this chapter is to analyze the characteristics of a teacher leader and examine the impact of teacher leaders on individual students, colleagues, and communities. We surveyed 11 principals in the Midwest and asked them to share stories of teachers serving as leaders in their schools. The data reveal the far-reaching impact that these teacher leaders are having. In the following sections, we provide some vignettes and an analysis of these examples in light of the current definitions, standards, and research on teacher leadership.

What Is a Teacher Leader?

Much research has been conducted in the area of teacher effectiveness. It has been estimated that at least 7.5% of the variation in student achievement results directly from teacher quality, and the actual number could be as high as 20% (Rivkin, Hanuschek, & Kain, 2005). Teachers are the single most important school-related factor in a student's academic achievement.

According to the Teacher Leader Model Standards, which were designed by the Teacher Leadership Exploratory Consortium (2008), a teacher leader displays outstanding knowledge and behaviors in the following domains:

- Knows how to develop a collaborative culture and uses that knowledge to promote an environment of collegiality, trust, and respect that focuses on continuous improvement in instruction and student learning. This is true for both the classroom environment and the school environment.
- Stays current in latest research and best practice and uses that new knowledge to improve teaching and learning
- Understands new paradigms and uses the new knowledge to promote continuous and embedded staff development
- Remains a continuous learner, modeling reflective practice based on student results
- Works collaboratively with colleagues to ensure instructional practices are aligned to a shared vision, mission, and goals
- Understands that families, cultures, and communities have a significant impact on educational processes and student learning

In addition to the achievement in these domains, teacher leaders carry out other practices. They advocate for student needs and for practices that support effective teaching and increased student learning. They are engaged with and demonstrate commitment to the school and community. They model effective practices and share those practices with other teachers. They take the lead in developing a positive climate and a collective responsibility in a community environment, ultimately benefiting students (York-Barr & Duke, 2004). In this way, they transform lives and become individuals of influence and respect within the school, community, and profession. In short, they focus on the children, display a positive attitude, collaborate, and know current research. They employ that current research to ensure highly effective instructional practices; use assessment to drive instruction; and aspire to high achievement for colleagues, the school, the district, and the whole learning community.

The Impact of Teacher Leaders on Students

During an interview, a principal relayed the following scenario that describes the impact of a teacher leader. He stated:

> Janie (all names are pseudonyms), a third grader [in the teacher leader's class], came from a solid middle-class family. She had been in this school since kindergarten. Her parents read to her nightly and encouraged her to read by taking her to the library.
>
> Given her background and all her parental support, the expectation when Janie came to school was that she would meet every grade-level benchmark. However, at the end of her kindergarten year, Janie reached the benchmark, but only at the lowest acceptable tier. In first grade, her teacher had numerous conferences with Janie's parents, outlining specific reading concerns and suggesting further testing for possible ADHD. Janie missed the first-grade reading benchmark by one level; she was now officially "on watch" for academic concerns.
>
> During Janie's second-grade year, her teacher went on maternity leave in March. A long-term substitute teacher completed the year. This was also the first year that Janie fell three levels below the district benchmark for reading, ending second grade in the "urgent intervention" category.
>
> Janie was then placed with Mrs. Crowthers for third grade. Before school began that year, Mrs. Crowthers met with me [the principal], wanting to know more about Janie. She then contacted Janie's second-grade teacher and found out as much information as she could. She called Janie's parents and had them in for a conference, not to go over the previous years' results but to find out what Janie's strengths were and what motivated her, what "makes her tick."
>
> During the first week of school, Mrs. Crowthers met with Janie for a few minutes after school every day, talking to her, building a relationship. During these conversations, it became evident to Mrs. Crowthers that Janie loved her dog, Maxi. Building on that conversation, Mrs. Crowthers created a motivation plan to increase Janie's reading achievement: earning treats for her dog.

Every day, Mrs. Crowthers would meet with her most struggling readers, including Janie. Great instructional practices were employed and stressed. Individual lessons were planned for each struggling reader. In addition, Mrs. Crowthers continued to meet with Janie after school, sometimes reading, sometimes talking. Mrs. Crowthers also implemented Janie's reading motivation plan of giving Janie dog biscuits wrapped in brightly colored ribbons when she reached her reading goal for the week. Janie loved it, her parents loved it, and Maxi loved it. The best part is that for the first time in Janie's school years, she was above the grade-level reading benchmark.

This story illustrates the first of six teacher leader characteristics identified by Stronge (2007): *the teacher as a person.* This characteristic means that the teacher treats children as individuals, has a positive attitude, and talks to students individually. By focusing on Janie's individual interests rather than simply reacting to the expectations that had been put on her, Mrs. Crowthers was able to motivate Janie to put effort into an important skill. During our interviews with other administrators, we heard the same idea repeated multiple times. For example, an administrator stated, "I had one of our best teachers tell me, 'I don't want any child to feel invisible. I won't let that happen in my classroom or in this school.'" There are many other ways that teacher leaders impact students. Here is a story from a different school:

> One of the teachers did a poetry unit. As you know, poetry usually isn't one of the most popular units. This teacher made the unit enjoyable, and the students learned more than they ever thought they would about poetry. The students could define alliteration, personification, and hyperbole. The class was brainstorming, and they decided to have a Poetry Night. During recess and lunch, they decorated their room to look like a beatnik place. Someone brought in a pair of bongos. The class put together a book of their original poetry and then read their poems aloud to their parents. The next year, every teacher in that grade level did a Poetry Night.

This story illustrates *openness,* a characteristic defined by York-Barr & Duke (2004) as the teacher's ability to be adaptable, open-minded, creative, and open to exploring options to gather the necessary resources to improve the state of education. These same researchers focused on another key attribute: *work ethic.* Having a work ethic means being perseverant, resourceful, action oriented, committed, and passionate. The following quote exemplifies a teacher leader's work ethic:

> One teacher tutors a student for close to an hour every night after school because the child is not performing at grade level. The teacher also knows that this family, headed by a single mom, hardly has any money, so she

> bought groceries for this family and then put the mom in contact with some social service agencies. She told me she wasn't going to let anything get in the way of this child's learning.

These resourceful, creative, and passionate teacher leaders do not give up on any individual. This unwavering commitment is evident in the following account from an administrator:

> I had a third-grade teacher ask to have a certain student placed in his class. This student had made his [current] teacher's hair turn gray. When I asked him why he wanted this student, he said he heard the teacher talk about the student in a derogatory way. He approached the [current] teacher and told her that some kids are tougher than others but they all have goodness. You could tell by listening to [this third-grade teacher] speak that he was dumbfounded that any teacher would talk about a student that way. He told me that student had to know his current teacher didn't like him. This teacher told me he wanted to make his third-grade year the best year of his life. This teacher had no idea that the mom of that student did come and talk to me about her son knowing the teacher didn't like him.

Teacher leaders display the kinds of behaviors exemplified here many times throughout the school day. What may seem like incidental or small behaviors, when displayed consistently by teacher leaders, can have a big impact.

The Impact of Teacher Leaders on Colleagues in Their Schools

Katzenmeyer and Moller (2001) wrote, "Teachers who are leaders lead within and beyond the classroom, identify with and contribute to a community of teacher learners and leaders, and influence others toward improved educational practice" (p. 5). Under any definition of a teacher leader, a teacher leader has influence beyond the walls of a classroom (Crowther, Kaagan, Ferguson, & Hann, 2002; Danielson, 2006).

In the earlier story, for example, Mrs. Crowthers shared her success about Janie in a staff meeting. She did it in a way that conveyed to colleagues that anyone could motivate struggling learners and that what she did was just what all effective teachers do. After the meeting a few teachers gathered around her and continued the conversation about motivation.

The following anecdote is yet another example of how teacher leaders can positively influence academic outcomes and the school environment, not only in their own classes but in an entire school and perhaps an entire district. A principal of an elementary school recounted this story:

Mrs. Barth is well known throughout the school as being an informal leader. She is not one of those teachers who dominate meetings, but when she speaks, people listen. She often backs up her opinion with research. The children in her class excel academically. Her words and actions toward colleagues, children, and parents are [words] of respect and collaboration. She has a "we're all in this together" approach to any situation.

She is also a mother of two children. Her children's school was doing something called "PIE Time," and her children were experiencing great success, coming home and sharing the latest activities with her. Mrs. Barth wanted to infuse this type of enthusiasm into the students in her classroom, [but first she] and I arranged to visit [her children's] school.

PIE time stood for Prevention, Instruction, and Enrichment. The program was based on the model of professional learning communities (DuFour & Eaker, 1998). The premise was that when teachers work together, pool resources, collaborate about children, and use assessment to drive instruction, great things happen for children.

All children of a grade level were given a preassessment of a grade-level standard. Based on that assessment, groups were formed and instruction was individualized for that group. The *prevention* group consisted of the most struggling learners, the *instruction* group consisted of children who mastered the skill at a level of 80% or better, and the *enrichment* group consisted of children who mastered the skill at 100%. Children in each group made gains, the largest gains coming from the children in the prevention group.

Armed with the data, Mrs. Barth [worked] with her grade-level team to create a half-hour block of time devoted to working with small groups of children needing different and individualized instruction to make academic gains. The team created pre- and postassessments for a variety of grade-level skills. Individual lesson plans were made, and parents were notified. After a few months of this practice, the assessment data were impressive. All the children met grade-level benchmarks.

Mrs. Barth [soon] had the whole school buzzing about professional learning communities and collaborating as a team and as a whole school about practices that work and about having all children reach grade-level standards. The teachers requested more staff development about this professional learning community concept, and it was offered in the form of a summer institute. Nineteen teachers participated for 3 full days in training, all on their own time.

The next year, all grade levels scheduled a half hour of time to work with small groups based on assessment data. I reallocated resources so that each grade level had at least two teaching assistants assigned to their grade level during this half-hour block of time. Once again, the assessment results were outstanding. Teachers began sharing across grade levels and requesting more time to meet on a formal basis.

In the preceding story, Mrs. Barth epitomizes two other characteristics of effective teacher leaders: *teamwork* and *leadership*. Mrs. Barth exemplified teamwork by working with many different stakeholders and building positive relationships. To build such relationships, she had to engender trust, work well with colleagues, communicate effectively, and resolve conflicts (Danielson, 2006; Killion & Harrison, 2006). She exemplified leadership, which is strongly interconnected with teamwork, by engaging, inspiring, and motivating others to improve and to become better through their actions (Bascia, 1996). Collaboration, leadership, vision, positive attitude, impacting children beyond the walls of a classroom, and teamwork are all evident in the story about Mrs. Barth. As a result of her efforts, individual student academic achievement increased in every grade level.

The Impact of Teacher Leaders on the Community

Just as Mrs. Crowther's work with Janie reached beyond her single classroom into the whole school, Mrs. Barth's focus on effective teaching and learning strategies soon reached beyond the walls of her school as well. As her principal claimed:

> Our school's success spread to the other schools in the district. Within 2 years of Mrs. Barth first asking to meet with me, every school within the district has implemented this structure. In addition, other area schools made visits to gather information and implement the model. None of this ever would have happened if it wasn't for Mrs. Barth wanting to do what was best for our students, our school, and our district.

As Danielson (2006) pointed out, this kind of *positive effect* on all around them is another defining characteristic of teacher leaders. These exceptional people seem to have a calling to have a positive influence beyond the walls of their classroom; and their optimism, enthusiasm, confidence, and collaboration are integral behaviors that contribute to their success. The point is aptly captured in the following story from an administrator:

> We have this phenomenal teacher who started "Math Night" about 3 years ago because the parents couldn't help their own children with their math homework. The response was so positive during the first year that he talked about it at a staff meeting, and now our whole math department is doing this. The community just loves it, and the kids can ask their parents for help on their math.

Conclusion

Teacher leaders are teachers who transform a learning community—one child, one teacher, one classroom, one school, and one district at a time. The traits of teacher leaders are numerous and varied, and this chapter has highlighted only a few of the key characteristics. A complete list of teacher leader characteristics is presented in Appendices 19.A and 19.B. In short, a teacher leader focuses on the children; displays a positive attitude; collaborates; knows current research and employs it to ensure highly effective instructional practices; uses assessment to drive instruction; and wants colleagues, the school, the district, and the whole learning community to achieve.

During the interviews, a principal, when asked why he chose a particular teacher as a teacher leader, replied "She makes everyone around her better—the kids, the parents, and especially the other teachers. She has this way of making things happen."

The key lesson is that every school has teachers who exhibit the qualities that contribute to student achievement, such as having a positive attitude, being dedicated to the achievement of every child, using assessments to create individualized plans, and keeping up-to-date on best instructional practices. Teachers who embrace these practices and behaviors become de facto leaders in their grades and schools by actively fostering a collaborative environment where colleagues work together to solve problems and leverage their creativity.

Teacher leadership is not really new. These exemplary teachers have always been a part of the educational system but have never received the recognition they deserved, nor were they given the power to organize and mobilize fellow teachers with new ideas and events for their students and schools. However, as demonstrated by the examples in this chapter, when principals recognize and support teacher leaders, the positive impact can quickly spread to entire grade levels, schools, and districts. Teacher leaders are, and always will be, *needed* in schools in order for students, schools, and districts to succeed. Because teacher leaders are so important, all teachers should foster and develop their inner "teacher leader." It is in there, and it has to come out because schools and society truly need as many teacher leaders as possible.

References

Bascia, N. (1996). Inside and outside: Minority immigrant teachers in Canadian schools. *International Journal of Qualitative Studies in Education, 9*(2), 151–165.

Crowther, F., Kaagan, S. S., Ferguson, M., & Hann, L. (2002). *Developing teacher leaders: How teacher leadership enhances school success.* Thousand Oaks, CA: Corwin.

Danielson, C. (2006). *Teacher leadership that strengthens professional practice.* Alexandria, VA: Association for Supervision and Curriculum Development.

DuFour, R., & Eaker, R. (1998). *Professional learning communities at work: Best practices for enhancing student achievement.* Bloomington, IN: Solution Tree.

Jackson, T., Burrus, J., Bassett, K., & Roberts, R. D. (2010). *Teacher leadership: An assessment framework for an emerging area of professional practice.* Princeton, NJ: Educational Testing Services.

Katzenmeyer, M., & Moller, G. (2001). *Awakening the sleeping giant: Helping teachers develop as leaders* (2nd ed.). Thousand Oaks, CA: Corwin.

Killion, J., & Harrison, C. (2006). *Taking the lead: New roles for teachers and school-based coaches.* Oxford, OH: National Staff Development Council.

Leithwood, K. A., & Riehl, C. (2005). What do we already know about educational leadership? In W. A. Firestone & C. Riehl (Eds.), *A new agenda for research in educational leadership* (pp. 12–27). New York, NY: Teachers College Press.

Rivkin, S. G., Hanushek, E. A., & Kain, J. F. (2005). Teachers, schools, and academic achievement. *Econometrica, 73*(2), 417–458.

Stronge, J. H. (2007). *Qualities of effective teachers* (2nd ed.). Alexandria, VA: Association for Supervision and Curriculum Development.

Teacher Leadership Exploratory Consortium. (2008). *Teacher leader model standards.* Retrieved from http://teacherleaderstandards.org/downloads/TLS_Brochure.pdf

York-Barr, J., & Duke, K. (2004). What do we know about teacher leadership? Findings from two decades of scholarship. *Review of Educational Research, 74*(3), 255–316.

APPENDIX 19.A

Teacher Leader Characteristics: Commonalities

Jackson, Burrus, Bassett, & Roberts (2010) surveyed the teacher leader research and identified several commonalities that are pervasive in the studies.

- **Work ethic.** This characteristic is defined as perseverant, resourceful, action oriented, committed, and passionate (York-Barr & Duke, 2004).
- **Teamwork.** A teacher must work with many different stakeholders and build positive relationships. To build such relationships, he or she must be able to engender trust, work well with colleagues, communicate effectively, and resolve conflicts (Danielson, 2006; Killion & Harrison, 2006).
- **Leadership.** Teacher leaders lead by engaging, inspiring, and motivating others to improve and become better through their actions (Bascia, 1996). The trait is strongly interconnected with teamwork.
- **Openness.** Teacher leaders are adaptable, open-minded, and creative. They are open to exploring options to gather the necessary resources to improve the state of education (York-Barr & Duke, 2004). Their relationships are filled with honesty and integrity.
- **Vision.** Teacher leaders have a vision to identify opportunities for improvement or fix problems within the school. They actively seek out opportunities rather than simply waiting for them to appear (Danielson, 2006). They have a calling to positively influence beyond the walls of their classrooms.
- **Positive effect.** Teacher leaders are positive. They are leaders who often succeed with the help of their positive effects of optimism, enthusiasm, confidence, and willingness to collaborate (Danielson, 2006).
- **Risk taking.** This characteristic allows teacher leaders to do whatever is necessary in order for children to learn. They do not mind if they fail or are criticized (Danielson, 2006).

APPENDIX 19.B

Teacher Leader Characteristics: Behavioral

Stronge (2007) also developed categories around specific behaviors of teacher leaders and used these behaviors to develop and implement new models for teacher evaluation. His characteristics for teacher leaders are the following:

- **Focused on the individual.** A teacher leader treats children as individuals and exhibits a positive attitude.
- **Effective at managing student behavior.** A teacher leader arranges children in groups rather than rows to facilitate conversations, emphasizes respectful interactions, covers the classroom walls with students' work, and guides students to behave appropriately.
- **Organized and oriented toward instruction.** A teacher leader's lesson plans are developed daily, students know the routine of the classroom, and assessment data are used to drive instruction.
- **Effective at implementing instruction.** A teacher leader allows children's questions to drive the lesson, adjusts the pacing to meet students' needs, effectively involves the whole classroom, and provides quick and specific feedback.
- **Aware of student progress.** A teacher leader guides children to track their own progress, gives multiple assessments to ensure skill mastery, and differentiates assessments for individual students.
- **Professional.** A teacher leader focuses on students, communicates with parents, volunteers to assist others, treats colleagues with respect, and works collaboratively.

EDITOR AND CONTRIBUTORS

Editor

Nathan Bond, PhD, is an associate professor in the Department of Curriculum and Instruction at Texas State University. He teaches graduate education courses in the areas of teacher leadership and curriculum development. His areas of expertise include teacher leadership, portfolio assessment, and foreign language pedagogy. Dr. Bond is a former president of Kappa Delta Pi, International Honor Society in Education.

Contributors

Shawn Christopher Boone, EdD, is University of Phoenix faculty development administrator for assessment and resource, and associate faculty for research and dissertation in the School of Advanced Studies. Named District Teacher of the Year for 2013–2014, he taught at Global Studies and Technology Academy in Los Angeles and led the South Area Teacher Collaborative. His research interests focus on school reform models, school culture, teacher education, and constructivist learning education.

Susan Trostle Brand, DEd, formerly a primary grade teacher and reading specialist, is a professor of education at the University of Rhode Island. She is the author of several books, book chapters, and articles addressing diversity, storytelling, multiple intelligences, and creative curriculum, and has presented at more than 150 conferences internationally. Dr. Brand has served on the Kappa Delta Pi Executive Council as vice-president and president-elect, and as counselor of the Iota Sigma Chapter.

Marsha L. Carr, DM, National Milken Educator, Teacher of the Year, and Fulbright Specialist, is on the faculty at the University of North Carolina Wilmington after previously serving as a school superintendent. Dr. Carr is author of *Educational Leadership: From Hostile Takeover to a Sustainable Successful System* and co-author of *The School Improvement Planning Handbook*. Owner of Edu-Tell, LLC, she is an international consultant to business and education on self-mentoring.

Mara Cawein, NBCT, is an instructor in the College of Education, University of Central Arkansas, teaching undergraduate education majors in an introductory course and a learning and development course. She is also a National Board Certified Teacher and has recently renewed her certification in AYA Mathematics. Ms. Cawein is currently a doctoral student with a research interest in community involvement at the secondary school level.

Terri Cearley-Key, MEd, is a senior lecturer in the College of Education at Texas State University. She teaches reading and elementary education courses in the Department of Curriculum and Instruction. Her research interests include teacher leadership, literacy instruction, and teacher research.

Marilyn Cochran-Smith, PhD, is Cawthorne Professor of Teacher Education and director of the doctoral program in curriculum and instruction at Boston College's Lynch School of Education. Dr. Cochran-Smith is an elected member of the National Academy of Education, a former president of the American Educational Research Association, and a member of the Laureate Chapter of Kappa Delta Pi. She has published nine books and more than 175 articles, chapters, and editorials on practitioner inquiry, social justice, and teacher education.

Barbara H. Davis, EdD, is a professor in the College of Education at Texas State University. She teaches reading and elementary education courses in the Department of Curriculum and Instruction. She also serves as co-director of the teacher fellows graduate program. Her research interests include teacher induction, teacher research, and literacy instruction. Dr. Davis is a member of the Eta Zeta Chapter of Kappa Delta Pi.

Laurie J. DeRosa, EdD, is a professor in the Education Department at Fitchburg University. She has been an educator for 35 years, both as an elementary art specialist and as a college professor training preservice teachers to value the arts in education through an interdisciplinary curriculum. She has presented at numerous conferences both regionally and nationally. Dr. DeRosa has served as counselor of the Xi Psi Chapter of Kappa Delta Pi and vice-president on the KDP Executive Council.

Nancy P. Gallavan, PhD, is a professor of teacher education at the University of Central Arkansas, specializing in classroom assessments, social studies, and multicultural education. With more than 120 peer-reviewed publications, Dr. Gallavan has served as president of the Association of Teacher Educators and in leadership positions with the American Educational Research Association, National Association of Multicultural Education, and National Council for the Social Studies. She is an inaugural member of the Kappa Delta Pi Eleanor Roosevelt Chapter.

Carol Gilles, PhD, is an associate professor in the College of Education at the University of Missouri. She teaches undergraduate literacy courses for middle level and graduate literacy courses for K–12. She is also the faculty coordinator for the teaching fellows program. Her research interests include teacher induction, using talk to learn, and struggling readers.

Christine Carrino Gorowara, PhD, is senior director of accreditation at the Council for the Accreditation of Educator Preparation in Washington, DC, and has worked in accreditation since 2005. She also has been a faculty member at the University of Delaware. She has a master of science in mathematics from The Ohio State University and a doctorate in curriculum and instruction with a concentration in mathematics education from the University of Delaware.

Lisa A. W. Kensler, EdD, is an associate professor at Auburn University. She earned her doctorate in educational leadership at Lehigh University. Her research interests include teacher leadership, democratic community, and whole school sustainability.

Joni M. Lakin, PhD, is an assistant professor at Auburn University. She earned her doctorate in psychological and quantitative foundations at The University of Iowa. Her research interests include educational measurement, test validity and fairness, and assessment of individual differences.

Ann Lieberman, EdD, is professor emeritus of education at Teachers College, Columbia University and a senior scholar at Stanford University. Previously, she was a senior scholar at The Carnegie Foundation for the Advancement of Teaching and president of the American Educational Research Association. Dr. Lieberman is widely known for her work in the areas of teacher leadership and development, collaborative research, networks and school—university partnerships, and the problems and prospects for understanding educational change. She was inducted into the KDP Laureate Chapter in 1995.

Angela Lupton, MS, NCC, serves as the assistant dean and an instructor of elementary education in the College of Education at Butler University. She has more than 20 years of experience in education as an elementary classroom teacher, middle school nonprofit director, consultant, and teacher educator, and is a National Certified Counselor. Applications for asset-based thinking in education, teacher leadership, and the dynamics of the clinical experience in teacher preparation are her areas of current interest.

Robin Haskell McBee, PhD, is a professor in teacher education at Rowan University, a state university in southern New Jersey, where she works with aspiring teachers as well as those already experienced in their practice. She coordinates graduate students in a master of education teacher leadership program. Her research interests include caring learning communities, teacher leadership, teacher educator standards, interdisciplinary instruction, and urban education.

Sheryl McGlamery, PhD, is professor of science education, co-director of the Office for STEM Education, and coordinator of secondary graduate programs for the University of Nebraska at Omaha. Her research interests include teacher development, induction programs, and inquiry-based learning.

Frank B. Murray, PhD, is H. Rodney Sharp Professor at the University of Delaware and was dean of its College of Education for 16 years. He has degrees from St. John's College in Annapolis, Maryland, and The Johns Hopkins University. Dr. Murray is a Fellow in the American Psychological Association, the American Psychological Society, and the American Educational Research Association. He was inducted into the Laureate Chapter of Kappa Delta Pi in 2009.

Sonia Nieto, EdD, is professor emerita of language, literacy, and culture, College of Education, University of Massachusetts, Amherst. She has written extensively on multicultural education, teacher education, and the education of students of diverse backgrounds, including *Finding Joy in Teaching Students of Diverse Backgrounds*. She has received many awards for her scholarship and advocacy, including four honorary doctorates, and is a member of the KDP Laureate Chapter and has served on the Society's Executive Council.

Edward Owens, MPA, has been teaching at Remington College for the past 7 years as a business administration instructor. He has held previous positions as a college department chair and university senior research associate. Mr. Owens currently is pursuing an EdD degree in higher education at Walden University. His dissertation topic is "Shared Governance: The Role of Student Advisory Committees in the Governance of a Higher Educational Institution."

Catherine Hagerman Pangan, EdD, is an associate professor in the College of Education at Butler University. A former fourth-grade teacher, she enjoys sharing ideas about hands-on science experiences with school communities. Her other interests include education policy, teacher education, and technology. Dr. Pangan is a columnist for the *New Teacher Advocate* and also published a children's book with her son titled *No Peanuts for Me!*

Patricia H. Phelps, EdD, is a professor in the College of Education, University of Central Arkansas, teaching graduate courses for the advanced studies in the teacher leadership program. She is also director of the Instructional Development Center for the university. Dr. Phelps is working with Mara Cawein as a mentor in the leadership studies doctoral program.

Saundra L. Shillingstad, EdD, is a professor in the College of Education at the University of Nebraska at Omaha. She teaches social studies education and foundations courses in the Department of Teacher Education. She also serves as faculty sponsor of Kappa Delta Pi. Her research interests include teacher induction, teacher development, and assessment for learning.

Clinton Smith, EdD, BCBA-D, a former practicing special educator and behavior intervention specialist, believes that educators can be most effective when they act as servant leaders in their schools and are involved in the lives of the students. Dr. Smith is an assistant professor of special education at The University of Tennessee at Martin and the advisor for KDP's Alpha Epsilon Epsilon Chapter.

Joanne Smith, PhD, is an assistant professor at Fontbonne University. She teaches courses in assessment and diagnosis of reading difficulties, content area literacy, and foundations of reading. She also supervises preservice teachers who tutor struggling readers. Her research interests are literacy and mental health, trauma informed instruction, and teacher education issues.

Jenny Stegall is a PhD candidate in reading/language arts in the College of Education at the University of Missouri. Her research interests include teacher induction, teacher education, and English language learning.

Rebecca Stern, MA, is a doctoral candidate in curriculum and instruction at the Lynch School of Education at Boston College, where she is studying educational policy, school leadership, and teacher education. She is a National Board Certified Teacher and has taught middle and high school social studies. Ms. Stern has been deeply involved in school reform efforts to increase equity for students both as a classroom teacher and a school reform consultant.

William Sterrett, PhD, a former principal and teacher, serves as a faculty member and program coordinator at the University of North Carolina Wilmington. He served as chair of the Kappa Delta Pi Public Policy Committee and is author of the ASCD book *Insights into Action*. Dr. Sterrett earned his undergraduate degree in education at Asbury University in Wilmore, Kentucky, and his MEd and PhD at the University of Virginia.

Yang Wang, PhD, is assistant professor of language and literacy education in the Department of Instruction and Teacher Education at the University of South Carolina. Her research interests include teacher induction, adolescent literacy, and English language learning.

Sue Lutz Weisse, PhD, has been in K–12 education for more than 25 years. Over the years, she was a teacher, supervisor, and building principal. Dr. Weisse has presented at numerous state and national conferences. Her undergraduate and graduate degrees are in special education, and she earned her PhD in education administration.

Elizabeth A. Wilkins, PhD, is a professor in the Department of Leadership, Educational Psychology, and Foundations at Northern Illinois University. She has been an educator in secondary schools and institutions of higher education for three decades and has given more than 150 presentations and workshops at the national, regional, and state levels. Her research agenda focuses on induction practices, pre-service education, student teachers, and supervision. She has served on the KDP Executive Council as vice-president and is the current president.

Pamela Scott Williams, PhD, is the title I teacher at Pick Elementary School in Auburn, Alabama. She earned her doctorate in administration of supervision and curriculum at Auburn University. Her research interests include teacher leadership, school/teacher effectiveness, and curriculum.

Suzanne M. Zentner, PhD, MBA, worked nearly 25 years in public education—from classroom teacher to superintendent. She has led a national P–20 effort for a Fortune 500 company, designed a parent engagement app, and is a business owner. Currently, she serves as the senior strategic advisor for Science Foundation Arizona, teaches for Arizona State University, and is a mentor for student entrepreneurs. She earned her PhD, MBA, MS, and BS at the University of Wisconsin.

INDEX

Page numbers followed by *f* indicate figures, by n indicate notes, by *t* indicate tables.

53012521R00156

Made in the USA
Lexington, KY
17 June 2016